THE PRIEST

MYSTERY OF LOVE

THE PRIEST
MYSTERY OF LOVE

Luis M. Martínez

Foreword by Bishop Daniel Flores

Translated with an Introduction by
Juan Macias Marquez, O.P.

Edited by Luke VanBerkum, O.P.

CLUNY
Providence, Rhode Island

CLUNY EDITION, 2024

This Cluny edition is a translation of *El sacerdote: misterio de amor*, originally published in 1958 by Ediciones Studium de Cultura.

All Scripture quotations are taken from the New American Bible, Revised Edition, unless specifically noted; all endnotes and footnotes are added by the translator or editor unless specifically noted.

The original work has been edited in order to reduce repetition and to make this edition more readable for a contemporary English-speaking audience.

For more information regarding this title
or any other Cluny Media publication,
please write to info@clunymedia.com, or to
Cluny Media, P.O. Box 1664, Providence, RI 02901

VISIT US ONLINE AT WWW.CLUNYMEDIA.COM

ISBN (paperback): 978-1685953225

Nihil Obstat: James Brent, O.P., *Censor librorum*

Imprimi potest: Allen B. Moran, O.P., *Prior provincial*
OCTOBER 25, 2023

Imprimatur: José María, *Ob. aux y Vic Gral.*
JANUARY 1958

Cover design by Clarke & Clarke
Cover image: Andrea Mantegna, *The Agony in the Garden of Gethsemane* (detail),
egg tempera on wood, between c. 1455 and c. 1456,
Courtesy of Wikimedia Commons

CONTENTS

FOREWORD

by Bishop Daniel Flores

THE SERVANT OF GOD Luis María Martínez grew up and served as a priest and bishop during a time of great upheaval in the history of Mexico. Despite both historical and often geographic proximity to the events of upheaval, we in the English-speaking world know little about the conditions during the persecution, the Cristero uprising, or the hierarchy's efforts to navigate the crisis. The Archbishop lived those times intensely. He knew the great protagonists on the various sides of the struggle to defend the Church's freedom to preach, to worship, and to act, while laboring at the same time to restore peace. He lived to see some sense of peace taking root and was in a singular position to describe the spiritual realities present in the midst of, not apart from, the flesh and blood struggles of his times.

Having said this, I would not suggest that the reader of this volume needs an in-depth study of the history of Mexico during the first half of the twentieth century in order to be affected by these sermons. On the contrary, it is more likely that someone reading these chapters will feel pulled to become more familiar with the history as a result of having read them. This is so because the first mark of a great preacher is thematic accessibility. The Archbishop preached the mystery of Christ, and this is accessible to us as soon as we begin reading. In this particular collection, he preaches it in relation to the ministerial priesthood. The focus is on Christ and then on the consequent consideration of the Trinitarian and ecclesial mystery conjoined in him.

He speaks of Christ first because this is the common tongue of the Church. Both by training and by intuitive resonance with the Tradition, the touchable Christ of the Gospel is the touchstone of the Archbishop's preaching. In these pages he frequently evokes the scene at the Lake of Tiberius where the Risen Christ calls for and receives the responsive love of Simon Peter. *Simon, son of John, do you love me more than these?* It is the premiere Scriptural allusion of these sermons, announced at the outset of this collection, giving us a lesson in where preaching the Mystery must begin and to where it must always return: *We are priests because we love*, says the Archbishop, *and because Jesus asked us the question of love* (Chapter 1). Neither the priest nor his preaching can prescind from the palpable particularity of Christ, and this is so because we are at the service of this mystery in the people to whom we preach: *On the day of our priestly ordination we surrender ourselves to Jesus so that he might make use of us. Our life is his, our thoughts are his, our words are his; our actions, work, time, and sacrifices are his; we do not live for ourselves; we live for him and we live for souls, but we live for souls because we live for Jesus Christ* (Chapter 7).

Within the fairly tranquil and elevated style of the various *predicaciones* in this volume, we find discourses preached at first Masses, at twenty-fifth and fiftieth anniversary jubilee Masses, and we encounter funeral orations for many of the Archbishop's contemporaries. In all of them, the overarching theme is gratitude for the Father's love manifested in Christ and gratitude for the call to surrender to him, in the form of a pastoral service to his people: *Feed my sheep.* Within this gratitude, there is room for the Archbishop to describe the manifold virtues and gifts that are meant to accompany and envelop the life of a priest.

If we find the language the Archbishop uses to describe the excellence of the priestly gift a bit too elevated for contemporary consumption, then we should take the time to think through the things he speaks about using our own particular idioms. The Archbishop does not, for example, enter the mystery of grace by first describing our failures; he begins always with the excellence of Christ's gift. Properly considered this has the singularly important effect of holding at bay moralistic reductions of the Gospel, reductions to which we are particularly susceptible. We do not speak enough of grace, and as a result our people are increasingly unsure of its referent in reality. This is a problem in our time. The gratuity of God's gift in the midst of our weakness (our *miseria,* to use the Archbishop's preferred word) is a central aspect of the Christian life, and of the Archbishop's preaching. We, too, need to find the appropriate language to speak of this in our *here* and *now.* This is as important to the life of the priest himself as it is to the Body of Christ we serve: *While we bear the divine treasures in the fragile vessel of our flesh, tell us your secret of love, as much as is necessary so that our poor hearts burn, but remember our misery and cover with a merciful veil your unfathomable mystery* (Chapter 1).

In these homilies and discourses on the priesthood there is a spiritual realism that never fails to announce the victory of the gift of Christ's love over the frailty of our wounded nature. The fidelity of Christ is what is praised. The *miserias* that hobble and drag us down are not denied. They are part of the mystery of love that gives life to the whole Body of Christ. *Lord, our brother, who celebrates twenty-five years of being a priest, has been faithful; if you will permit me a word from everyday language, he has been haphazardly faithful,* [ha sido fiel a lo pobre] *Lord, but he has been faithful.* He uses the concise colloquialism (*a lo pobre*) to emphasize the distance between the Lord's fidelity and our own. And this he describes in a variety of ways throughout. *We can be the smallest and most miserable, but, nonetheless, we form the saints. Our word is the one that has divine efficacy to sanctify; the public word that, like sowers, we scatter from this holy chair* (Chapter 2).

He approaches the preaching and teaching ministry as progressively epiphanic in form. His preferred organizing principle is affirmation, description, and negation, followed by further affirmation. In this way, he takes us deeper into the mystery. "It is this," he says; and then after describing what "this" is, says later, "It is not this, it is more than this; it is this." He uses this manner of exposition throughout, as is exemplified in this passage from the funeral oration for Bishop Rafael Guízar y Valencia: *And, nevertheless, it is not his confidence that is the most characteristic part of his soul. Ah! The secret of Bishop Guízar is deeper, we still have not found the key of his soul and of his life* (Chapter 15).

The Archbishop's style involves drawing us into accompanying him in the search for the deeper key that sheds light on Christ's action in our midst. In his particularly remarkable sermon, *The Epiphanies of Jesus to the Priest*, Chapter 6 in this volume, he unfolds a fourfold way into perceiving Christ in and with us. The Archbishop traces a path that starts with the Gospels, and proceeds to unveil the manifestations of Christ in the Eucharist, in the lives of the people the priest serves, and then in his own soul. At work here is the splendidly Catholic principle, as old as the Gospel itself, that perceives the aim of the Incarnation to be progressively epiphanic. Redemption in Christ entails, among other things, a graced showing of the love of God in Christ that engenders a graced seeing and a graced participatory love given in response. At its root, the soul's engendered response to the love of Christ manifested is both generous and particular.

The epiphanic is a presently lived dynamic of priestly and Christian life. *The priest is constantly studying the Gospel, and the Gospel is constantly revealing Jesus to him,* the Archbishop says (Chapter 6). Speaking next of the Eucharist, he touches upon the sacramental, bodily presence: *How many times do we say to Jesus: "Lord, do not allow me to be separated from you; let me live near your tabernacle, near this tent that I myself have raised for you, so that I may always live in the eternal Tabor of the Eucharist* (Chapter 6). The Gospel Word and the Eucharistic mystery, in turn, lead to a living presence and transformation of the soul by Christ. Thus the actions of Christ in the souls of the faithful are a further epiphany. Such souls give witness to something only God can do by the grace of the Spirit. *For the priest, souls are the complement of the Gospel, and, I will dare to say it, they are the complement of the Eucharist; the epiphany in souls is the splendid epiphany that makes us know Jesus marvelously, that makes us discover his intimate way, his mercy, his love, his goodness, his greatness, his omnipotence* (Chapter 6). The graced eye sees in God's work among his people mysteries that are hidden; hidden, that is, until they are seen. And then, speaking of how the Lord manifests himself in the priest's self-knowing, he situates even the priest's failures: *Men,* he says, *when they discover our defects, move away; they are to some extent right to do so, our defects are so repugnant! The only one who does not walk away because of our miseries is Jesus* (Chapter 6). The epiphanic should be a constant in the life of a priest, not for himself alone, but for the sake of forming in the Church he serves a people capable of seeing the Lord present and at work in our midst.

Yet, there is more here. When the Archbishop speaks of the epiphanies of the Lord in the Church, he is actually pointing us to the source of these manifestations. We are invited to see Christ in all of these ways so as to cultivate a true contemplative gaze of love that sees the *something always more* within the mystery of Christ, who shows us the Father by the gift of the Spirit. *In what, then, does the mystery of preaching consist? The preacher is a man who has ascended to the heights of contemplation, who has felt his spirit and his heart bathed with the divine light, and who from the plenitude of contemplation allows some words to fall on the earth* (Chapter 2).

What we see in the contemplative gaze is determined by the graceful dispositions of providence, of course, yet it is generative of what the Archbishop calls the *physiognomy,* or particular graced conformity of the soul to the mystery. *To know a man interiorly, one has to discover his spiritual physiognomy, just like to know him exteriorly it is necessary to look at his face. And the physiognomy of souls is what is highest and most beautiful in them, what rises to the heavens, what communicates with God, what is bathed in the light of the divine face. . . . What those eyes see in the divine splendor marks the physiognomy of a soul. There are souls who see nothing: they are blind, and their face has no expression. There are souls who sink their pupils in the ocean of light, and from* glory to glory *they come to be transformed into that same divine image (2 Cor 3:18)* (Chapter 14). Transformed by what we see, we see with eyes transformed.

There is much to perceive within the Archbishop's exposition of the fruits of his own contemplation. The reader will discover a meditative joy while receiving what the Archbishop's words attempt to unveil. In a spirit of gratitude, I will mention three striking themes in particular.

The first is the Archbishop's love for, and his spiritual vision of, the Blessed Virgin in the life of a priest. Particularly in the fourth sermon, the Archbishop carefully describes the maternal role of the Blessed Virgin Mary in the life of a priest, if I can use an audacious phrase, as a kind of spiritual midwifery. Even as she accompanied and facilitated and participated in the three principal stages of the Lord's life, so also she does for the priest. *And, indeed, Mary does with us what she did with Jesus* (Chapter 4). The priest, like Christ, has a hidden life. Ours, however, is marked by distinct characteristics proper to the struggling servant. The priest's interiority is his hidden life: his prayer, his silent suffering, his awareness of the failures and weaknesses that are in him. Mary is there. The priest has also a public life of preaching, celebrating the mysteries, of guiding souls. Mary is there. And, at length there is always in the priest's life the unfolding, inevitable encounter with Calvary. Mary is and will be there. The mysticism of Mary at the foot of the Cross is not a flight of fancy in an age of martyrs: *And when Calvary comes for you, which has to come—you would not want to remain eternally on Tabor, knowing that Jesus, the beloved of your soul, is on Calvary—when the immolation and the bitterness come for you, think how close Mary is to that cross, and turn your eyes to her, and in her eyes you will find strength, consolation, and peace* (Chapter 4).

Secondly, the Archbishop lived in a time and place where great sacrifice was needed. His was a time dominated by persecution, and, more dangerously, a time of division and of polarized approaches within the Church herself. In light of this, of particular importance are the funeral orations preached upon the death of Leopoldo Ruiz y Flores, Archbishop of Michoacán and Apostolic Delegate of Pope Pius XI to Mexico during the most intense years of the crisis. For the Archbishop he was a friend, and for the Church he was a man sent on a mission of peace. The two funeral orations describe a man of deep interior peace and sacrifice who was also given a mission to help reestablish peace for the Church in Mexico. The peacemakers pronounced blessed in the Gospel, and described by the Archbishop, however, are not primarily persons of political calculation. For if Archbishop Ruiz and others are praised for having promoted a kind of reconciliation between Church and state, the Archbishop saw the Apostolic Delegate's work from the perspective of a deeper spiritual vision. The funeral orations are occasions to instruct us about supernatural prudence and the related gift of counsel. And, in one of the many poignant passages in this collection, the Archbishop speaks gently of what it cost the delegate to plant seeds of peace: *In a certain way, the gallant attitude of intransigence and combativeness has its flatterers; but when prudence asks that gallantry depart, then it is necessary to have the courage to appear before others as weak. Condescending and having the necessary strength to appear weak before others when duty requires it, is a glorious fortitude, bordering on the heroic* (Chapter 17).

Thirdly, and perhaps most near to the heart of the Servant of God, the Archbishop often speaks of the sorrows that are properly, unavoidably, and intrinsically a part of the priestly vocation. *We live,* he says, *from Calvary, we live from the cross, and we should for the same reason understand Jesus Christ crucified. But this does not simply mean that we are filled with compassion when considering his cruel sorrow. . . . We should know the depths of the sorrow of Jesus because we have to bear in our souls and in our bodies the marks of the sacrifice* (Chapter 8). To hear him say these things draws us close to the secret that the Servant of God very much spent his life publicizing. I hesitate to say there is a theology of the priesthood in these pages; there is, but there is more than that. There is an experiential perception of the mysteries of Christ, of his glories, of his gifts, and of the wounds in his Body. These are the things he himself saw in the Mystery he contemplated.

I did say at the outset that the mark of a great preacher is the accessibility of the Christian thematic. That was clumsy of me, and taken by itself, hardly true; there is more. There is the grace that nourishes the poor priest and that can make him a generous recipient of the grace that Christ offers at the sea of Tiberius. And so it is that from the vantage point of these homilies and discourses, we can begin to appreciate the spiritual physiognomy of the Servant of God, Luis María Martínez, to catch a glimpse of what he saw in the Mystery that transformed and guided him. He was a man who saw the gratuity of Christ's generosity, who heard the vivacity of Jesus's voice, was docile to the gifts of the Spirit, who knew the spiritual assistance of the Blessed Virgin. He was a man who knew the frailty of the vessels that bear the grace given, and was attentive to the epiphanies of Christ in the Gospel, in the Eucharistic sacrifice, and in his own people. And he was a man of suffering, a man of peace, a man of hope, a priest who loved. A great soul, by the grace of God.

INTRODUCTION

by Juan Macias Marquez, O.P.

THE SERVANT OF GOD Archbishop Luis María Martínez was a Renaissance man. According to his close friend and biographer, Martínez was a "philosopher, theologian, educator, superior, sociologist, sacred orator, writer, poet, spiritual director, humorist."[†] Martínez, like a good pastor of souls, was all things to all men (1 Cor 9:22). Above all, however, Martínez was a father and a priest of Jesus Christ. Martínez could expound the intricacies and delights of the sacred priesthood in an unparalleled manner—as is evident in this collection of homilies—because the mystery of supernatural fatherhood formed his core identity.

To become a father, however, a man must first be formed by other fathers. Luis Gonzaga María Martínez y Rodríguez was born to Rosendo and Ramoncita on June 9, 1881, in a small town northwest of Mexico City in the state of Morelia. No sooner had eleven days passed than his father died, leaving his mother to move in with her brother Casimiro, a priest and the vicar of the local parish. "Papa Mirito," as little Luis affectionately called him, would be a tremendous fatherly influence on the boy in his early years. Fr. Casimiro would be the first of many influential priests in Martínez's life,

† Joseph G. Treviño, *The Spiritual Life of Archbishop Martínez*, trans. Sr. Mary St. Daniel Tarrent, Cross and Crown Series of Spirituality, no. 33 (St. Louis: B. Herder Book Co., 1966), xi.

cooperating with God to sow those first seeds of the priestly vocation in the future archbishop. But his fatherly care would also be all too short.

Martínez had scarcely turned seven when Fr. Casimiro died. Once Ramoncita secured support for herself and Luis from her other brother, Sabino, Martínez matriculated in the seminary in Morelia at the tender age of nine and a half. At that time, seminaries offered an education at all different levels. This point marks the beginning of his thoroughly ecclesiastical and clerical life. During this time in seminary, Sabino would also make his fatherly mark on the character of the young Martínez, forming him as he did the other seminarians by his manner of life. Martínez would end up spending decades at this seminary both as a student and as a formator of young men and seminarians.

When Martínez was fourteen, he entered the major seminary to study theology in preparation for the priesthood. After turning twenty-three and having received an indult from the Holy See (because a man had to be twenty-five to be ordained a priest), Archbishop Atenógenes Silva ordained Martínez to the priesthood of Jesus Christ on November 20, 1904. Conformed to Christ, Martínez became a father and began forming other men to be priests of Jesus Christ. Soon after he was ordained, Martínez became the seminary's prefect of discipline. In this position, Martínez, formed as a father, began to act as a father for the men in the seminary.

Archbishop Silva, with high aspirations for his seminary, appointed Monsignor Francisco Banegas the rector in 1906, who in turn named Martínez vice-rector. Banegas had had an enormous fatherly influence on Martínez throughout Martínez's time in seminary. Treviño claims that "Martínez was the masterpiece of Bishop Banegas."[†] Together, Banegas and Martínez marked out a new vision for the seminary and priestly formation, even as Martínez

† Treviño, *The Spiritual Life*, 10.

became rector in October 1919. They battled and overcame many obstacles—including the seminary's closure—during the religious persecutions of 1926 1929. Banegas would remain a close friend of Martínez throughout his life, even assisting as Martínez's co-consecrator at Martínez's episcopal consecration. Banegas transcribed many of Martínez's sermons, some of which are preserved in this collection. In 1953, when the *Academia Mexicana de la Lengua* made Martínez one of their members, the Archbishop gave an homage to his longtime friend and mentor Banegas in thanksgiving. Finally, God granted Martínez the opportunity to attend to Banegas at the end of his life.

Martínez was not only an administrator in the seminary. He always loved to teach. He captivated his students with clear and authoritative lecturing.[‡] Martínez also used much of his free time to study and read widely. Philosophy remained one of his greatest loves, and he became a revered philosopher.

Ordained a bishop on September 30, 1923, Martínez was more perfectly configured to Christ and also took on a new fatherly role of a much larger flock as auxiliary bishop of the Archdiocese of Morelia. Later, he was appointed coadjutor to the Archbishop of Morelia on March 10, 1934. Martínez would be called to his final post as Archbishop of Mexico City, the first Primate Archbishop of this see, on February 20, 1937, where he would remain and serve until he died.

The first task Martínez tackled upon ascension to the see of Mexico City was the restoration of the battered seminary. Once again, we see the enormous importance Martínez placed on forming priestly fathers. He even attended to the seminary personally as its rector while still the bishop of the capital city.

‡ Luis Martínez, "Mons. Martínez y la santificación del sacerdote: discursos y otros textos en el Seminario de Morelia (1906–1937)," ed. Pedro Fernández Rodríguez, O.P. (Mexico City: Sede de la Postulación, 2005).

As Archbishop of the primatial see of Mexico, he was a consummate shepherd. He possessed a rare and shrewd political acumen, fathering not only Catholics, but all Mexicans, as he slowly ameliorated the relations between the Church and state during the presidency of Lázaro Cárdenas, a childhood friend. Even as Archbishop of Mexico City, he allowed himself to receive the paternal love of brother bishops. In a letter, he expresses his sorrow upon the death of his friend Archbishop Leopoldo Ruiz, whom Martínez said was like a father to him. Four of the sermons in this collection honor Ruiz in some way.

As his fame and pastoral scope spread throughout his life, God sent him chosen souls to direct to the heights of the spiritual life. He was the spiritual father of Blessed Concepción Cabrera de Armida, affectionately known as "Conchita." This young, widowed mother of nine started many apostolates and wrote thousands of pages on the spiritual life. Martínez directed her in these works for the last twelve years of her life. Always deeply connected with his brother priests and bishops, Martínez also directed some of them. One bishop whom he directed, Rafael Guízar, would be canonized a saint. The fifteenth sermon in this collection is Martínez's funeral oration for St. Rafael.

The indefatigable Martínez worked tirelessly in the apostolate even in the last years of his life. With great devotion to the holy sacrifice of the Mass, he celebrated it until he was physically unable to carry out all the rubrics correctly. Archbishop Martínez died on February 9, 1956, in the odor of sanctity. Within hours of his death, hundreds of thousands of pilgrims from all over Mexico flocked to pay their respects to the holy pastor of the whole country. Currently, Martínez is a Servant of God, and his cause for canonization is in process.

There is a word that Martínez uses constantly that captures the fatherly soul of this priest of Jesus Christ: *fecundo* or *fecundidad*. English speakers do not commonly use the term fecundity. Still, we decided not to use the more common English translation "fruitfulness" for *fecundidad* because fecundity denotes more than generic fruitfulness, though it does include this signification. Fecundity signifies both generation or giving life—the beginning of the process—and also extends to the meaning of fruitfulness, which especially signifies the result of the process of giving life. For Martínez, the great spiritual father, the spiritual life was about rebirth in Christ and, for priests, about spiritually begetting others in the faith by grace after the manner of St. Paul (1 Cor 4:15).

Another uncommonly used English word that we translate is vicissitude. Martínez uses *vicisitud* in a manner similar to *miseria*, which Bishop Daniel Flores explains well in the Foreword. It is a common term the Archbishop uses to convey life's chaotic change, disorder, and unsteadiness. Martínez uses it so frequently that we thought it necessary to translate the word consistently so that readers would be able to track when he uses the word and understand the nuances he places on it. Martínez recognizes the messiness of life but also the power of grace that operates in human weakness. In fact, Martínez chose as his episcopal motto 2 Cor 12:10: *Cum infirmor, tunc potens sum; for when I am weak, then I am strong.*

As for dating, some of the sermons are dated in the original collection but some are not. Nonetheless, we know that the sermons collated in this volume span most of Martínez's life. Thus, the reader enjoys a grand survey of Martínez's thought throughout the years and can appreciate the consistency and depth with which he teaches about the sacred priesthood.

By now, from his biography, it should be evident that Martínez studied, experienced, and lived out the priesthood in a unique and mystical way. The wealth of his experience shines all the more brightly through his preaching in these sermons. He was spiritually fecund in the lives of many. The translator hopes this work may perpetuate his fecundity and produce holy priests of Jesus Christ. May the anointed words of Archbishop Luis María Martínez help all the faithful of Christ's Church understand more fully the great wonder that is the priesthood of Jesus Christ.

THE PRIEST

MYSTERY OF LOVE

CHAPTER 1

The Mystery of the Priesthood

A DISCOURSE ON THE PRIESTHOOD

I

Diliges me plus his?
Do you love me more than these?
(John 21:15)

It was a radiant morning. On the waters of Lake Tiberias, rosy by the light of dawn, the boat of St. Peter lazily approached the shore, and over the ruddy bank the figure of Jesus began to rise, noble and so sweet. St. John spotted him before everyone else, the apostle with virginal soul, pure gaze, and loving heart. *It is the Lord!* he said to Peter (John 21:7), and Peter, always impetuous and audacious, did not wait for the boat to touch the shore but threw himself into the water to get closer to Jesus more quickly.

The divine resurrected one asks his friends for food, and they serve him a simple meal with immense love from what they have just caught. Like the old patriarch blessed Jacob after eating what his son had prepared for him, Jesus, after that hearty meal, strikes up with Peter the ineffable dialogue of love, the unforgettable and immortal dialogue that extends throughout the centuries, vivifying with its ardor, its aroma, its divine efficacy the Roman pontificate (John 21:15-19).

Simon, son of John, do you love me more than these?

With what emotion would the divine lips pronounce these words! What ineffable accent, what inflection from heaven, Jesus would put in this loving question!

The heart of the great apostle throbbed with unfamiliar violence. Yes, he loved him! Neither the remembrance of his falls, nor the conviction of his misery, nor the distrust of his fragility was able to dissipate the holy confidence of his immense affection. Ah! The love that doubts itself is not love! Humble, but sure, Peter discovers the profundity of his love before the unfailing light of divine knowledge.

Yes, Lord, you know that I love you!

And Jesus, satisfied, says to Peter:

Feed my lambs.

Three times that question of love resounds on the shores of Lake Tiberias, which "always being said is never repeated again,"[1] and three times St. Peter repeats the victorious word of love that is sure of itself.

What deep emotion, what variety of sentiments the apostle would experience when he said, *Lord, you know everything; you know that I love you!* And Jesus, completely sure of the disciple's love, expands his divine response, saying, *Feed my sheep*, which is the full priestly blessing, the gift of perpetual fecundity, the supreme reward of love on earth.

Observing a due proportion, that sweetest dialogue of love is mysteriously repeated in the intimacy of all priestly hearts. Since we are cooperators with Peter, since we participate in his priesthood and in his mission to the degree that corresponds to us in the place that we occupy in the hierarchy, the mystery of love and fecundity that lies in the depths of the priesthood is brought about in our souls. We are priests because we love, and because Jesus asked us the question of love and we ourselves gave him Peter's sweetest response of love, he puts in our consecrated hands and in our priestly hearts his precious treasure of souls.

Do you love me more than these? This question is a very sweet confession of love, since no one but he who loves has the right to make such an interrogation, to ask if he is loved. And if he asks of us a singular love, it is because he loves us with predilection as well. Ah, yes! Jesus singularly loves us priests; we sprout from the depths of his heart at the impulse of a most fine love and at the expense of an exquisite sorrow.

Jesus left his precious treasures on earth—the Gospel, the cross, the Eucharist, souls—and he needed the fidelity of a unique love in order to guard those treasures. That is why from the intimacy of his heart he brought out the mystery of the priesthood—the complement of all his mysteries, the deposit of all his secrets, the most faithful guardian of all his mysteries.

Yes, he loves us more than the rest, he loves us tenderly, with heavenly love, with divine passion, with incomprehensible delicacy, with ineffable self-denial. If we knew how much he loves us!

But no, most sweet Jesus, you do well to veil discreetly for us the loving mystery, because if you told us with complete clarity how much you love us, if you gave us the full revelation of your most sweet secret, we would die, and we need to live in order to guard your treasures, to feed your souls, to suffer for you. Tomorrow, in the eternal fatherland, in the place where no one dies, you will give us the marvelous revelation. But now, while we bear the divine treasures in the fragile vessel of our flesh, tell us your secret of love, as much as is necessary so that our poor hearts burn, but remember our misery and cover with a merciful veil your unfathomable mystery...

On the day of our priestly ordination, the bishop said to us in the solemn moments in which our first sacrifice was consummated the same words that Jesus said to his apostles on the night of the mysteries: *I no longer call you slaves, because a slave does not know what his master is doing. I have called you friends, because I have told you everything I have heard from my Father* (John 15:15).[2] Sweetest love, founded in the full communion of the divine secrets! All he heard from the Father he has told us. He opened his heart to us and poured into ours all his secrets: the secret of his light and the secret of his glory, the secret of his joy and the secret of his sorrow, the secret of his fecundity and the secret of his love.

He named the love he gave us friendship, but it is not only friendship. It encloses all the nuances of human affections, and, like the manna in the desert, for the soul it has all the celestial savors of love. What does it matter that to be priests we have had to renounce all the affections of the world, even the legitimate and noble ones, if, in exchange for all that we asked, we found the precious pearl of this ineffable love of Jesus? He is everything for us: father, mother, son, brother, friend, and something more that has no analogy with earthly things, something that language does not express nor intelligence defines, but that the heart enjoys in intimate silence.

In order to make out him who loves us, it suffices to look at what he gives us: his Eucharist, the compendium of all his wonders, close and eternally united with our priesthood; and the souls which he bought with his blood, which are destined for the loving embrace, for the eternal union of heaven. All that he has and all that he loves, even all that he is, he put in our hands, he deposited in our hearts.

And because he loves us in this way, he asks us if we ourselves also love him with predilection. In order to hand the Church over into the hands of Peter, he asked him no more than one question three times repeated: *Do you love me more than these?* If we would have had to confide to Peter the mission that Jesus confided to him, we would have asked him, without a doubt, innumerable questions, a whole exam, to assure ourselves of his prudence, of his fortitude, of his fidelity. Jesus asked nothing of him but love because he knows that it is enough. "Love and do what you will," said St. Augustine,[3] and the Apostle teaches that charity coordinates all the virtues and brings about all miracles: *Love is patient, love is kind...It bears all things, believes all things, hopes all things* (1 Cor 13:4,7).

The first and, in a certain way, the only thing that Jesus asks of his priests is that we love him. The simplicity of divine things disconcerts us; that is why we cannot understand that, more than our words, more than our sacrifices, Jesus asks of us our love, and of all the many great things that a priest can do, the greatest is to love Jesus. Without this love our words are hollow and sterile, our works and even our sacrifices are nothing. Is it not this that the Apostle teaches us in his magnificent praise of love?

If we love Jesus, from the abundance of our hearts our lips will speak and from the plenitude of our interior life our exterior apostolate will overflow, fecund like the word of God, burning like the fire Jesus came to earth to bring, fast-flowing and full like the torrents that come down from the mountains, and the apostolate, like those things, will leave precious seeds from heaven so that souls will have life and have it in abundance.

Do you love me more than these? Jesus says to us with the yearning of one who loves infinitely, with the ardor of one who seeks to be loved without measure, with the vehemence of one who has placed his whole soul in a love, with the tenderness that can only exist in his heart.

Do you love me more than these? As if he said: Do you love me even to the extreme of renouncing for my sake all the things of this world and all the affections of this earth? Do you love me even to the degree of emptying your heart so that my love fills it, so that it becomes the sovereign of your soul, the only one of your heart? Do you love me with inviolable, eternal, and victorious fidelity? Do you love me even to sacrifice, even to death? Do you love me so that I am your allotted portion and your cup (Ps 16:5)? Do you love me with this priestly love, which is like a reflection of the love of my Father, like the likeness of that virginal tenderness that enveloped me on the earth when the miracle of the Incarnation came about?

Do you love me more than these? Many souls love me on earth with a passionate ardor, with exquisite tenderness, with heroic self-denial. The virgins love me in inviolate purity, living on the earth as the angels of God live in heaven; the martyrs love me in pain and in blood; the contemplatives love me in silence and in light; penitents love me in roughness and in sacrifice; and some souls love me, like Mary, in rest, and others, like Martha, in activity; some with delicacy, others with tenderness, still others with humility. Oh, my priest! *Do you love me more than these?* More than the simple faithful, more than religious? Do you love me as I have loved you, with a singular predilection?

We told him on the day of our ordination, in the splendor of our youth, in the plenitude of our strength, in the simplicity of our heart, in the most pure and virginal candor of our soul: *Yes, Lord, you know that I love you!*

And our word was sincere, and our promise broke out from the depths of our soul! How could we not have told him that we love him? True love is always sure of itself. And I think that, although we could have probed the future and in him we could have contemplated our struggles and pains, our vicissitudes and even our frailties, we always would have said to him the word of love, as after many years of priestly life, in which we have had the experience of pain and joy, of triumph and defeat, of our love and our frailty, still we snowy-haired men tell him, and despite the memories of our miseries, what we told him in the radiant spring of our life: *Lord, you know everything; you know that I love you!*

Of course we love you, most sweet Jesus, as poor creatures, not with your always faithful, always full, always victorious love with which you love us. We love you with all the vicissitudes of time, with all the ups and downs of human life, with all the deficiencies of our frailty. But we love you, Lord, you yourself know it; and you, who pardon our falls, who forget our ingratitude, who loved Peter after his denials and Paul after he persecuted you, you love us also, poor and imperfect, and you accept the heavenly elixir of our love, although it is poured out in the fragile and earthly chalice of our misery!

In this mutual love of Jesus and his priests is the intimacy and secrecy of our priesthood. Those who look at us from the outside cannot guess what we carry inside, nor do they even suspect our sweet secret. For enemies, we are hypocritical exploiters of the people; for the worldly, we are worthy of pity because we do not sit at the loud and empty feast of the pleasures of the world. Some respect us, but they do not understand us; others love us without knowing why; even those who know that we are *servants of Christ and stewards of the mysteries of God* (1 Cor 4:1) have no idea of the intimacies of our heart.

There are still priests forgetful of what they are, who do not recognize the gift of God, and who do not enjoy the hidden manna anymore, which should be their food. But in the eyes of God and in the illumined eyes of faithful priests, the priesthood is a mystery of love, of mutual and singular love, of a unique love that encloses the charm of all the affections of the earth and that is the likeness of the love of the Father, the virginal reflection of the tenderness of Mary.

And this unfathomable mystery conceals itself in the delightful dialogue of Lake Tiberias between the divine Jesus and the fervent apostle, in that radiant morning in which the sun shone brightly over the crystalline lake, and the perfumes of the spring permeated the air, and the canticles of love of the birds of heaven resounded in the clear air...

II

Pasce agnos meos...pasce oves meas.
Feed my lambs...feed my sheep.
(JOHN 21:15,17)

TO the precious confession of love from St. Peter, Jesus answered with the gift of fecundity.

These profound phrases of Jesus—*Feed my lambs...feed my sheep*—are the ineffable reward of that cry of love: *Lord, you know that I love you!* And those words of Jesus, efficacious because they are divine, envelop the mystery of that fecundity that has diffused true life into the world for twenty centuries and will continue diffusing it until the end of time, as those words of Peter keep the secret of that love, unique and victorious, which is not extinguished, which does not lose heart, and which keeps with immense tenderness and with exquisite solicitude the divine treasures of Jesus. Upon that confession of love and that mystery of fecundity rests the unfailing and immortal Church.

As the priest participates in Peter's love, he also participates in his fecundity. The reward of priestly love is souls; because the priest loves Jesus, he has the celestial gift of giving life to souls.

Judging superficially, it would seem that to feed souls is a burden, a trial that Jesus imposes on priestly love in order to appreciate its sincerity, to measure its strength, to reward it at the end. As if Jesus, upon saying to the priest *Feed my lambs*, wanted to say to him: since you love me, you will help me carry my cross and you will take upon your shoulders the very heavy burden of souls that love will make sweet and light.

But it is not like that; souls are not the trial that the priest has to bear in order to achieve the fulfilled joy of his love, like Jacob had to work for fourteen years in order to win the hand of Rachel. No, souls are the earthly reward of priestly love and its eternal crown.

For a mother, are not her children the reward of her love? Are not souls the prize of Jesus's love and the fruit of his sorrow?

All fecundity comes from the Father, the principle of every being, of every life, of every perfection, in heaven and on earth; and the Father, in the excess of his love, communicated to the Son with whom he is well pleased, to Jesus, his divine fecundity: *You gave him authority over all people, so that he may give eternal life to all you gave him* (John 17:2). The Father loved Jesus, he sent him to the world, and he gave him the power to give life.

In the priestly prayer that Jesus directed to the Father on the night before his Passion, he expresses the supreme longing of his soul, the reward of his fulfilled mission, and it is that all whom the Father gave him might be enveloped by the same glory and the same love: *I have given them the glory you gave me* (John 17:22), *that the love with which you loved me may be in them and I in them* (John 17:26). The reward of Jesus is his perfect fecundity in souls.

What is more, he shared with his priests the love and mission that he received from the Father: *As the Father loves me, so I also love you* (John 15:9), *as the Father has sent me, so I send you* (John 20:21). And as a divine corollary of that love and of that mission, he communicated to them the magnificent gift of fecundity, which is the highest end and the precious reward of the priesthood.

Because Jesus loves us like the Father loved him, because he has sent us like the Father sent him, for that reason he gave us the wonderful power of giving life to souls, of having the marvelous fecundity enclosed in these brief words: *Feed my sheep.*

We are not only shepherds, we are fathers. That is what the faithful call us, and rightly so, because we truly are. St. Paul boasted of this eminently priestly title when he said to the faithful in Corinth: *Even if you should have countless guides to Christ, yet you do not have many fathers, for I became your father in Christ Jesus through the gospel* (1 Cor 4:15). And this sentiment of his spiritual paternity swells the heart of the apostle with tenderness when he writes to the Galatians: *My children, for whom I am again in labor until Christ be formed in you!* (Gal 4:19). And with his familiar audacity, St. Paul declares that his children are his *joy and crown* (Phil 4:1), that is, the reward of his heroic and glorious apostolic ministry.

We are fathers because Jesus shared with us the gift of giving life to souls, the true life that he brought us, eternal life. Each one of our ministries is to give life. We give it when baptizing because baptism is a rebirth *of water and Spirit* (John 3:5); we give it in the sacrament of penance to those souls who lost it through sin; we give it, above all, in the Eucharist, since through this wonderful sacrament we give Jesus, who is life itself.

Even in preaching we give life, because our words are not, nor should they be, *persuasive words of wisdom* (1 Cor 2:4), like St. Paul said, but rather they should be the very words of Jesus, those which, as he said, are *spirit and life* (John 6:63). Precisely by his preaching, the apostle engendered the Corinthians, of whom he declares himself to be their only father in Christ.

More principally, where we give life to the world, where our fecundity takes on sublime characteristics, is on the altar. The prophet Ezekiel, by the mandate of God, called the Spirit to come from the four winds to vivify the heap of dry bones that were strewn about on the field of death. And from those most sad mortal remains arose a living and powerful army (Ezek 37:1-14). On the altar we effect a greater marvel: we make the Word made flesh come down from heaven, and from the material substances of bread and wine we make rise the splendor of the Father, the substantial glory of God, he who is life. And we offer life to the Father so that he might be glorified, and we give life to souls so that they are nourished, satiated, sanctified, and happy.

The only other similar fecundity is that which the world contemplated astonishedly in Bethlehem, when a Virgin showed men, in her immaculate hands, Jesus, the blessed fruit of her womb; and that other ineffable and eternal fecundity that constitutes the divine joy of the Lord, whose secret the psalmist revealed to us with these unfathomable words: *You are my son; today I have begotten you* (Ps 2:7).

Who would believe it! We can repeat the echo of those words on the altar when we say the words that Jesus taught us to say in the Upper Room. In our consecrated hands, the Father engenders his divine Word, and he, who did not use an instrument to accomplish the wondrous work of creation, takes our fragile, creaturely lips in order to accomplish a work greater than the creation of the universe: the marvel of the Eucharist.

Ah, yes! The priest gives life. Better yet: the priest does not know how, is not able, to do anything other than give life. If he is wise, eloquent, artistic, a man of heart or of action—all this is accidental to his priesthood. His proper function, his unique function, is to give life.

Our priestly word gives life, our apostolic action is vivifying, and the priestly sentiments of our heart, which should be the same as the heart of Jesus, are the life that overflows in torrents of divine love and fertile sorrow.

And to give life is always a joy, a joy and a reward of love. The eternal joy of the Lord is the ineffable mystery of his divine fecundity: the joy of the Father, which engenders the Word; the joy of the Father and of the Son, which spirates the Holy Spirit. The mystery of the august Trinity is the mystery of the intimate life of God and of his eternal joy.

And whoever participates in the love of the Father participates in his fecundity; that is why the shadow of the Father casts itself over all that lives, communicating to it the reflection of his love, fecundity, and joy.

But more than over every other creature, if we exclude the Virgin Mary, that shadow of the Father—intense, majestic, divine—casts itself over every priest, enveloping him in love and fecundity.

The mystery of the priesthood is a mystery of love and fecundity, and it is a mystery of fecundity because it is a mystery of love.

The dialogue of Lake Tiberias expresses all the secrets of the priesthood. When St. Peter says to Jesus, *Lord, you know that I love you*, he made the formula of priestly love. But that love is the fruit of other loves, the love of Jesus and the love of the Father; it is the oasis of that divine waterfall of love that springs from the bosom of the Father and that springs from the divine heart of Jesus to flood the heart of the priest, who must in turn pour it out into souls. And the formula of fecundity answers the formula of love: *Feed my lambs*, the divine formula that contains with the secret of giving life the sweetest promise, the most copious blessing, and the most perfect reward.

The patriarchs of the Old Testament considered themselves happy and judged their fidelity to the Lord rewarded when they heard the mysterious word of fecundity in the midst of mysterious dreams: *I will bless you and make your descendants as countless as the stars of the sky and the sands of the seashore* (Gen 22:17). The priest receives a more perfect blessing: that of innumerable souls who will gather around him like olive shoots, to whom he will give, not the life of time, miserable and fleeting, but eternal life, which consists in *know[ing] you, the only true God, and the one whom you sent, Jesus Christ* (John 17:3), which brings with it the possession of God through Jesus Christ our Lord.

Jesus, generous, benevolent, who promises eternal life to him who gives a glass of water in his name (Matt 10:42), could not leave the love of his priests without a reward worthy of him. And at the cry of a unique and victorious love—*Lord, you know that I love you*—he responds with an unutterable promise of fecundity, with the divine gift par excellence, with the reflection of the heavenly Father, which was the reward of the same love of Jesus; and from the shores of Lake Tiberias, infused with heavenly perfumes, the divine promise comes forth and spreads into priestly hearts throughout the centuries: *Feed my sheep*...

III

Cum esses junior cingebas te... cum autem senueris... alius te cinget.
When you were younger, you used to dress yourself...
but when you grow old... someone else will dress you.
(John 21:18)

Three times Jesus asked Peter if he loves him; three times the apostle made his sincere confession of love; and three times the divine Master gave him the supreme blessing of fecundity.

All appeared to be finished, because what can love lack when it is mutual and fecund? What does he lack who has said the word of love, without ever repeating it, like Father Lacordaire said?

And, nevertheless, Jesus has not finished: on that same bank of Lake Tiberias, in that same hour of love, and under the impulse of the same holy emotion, he continues saying to St. Peter, if possible with greater solemnity because he uses a formula that in the language of Scripture involves an oath, the following very profound words: *Amen, amen, I say to you, when you were younger, you used to dress yourself and go where you wanted; but when you grow old, you will stretch out your hands, and someone else will dress you and lead you where you do not want to go.* And the evangelist explains the meaning of these words, saying*: He said this signifying by what kind of death he would glorify God. And when he had said this, he said to him, "Follow me"* (John 21:18-19).

In the school of Jesus, after the word of love, another word can be said, that of sacrifice; after the blessing of fecundity, which appears to be the supreme one, comes another more perfect blessing, the blessing of the cross.

And this word and this blessing, which are the last and definitive ones on earth, flow from the lips of Jesus and envelope the Prince of the Apostles as the breezes full of the perfumes of spring enveloped him in that radiant and unforgettable morning.

The mystery of the august mission of Peter was not fully expressed with the immortal dialogue, because in order to consummate that highest mission it was necessary that the confession of love and the blessing of fecundity be crowned with the promise of martyrdom made with the solemnity of an oath. And when Jesus gave the cross to Peter as a supreme sign of his pontificate, he could already tell him the divine conclusion of that inexpressible poem: *Follow me!*

And Peter has gone in pursuit of Jesus for twenty centuries, continuing the most beautiful scene of Lake Tiberias by his perennial confession of love, by his inexhaustible fecundity, and by his perpetual martyrdom.

If we priests share in the love and the fecundity of Peter, it is logical that we share in his cross. Jesus promised it to us many times, above all on the night of the Upper Room. Even to the simple faithful he offered the cross! But if he had not promised it to us, we would be crying out for it. What would become of us without the cross?

I have just said that the cross is above love and fecundity. This is inaccurate; it would be better to say that the cross is the supreme expression of love and fecundity, and therefore that our love would not be priestly love if it did not crucify us, and our fecundity would not be the divine fecundity that gives life to souls if it did not flow from martyrdom.

Human love knows about sacrifice, because if it did not know it, it would not be love; whoever loves with that love is immolated, but with what timidity, with what weakness, with how many reservations! Divine love reaches to the bottom of the mystery of sacrifice; whoever possesses this love does not stop until the cross, until he is immolated, and until he is immolated without measure! That divine love throbbed in the heart of Jesus, and Jesus nailed himself to the cross; the Father infinitely loves the Son with whom he is well pleased and delivered him to the cross.

Our judgment is confused and our hearts tremble before this love *strong as death* (Song 8:6). What love is that which, having proposed joy, prefers the cross?

When divine love comes to possess a heart, it infallibly encloses within it the burning thirst for sacrifice. Mary loved as even the seraphim have not come to love, and at the foot of the cross she offered the immolation of Jesus to the Father and opened the bosom of her soul to be pervaded with the perfume of myrrh of her beloved Son. St. Andrew loved and greeted the cross of his martyrdom as the most passionate husband greets the chosen one of his heart. St. Ignatius of Antioch loved, and with all the ardor of a soul impatient to suffer, he wrote these inimitable words: "I am the wheat of Christ, I will be crushed by the teeth of wild beasts to become immaculate bread."[4] St. John of the Cross loved, and as the only reward of his life he asked "to suffer and be despised for Jesus."[5] And for the incomparable love of St. Thérèse of the Child Jesus all the martyrdoms that have been suffered and will be suffered in the world were not enough.[6]

What is it about love that yearns for sacrifice like that? It could be said that love is a thirst for suffering.

Now then: if we priests have to love more than others, we need to suffer more than them. If all love were not a desire for sacrifice, priestly love would be, as a copy and participation of that inexpressible love of Jesus, whose constant yearning was to drink the chalice of the Passion, whose supreme fruit was the cross, and whose perpetuation was the Eucharist.

Neither the sweet words on our lips, nor the tender tears in our eyes, nor the passionate sentiments of our hearts, nor even the fruitfulness of our apostolic life are enough to manifest our priestly love to Jesus, to fulfill what we promised to the Lord when we told him like Peter: *Yes, Lord, you know that I love you!*

Priestly love demands the cross and impels him to embrace it, exclaiming like St. Andrew: "Hail, oh precious cross! Receive the disciple of him who was nailed to you and who in you receives me, who in you redeemed me."[7] In these words are enclosed the supreme motive of the priestly cross; we embrace it with joy, because we ardently love Jesus; we embrace it, because on it Jesus loved us.

The priesthood is a mystery of sacrifice because it is a mystery of love.

The supreme act of Jesus's priesthood was to immolate himself on the cross out of love; the supreme act of priestly love is to immolate Jesus mystically on the altars, but to immolate him by carrying in our hearts the same sentiments of the divine heart, offering ourselves as a victim with him, joining our poor immolations with the divine ones of Jesus.

The fecundity of the priest also requires the cross, because sacrifice is the key to fecundity.

This is how Jesus taught us, saying: *Unless a grain of wheat falls to the ground and dies, it remains just a grain of wheat; but if it dies, it produces much fruit* (John 12:24). To give life it is necessary to suffer:

wheat dies to multiply itself; the woman suffers terrible pain to give birth; Jesus, to give us true life, died on a cross. From that blessed cross, from his torn heart, flowed streams of life that fill the world. The Eucharist, which is a sacrament of life and fecundity, is a sacrament of sacrifice. *For as often as you eat this bread and drink the cup, you proclaim the death of the Lord until he comes*, says St. Paul (1 Cor 11:26). And the marvelous fecundity of the Church, has it not developed in the Calvary of constant persecutions?

He who does not know how to suffer will remain alone in the sad isolation of sterility; to give life it is necessary to be nailed to the cross.

And the priest has to give his life, this is his proper function, his highest mission, and his ineffable reward; like Jesus, the priest can say: *I came so that they might have life and have it more abundantly* (John 10:10).[8]

There is no other life-giving knowledge than what Jesus taught, the knowledge of the cross; there is no other method to save souls than the one that Jesus practiced, ascending the tortuous ascent of Calvary and being nailed to the cross.

Of course, before going up to Calvary, Jesus began to work and to teach (Acts 1:1), but neither his words of eternal life, nor his stupendous wonders, nor his admirable examples were anything other than seeds that only bore fruit when the divine blood watered them. The priest, like Jesus, must teach and give holy examples; but for his teachings and his action to be fruitful, he must water them with his tears and with his sacrifices.

There is nothing more fecund than suffering; Jesus put his omnipotent efficacy in it. To joyfully collect the piles of the opulent harvest, one must water with tears the furrow in which the seed is deposited. To have numerous offspring, like *the stars of the sky and the sands of the seashore* (Gen 22:17), one must make the supreme sacrifice like Abraham on Mount Moriah (Gen 22:2).[9]

St. Thérèse of the Child Jesus could not comprehend how good was done for souls without sacrifice, and for this reason she used the weapons of prayer and sacrifice to do good for her novices. When will we understand this capital doctrine? When will we be convinced that the best thing we can do for souls is to suffer for them?

St. Paul expressed the burning zeal of his immense heart as an apostle in this energetic formula: *I will most gladly spend and be utterly spent for your sakes* (2 Cor 12:15). The priest must give everything for souls: his goods, his time, his tastes, his words, his actions; but after giving everything, he must give the supreme gift to souls, the gift of himself, giving them his heart on fire and torn with sorrow, like the heart of the Eternal Priest.

Suffering gives effectiveness to all our ministries, and the supreme ministry of the priest is to suffer for souls, just as the supreme ministry of Jesus was the sacrifice of Calvary.

To give life you have to suffer, as a woman suffers terrible pains to give birth to her child; the priest needs to suffer the anguish of death to give birth to souls until Jesus is formed in them.

Earlier, I had said that it is the supreme joy to give one's life; now I affirm that one cannot give life without suffering; and although superficially considered these affirmations seem incompatible, in reality they are not but rather they form a divine paradox of the mystery of fecundity. Jesus gave life to souls, carrying in his heart the joy of heaven and the suffering of hell, and the life he gave us is at the same time the fruit of his joy and his suffering.

When the priest received a share of the power to give life, Jesus gave him a share of the secret of his suffering and his joy; that is why the priest carries in his heart the fecund martyrdom and the heavenly joy of giving life. The priestly joy *par excellence* is the exquisite joy of suffering deeply so that souls may have life, and in a lofty sense one can say what the psalmist says: *When cares increase within me, your comfort gives me joy* (Ps 94:19).

Souls are the joy and the martyrdom of the priest, as they were the joy and the martyrdom of Jesus.

The Beloved Disciple, the evangelist of life and of love, kept for us in an exquisite page the heavenly scene of Lake Tiberias.

All the mysteries of the priesthood are there: the deep and sincere confession of love, the divine promise of fecundity, and the mysterious announcement of martyrdom. With these perfumes from heaven the priestly anointing is formed, which, poured out on Aaron's head, gently descends through his ruddy beard and reaches the hem of his cloak (Ps 133:2).

Would to God that the fragrance of those aromas spread throughout the world and pervade all priestly hearts, just as the breezes of Lake Tiberias spread the perfumes of spring on that splendid morning in which love passed along the shores of that unforgettable sea like a burst of light from the eternal fatherland!

CHAPTER 2

Jesus and the Priesthood in the Mystery of the Ascension

AT A FIRST MASS

Ascendens in altum, captivam duxit captivitatem:
dedit dona hominibus.
He ascended on high and took prisoners captive;
he gave gifts to men.
(Ephesians 4:8)

All the mysteries of Jesus are linked and harmonized wonderfully with the unfathomable mystery of the priesthood.

And it is logical that it be this way. On the one hand, the priest is another Christ, and if he is, he has to reproduce mystically in his priestly life the mysteries of Jesus's life. On the other hand, the center of the life and mission of Jesus Christ is his priesthood. And that is why all the mysteries of Christ have a priestly savor, a priestly sense. That is why we can, naturally, unite in a single thought the two mysteries that at present call our attention and excite our piety.

With Holy Church we celebrate the mystery of the wonderous Ascension of the Lord, of that mystery that is like the consummation of his entire mortal life. Can we cease to rejoice with the Church and with the supreme triumph of Jesus? Can we cease to fix our eyes on that mysterious height where he took our hearts?

But, on the other hand, a brother of ours goes today for the first time to celebrate the most sacred sacrifice of the Mass. Can we allow ourselves to fix our gazes on him? Can we allow ourselves to rejoice with him today, which is the day of his nuptials and the joy of his heart?

Then let us unite the two mysteries, and let us not fear for one instant that we might lose the unity of the thought: because the two are united, because they are like two facets of the same diamond. Both mysteries, that of the Ascension of Jesus and that of the priesthood, can be expressed in one formula, the one that St. Paul takes from the psalms and explains admirably: *He ascended on high and took prisoners captive; he gave gifts to men.*

I

THE whole mystery of grace, of redemption, and of the sanctification of souls is enclosed, if you will allow me the word, in two journeys, in two divine pilgrimages: the Word of God who descends, and the Word of God who ascends, who ascends taking what he gathers from the earth. Thus says the apostle St. Paul: *What does "he ascended" mean except that he also descended into the lower regions of the earth?* (Eph 4:9).

In order to ascend to heaven, it is necessary first to descend from heaven. We miserable, impotent sinners, carrying in our flesh and in our soul the saddest marks of the first sin, would never have been able to know the way, nor would we have had the necessary strength to ascend to heaven; but he who was in heaven descended to us and took us in his hands, he took us with him.

Have we not seen what the birds do, who hover in the heights and with a penetrating gaze see their prey in the bottom of the valleys and descend rapidly and snatch it and take it up with them? This the Word of God did: from the heights of his divinity he looked upon us as his prey, his prey of love, his prey of mercy, and his infinite heart was not only filled with compassion, with tenderness, with love for us but also had the crazy idea to enamor itself with our littleness and our misery. And he came down to earth, and took with his most holy hands that prey, and put it on his heart, and returned to ascend to the divine heights from which he had descended.

Because when Jesus Christ ascended to heaven, he did not ascend alone: he lifted us up with him. Because the Word of God came to this world and united himself to our poor nature, Jesus's destiny and our destinies cannot be separated: he shares our destiny and we share his to such a degree that we truly participate in all his mysteries.

Holy Church is careful to tell us in its liturgy that the mysteries of Jesus are for us, not simply memories but realities. Thus, in the joy of Christmas we intone this most beautiful canticle: "Christ was born for us,"[1] and for us he lived thirty years on earth, for us he hid in Nazareth, for us he preached on the shores of Lake Tiberias, for us he died on Calvary.

St. Ambrose says that in Christ the universe resurrected, heaven resurrected, and earth resurrected.[2] No longer will Jesus be able to do anything alone. We are united with him, and all that he does we will do, and wherever he goes we will also go with him.

So, when he ascends to heaven he does not go alone; the Word of God takes, of course, our own nature, with which he united himself hypostatically. For the first time, this fruit of the earth appeared in heaven: a human body, a human soul. In those lofty and mysterious places, there was nothing more than spirits; since the day on which Jesus rose, there has been a body and a soul, our poor human nature, and a company of souls that had waited for their redemption in the bosom of Abraham.

When we ascend, we all ascend—in principle and justly—to heaven; if Jesus had not ascended, no one would have been able to ascend. Because he ascended, we ascend; for this reason, Holy Scripture says that upon ascending to heaven he took captivity captive.

We were held captive by the devil because of sin; but Jesus, conquering the devil, snatched his prey from him; and just as the victors bind the vanquished to their triumphal cart, Jesus, with his bonds of love, with the holy ties of charity, bound us to his triumphal cart, and thus we accompany him in his victorious entry to heaven. We are captives of love. Jesus came and robbed our hearts from us.

But Jesus not only elevated poor humanity—he also took to himself certain fruits of our nature that we did not even suspect were able to ascend to heaven: he took, in a certain manner, our suffering. Do we not see in the resurrected humanity of our Lord Jesus the most holy wounds of his hands, of his feet, of his side, the marks of suffering? It is the perpetuated, sanctified, in a certain manner, divinized suffering that rises to heaven. In heaven there were flowers of perennial love, flowers of everlasting joy—but suffering had never appeared. Jesus, when he descended to earth, took it upon himself and desired that it be eternally in heaven, crystallized and perpetuated in his most holy wounds.

And I believe that with his own suffering he took also all our sufferings, that in those most holy wounds all our pains, all our sufferings, are, in some manner, sanctified.

And whenever we go to heaven, on the day of the resurrection, when our mortal bodies resurrect at the all-powerful voice of the Lord, we will enter also carrying in our poor bodies the mark of our sufferings. Heaven will be like a kind of garden with all the flowers of love, of suffering, and of purity.

Like the wayfarer who goes to a far off and mysterious country and brings back exotic flowers that he has cut and carefully preserved so that his family can admire them, thus Jesus, upon rising to heaven, took with himself the flowers of the earth, the exquisite flowers of suffering.

But I hasten to affirm that it was not only a memory that Jesus wanted to take in his most holy wounds upon entering heaven. His wounds have a priestly meaning, they are, in a certain manner, the crowning and culmination of the sacrifice of the cross.

St. Paul is careful to explain this mystery (Heb 9). The Apostle says that, just as in the old law the High Priest would offer a special sacrifice one day of the year, and having in his hands the blood of the victim he entered the *Sancta Sanctorum*, so Jesus, not by the blood of common victims but by his own blood, entered one day into the *Sancta Sanctorum* (not into the one made by the hands of man, but into the bosom of the heavenly Father), carrying in his hands, in his side, in his feet his precious blood shed in the sacrifice of Calvary, so that from there he would descend transformed with magnificent gifts.

The Ascension of the Lord is the entry of Jesus into the *Sancta Sanctorum*; and as in the Old Law, Jesus needed to take in his most holy body the marks of his blood. And until he presented that precious blood to the heavenly Father upon his entry into heaven, his sacrifice remained unconsummated, and only when his sacrifice was consummated could the Holy Spirit be sent

On the eve of his Passion, Jesus said to his disciples: *Because I told you this, grief has filled your hearts. But I tell you the truth, it is better for you that I go. For if I do not go, the Advocate will not come to you* (John 16:6-7). The coming of the Holy Spirit is the precious fruit of the sacrifice of the cross.

And so that this fruit might come off mature and seasoned, it was necessary that the sacrifice was consummated fully, that Jesus entered into the *Sancta Sanctorum* of heaven. For this reason, ascending to the heights he not only took captivity captive: he also sent his gifts to men from there, or, to say it better, the gift of God, the gift par excellence, the Holy Spirit.

II

THESE slight indications are already enough in order to understand that the whole economy of grace and redemption is contained in these two divine pilgrimages: in the Word of God who descends from heaven and in the Word of God who ascends to heaven, carrying all of humanity with himself.

But Jesus, ascending to heaven, left on earth the secret of these two divine pilgrimages: to priests he taught the way to descend and ascend to heaven to him.

And the priesthood, the reproduction of the life of Jesus, is nothing other than those two pilgrimages: the priest ascends to heaven, and the priest descends from heaven. He also ascends to heaven bearing captivity captive; he is the eaglet, in the likeness of the divine Eagle, who descends and snatches his prey and lifts it up in his heart, and then descends from heaven, his hands bursting with the Spirit of God.

The ministry of the priesthood is nothing other than this ascent and this descent. In the younger days of this priest, when the hands of the bishop had not yet been placed on his head, he knew the ways of life, the paths of science and art, the paths of joy and suffering, and perhaps he walked in the path of iniquity. Now he has no right to know anything more than one way, the way that leads from earth to heaven.

The priest does not really have more than two functions: to ascend and descend, to ascend to heaven and descend to earth. To ascend to heaven carrying souls, bearing suffering, bearing disgraces, carrying in his body and in his soul the marks of sacrifice; to ascend in order to carry with himself all souls and hearts to Jesus.

The second function of the priest is to descend from heaven, bringing the Holy Spirit in order to pour him out into souls. The priestly function *par excellence* is to give Jesus, is to give God; the priest does not know, should not know, anything else; he should only know how to give God. Some give him under the magnificent guise of eloquence, others in the crude cover of simplicity and even of platitudes. What does the cover matter, when that cover encloses God!

Within a few moments this new priest is going to ascend to the altar. Is it not true that ascending to the altar is just like ascending to heaven? Is heaven not God? Is it not the bosom of the Father? Is it not the Most Sacred Heart of Jesus? Is it not the unction of the Holy Spirit?

"To be with Jesus is to be in paradise," the author of *The Imitation of Christ* would say,[3] and he said it because of an intimate and very sweet experience he had. On the altar, the all-powerful word of the priest is going to make the Word descend, like he descended twenty centuries ago into the immaculate womb of Mary, in order to return and ascend to heaven laden with hearts and souls. To that altar, Jesus will descend, and with him the Father and the Holy Spirit; on that altar heaven will be veiled, but heaven nonetheless.

After the consecration there is a mysterious prayer, in which the priest, with hands joined over the altar and making a profound bow, beseeches the Lord to descend and elevate those gifts and present them before the sight of the Most High, so that afterwards a torrent of heavenly blessings might descend over all those who are present at the Holy Mass: "Command that these gifts be borne by the hands of your holy Angel to your altar on high in the sight of your divine majesty."[4]

It is the mysterious revelation of the heaven of the altar. The angel of the Lord ascends to heaven, but he does not ascend alone. When the priest goes up to the altar, the Church goes with him, and so do souls with their prayers, their needs, their sufferings, and their tears. The priest ascends to the altar under this overwhelming weight, but he discharges it onto the heart of the immaculate Victim, and then he beseeches the holy angel of God to descend and take all those gifts to the sublime altar of heaven.

At this point of the Canon, the consummation of the eucharistic sacrifice is realized.

Then the priest descends.

This priest, our brother, will descend in a few moments from the altar with his hands laden with gifts, with a heart full of the Holy Spirit, and will pour him out upon the faithful so that they might be full of the blessing of Jesus Christ.

And let us not think that this ascension only takes place on the altar; no, it always takes place. What else should the mystery of preaching be? Many will think that it is a form of oratory, that to preach is nothing more than to apply to spiritual things what rhetoricians have taught. That is not Christian preaching.

The apostle St. Paul says: *It was the will of God through the foolishness of the proclamation to save those who have faith* (1 Cor 1:21). Common rhetoric, the oratory of the earth, can even be described as quite ridiculous or a bit tiring; but, why did they call it folly if it is in accord with reason? But the priest, as St. Paul says, never speaks with the persuasive words of men but rather with the manifestation of the power of God. If he possesses some eloquence of the earth, it is a secondary matter.

In what, then, does the mystery of preaching consist? The preacher is a man who has ascended to the heights of contemplation, who has felt his spirit and his heart bathed with the divine light, and who from the plenitude of contemplation allows some words to fall on the earth. Preaching must not be something other than fallen crumbs from the magnificent and divine banquet of contemplation; that is, preaching should be the mystery of ascending and descending from heaven. In order to preach, the priest needs to go up to the heaven of contemplation.

Contemplation is heaven because God is there, because there we see him with the eyes of our hearts, because there we feel our way around with the hands of our hope, because there we cling to him with the strongest embrace of love. And from that heaven of contemplation the priest descends, like Moses descended from the burning summit of Sinai, bearing on his head the signs of his contact with God, bearing something divine within his heart. Has it not ever happened that we approached a priest and felt some mysterious glimmer of glory? It is because he comes from heaven and still carries the memories of that land, and comes in order to give men gifts of love. The mystery of preaching is nothing other than the mystery of an ascent and a descent from heaven.

And what is the mystery of the direction of souls other than this same mystery? It might have been thought at first glance that priests can direct souls because they are intelligent, learned, full of experience, able, sagacious, spiritual pedagogues, who have learned classifications in order to know souls and formulas for advising them.

Certainly not. The priest is able to direct souls, as he is able to preach and say Mass, because he has descended from heaven and bears something divine in his soul. In order to direct, he needs first to ascend to heaven, ascend to the peak of perfection, to that heaven wherein God is found, to that summit about which the words of St. Paul can be repeated: *What does "he ascended" mean except that he also descended into the lower regions of the earth?*

And only when he has come down from that peak can he take by the hand the souls who are little, yet eager for perfection, in order to lead them by those paths full of mysteries unto the summit from which the priest has descended.

And so one may be able to continue explaining how all the functions of the priest are reduced to this: the priest must live in heaven, and he can only descend to the earth in order to bring to souls and pour into them the magnificent gifts of God.

You already know your mission, oh priest! Your priestly life should not be anything other than this ascent and descent.

If you learned before today other paths, forget them, because you must not know anything more than this royal way: the one that leads to heaven. You must ascend to the heaven of the altar constantly, ascending each day more lovingly, more saintly. You shall also ascend to the heaven of contemplation, and it is necessary that your wings grow so that each day your flight might be more rapid, more powerful and happy. You shall ascend, finally, to the heaven of perfection, for which you must work without rest until you fully realize the divine ideal.

But you will not ascend alone; priests, like Jesus, cannot be alone because with them is linked the fate of other souls, and wherever priests go it is necessary to take them.

Descend to earth, descend so that you can take the beloved prey of Jesus and carry in your heart the souls that you have to lead to heaven unto the sight of the Most High, to the immense bosom of the Father.

Descend, descend in order to bring souls the gifts of heaven, the unique gift of God, the Holy Spirit, who is the unfathomable font of all gifts.

Ascending and descending you will make souls very wonderful, you shall imitate Jesus, you shall console his divine heart, and you shall glorify the heavenly Father.

And one day, that will not be too far off, when you try to traverse for the last time the way from earth to heaven, you shall listen to a most sweet voice that will tell you: *Well done, my good and faithful servant. Since you were faithful in small matters, I will give you great responsibilities* (Matt 25:23). And then the divine Eagle, who is Jesus, will take your soul purified by suffering and will present it in the sight of the Most High so that you can enter perpetually into the joy of your Lord.

CHAPTER 3

The Outpouring of the Holy Spirit on Mary and on the Priest

AT A FIRST MASS

Spiritus Sanctus superveniet in te
et virtus Altissimi obumbrabit tibi.
The Holy Spirit will come upon you, and the
power of the Most High will overshadow you.
(LUKE 1:35)

GENIUSES have the mysterious privilege of putting their intangible mark, their unmistakable stamp, on their masterpieces; and great considerations are not needed for us to understand the mysterious connection, the artistic connection, that the masterpieces from the same genius have among themselves.

There are in the Church of God two marvelous works of divine artistry that have between them a mysterious connection, and in order to understand it, it suffices to contemplate the divine trace that the creating hand put in them. These two works of art are: Mary and the priesthood.

As a lily among thorns, the Virgin, beautiful, pure, carrying in her heart and in her hands the divine Jesus, emerges in the midst of this corrupt world; and also in the midst of the sea of life, the sea of history, arises solid, unchangeable, glorious, the Catholic priesthood, light of the world, salt of the earth, the divine likeness of Jesus.

These two masterful works of God have the divine trace of their author; the illumined eyes of our hearts discover their connection and the unity of their origin; both are masterpieces of wisdom and power, but, above all, of divine love.

Their origin is the infinite love, the personal love, of God. The Holy Spirit was the supreme craftsman who forged the heavenly form of the Most Holy Virgin and the monumental form of the Catholic priesthood.

We see these two mysteries united on top of Calvary, at the foot of the bloody cross, when two almighty words of Jesus resound over the earth: *Behold, your son.* And then: *Behold, your mother…* (John 19:26-27). And united, marvelously connected, these two mysteries have traversed history and will last until the consummation of the ages.

Mary and we are united, and no one will be able to separate us, because God united us.

And in a special way we feel today the necessity of uniting these two mysteries in one and the same solemnity, in one and the same joy: with the Church we celebrate the mystery of the Assumption of the Blessed Virgin, the mystery of her glory, of her consummation, the ultimate touch the divine craftsman put on her that her perfection would be complete; and the mystery of the priesthood enters into the deepest depths of our hearts, so to speak, when we see one of our brothers who, in the splendor of his youth, in the fullness of life, comes for the first time to approach the august altar to immolate the holy Victim, to enact the greatest act that one can celebrate on the earth.

And to connect these two mysteries that are connected in the Church and in our hearts, let us lift ourselves to the eternal love, and in the unity of the Holy Spirit, creator of Mary and creator of the priesthood, let us glimpse the marvelous harmony that the Spirit of the Lord established in those two masterpieces.

I

THE life of the Ever-Virgin Mary was a continuous Pentecost: day after day, instant by instant, the Spirit of the Lord was poured out into the most pure and immaculate soul of the Virgin. The outpouring of the Holy Spirit was not an intermittent occurrence but a perpetual spring, a font that gushed up in the depths of her being and leapt up to eternal life, like a mighty river that fills the city of God with rejoicing, according to the expression in the Scriptures (Ps 46:5). The Holy Spirit with his heavenly impulse, with his divine vigor, infused and filled the immaculate soul of the Virgin Mary with his charisms and graces.

But just as here on earth a river, whose crystalline waves are abundant, suddenly receives special floods, immense torrents of water that come from far away, from the high mountains, and the waves of the river swell, and its crystals expand, and its flow leaves the riverbed and floods the surrounding pasture, filling it with fecundity; just so, although the life of Mary was already a mighty river from when the Holy Spirit descended upon her with his grace, with his life, and with his fecundity, from time to time an exceptional flood, most abundant and impulsive, came from heaven, came from the very heart of God, swelling its flow; and the Holy Spirit poured himself out with growing vigor, with gentle vigor, upon the exceptional soul of the Blessed Virgin Mary.

The Scriptures and the teaching of the Church show us some of those exceptional floods that the Holy Spirit poured out into the soul of the highest Lady.

The first is a flood of purity. The Holy Spirit descended upon the soul of the Blessed Virgin Mary in the first instant of her conception—a mystery hidden to all human perception but manifest to the profound eyes of God.

What would that solemn mystery be like, the only one in the history of humanity? With what love, with what rapidity, with what vehemence, to speak in our language, did the Holy Spirit descend upon the soul of the Virgin Mary, and descending prevent the stain of original sin from sullying, even with an intangible breath, the soul of the sovereign Queen who by a stupendous wonder was going to be conceived without guilt, the only one among the daughters of Adam?

But the outpouring of the Holy Spirit did not only produce this negative effect of turning away from her the stain of malignancy, no; the theologians teach that the Holy Spirit poured into Mary such an influx of life that our poor spirit is helpless to glimpse it.

Let us think about the consummation that the saints receive from God after a long life of heroism and grace. Let us think about the men like St. Paul, like St. Francis Xavier, who after a long life of apostolic hardships arrive at the end of their existence and say with the audacity of the Apostle: *I have competed well; I have finished the race; I have kept the faith. From now on the crown of righteousness awaits me, which the Lord, the just judge, will award to me on that day* (2 Tim 4:7-8). Let us consider the consummation of the holy virgins, like St. Thérèse of the Child Jesus, who, after an immaculate life of self-emptying and of love until holocaust, release their spirits under the ardor of a heavenly caress of God. Let us consider all the saints, bring them together, sum up the abundance of the gifts that they received when their lives were consummated—and with this we will have an idea of what Mary Most Holy received in the very instant of her Immaculate Conception.

Unlike the saints, whom we celebrate on the day of their consummation, the Church celebrates Mary on the day of her Immaculate Conception, since the foundations of her perfection were then laid, and at that point she received more graces than the saints receive in their consummation. The outpouring of God was this, most pure and exceptional, that he poured out the plentitude of his graces and his gifts with a munificence truly divine.

This is the first outpouring of the Holy Spirit, the first flood that arrived at that immaculate soul: the outpouring of purity.

Time passed, and one day, in the silence of Nazareth, the Holy Spirit returned, if it is even possible, with greater love and with more vehemence than in the mystery of the Immaculate Conception, to descend upon the Most Holy Virgin.

An angel announced to the maiden of Nazareth the divine mystery. The words that he used are those that I have already cited: *Spiritus Sanctus superveniet in te et virtus Altissiimi obumbrabit tibi. The Holy Spirit will come upon you, and the power of the Most High will overshadow you*... And the mystery was fulfilled; and something very intimate, very holy, something divine, took place in the soul and in the body of Mary Most Holy: a new outpouring, ineffable and resplendent—the outpouring of fecundity.

We, with our narrow criteria, with our near-sighted eyes and our petty hearts, think sometimes that fecundity and purity are incompatible things. For us, the height of purity is virginity, and earthly virginity seems before our inept concept entirely incompatible with fecundity. But it is not like this: there is nothing more fecund than purity, there is nothing more fecund than virginity.

That is why God, who is infinite purity, who is—if you will allow me the expression—eternal virginity, is also fecundity without limit, all-powerful fecundity, infinite fecundity. That is why the Father, who is holy, who is most pure, not earthly, without composition in his divine, in his sovereign simplicity, eternally begets his Son, and from his most pure lips flow this unfathomable expression: *Filius meus es tu: ego hodie genui te. You are my Son; today I have begotten you* (Ps 2:7).

Who would have thought it! That fecundity of the heavenly Father was reflected in the most pure soul of Mary when the Holy Spirit descended upon her and communicated to her the secret of the divine fecundity.

Earthly fecundity—how narrow, how petty it is! The artist

produces a work of art, sterile and cold; the wise man makes a great discovery, ordinarily sterile; man is able to arrive at the glory of communicating life, of producing a being similar to himself.

The height of our fecundity is a man. The fecundity of the Most Holy Virgin had as its end Jesus! That is why the angel said to her: *The Holy Spirit will come upon you, and the power of the Most High will overshadow you. Therefore the child to be born will be called holy.*

And in that unforgettable moment, and under the impulse of that divine word, Mary became the Mother of God, and the world contemplated in her hands Jesus, and the world has received him from those blessed hands in every age.

Thirty years later, the influx of fecundity was completed. What are thirty years for God, before whose presence *a thousand years in your eyes are merely a day gone by* (Ps 90:4)? Between Nazareth and the Upper Room there is time, there is distance, but in the supernatural order they are a perfect unity. The Upper Room is the natural complement of Nazareth.

In Nazareth, Mary received the fecundity that made her the Mother of God; in the Upper Room that fecundity comes to completion, making her Mother of men, mediatrix of every grace, diffuser of Jesus in every heart.

A mysterious noise came about in the holy place. Tongues of fire appeared over the heads of Mary and the apostles, and all those exterior signs in the holy enclosure symbolized the intimate influx, the prodigious influx that descended upon Mary and upon the apostolate.

Some people think that the Holy Spirit descended directly upon the Most Holy Virgin and that from there he spread to the souls of the disciples, because to her the words of the evangelist St. John are able to be applied in some way: *From his fullness we have all received*

(John 1:16).

But the influx of the Upper Room was not the last influx of the Holy Spirit that the Virgin Mary received. After the one in the Upper Room came the influx of the consummation, the definitive, the perfect one.

One day, many years after the death of Jesus, Mary passes, calm and tranquil, as if she surrendered to a most sweet dream; her face turns pale, her body chills...

She is a plucked lily that withers, an amphora of alabaster that breaks and the exquisite perfume that it contains rises to the heavens in mysterious spirals.

Mary died; but her death is not like our death, full of horror and sadness and pain. Her death was a Mass, her death was a canticle of love, her death was a mystery of glory.

What mysterious evil, as we call that which produces death, what mysterious evil invaded the virginal body of the Most Holy Lady and broke the heavenly amphora?

I just said that Mary's death was like a Mass, an image of the sacrifice of Jesus, but without blood, without disgrace, a most sweet sacrifice, an oblation full of peace, a guileless host that was raised to the heavens.

But who was the one making the sacrifice? Could it be the emissaries of Satan, as were those who sacrificed Jesus on Calvary? Could it be the wild beasts, like those that were thrown upon the exalted martyrs in the arena of the Roman circus? Who immolated Mary? Some words from the Christian liturgy come to my mind: the priest-love immolated her, "amor sacerdos immolat."[1]

Why did the Virgin die? Because upon her, in a new, vehement, ineffable way, the Holy Spirit descended: the priest-love immolated her...

But in order to understand my thoughts, it is necessary to observe that when the Holy Spirit descends upon our souls he needs to restrain himself. Have you ever seen a passionate mother, most vehement, who hugs her tiny and fragile son to her heart? If she followed the impulses of her maternal heart she would kill him, she would kill him out of love! But she is a mother and knows to restrain herself. By the intuition of her heart, she knows well how much she is able to hug her son, and she contains the force of her tenderness so that her son does not die, so that her son does not suffer.

So the Holy Spirit is with us. Each time he descends into our souls he would love, ah!, he would love to hold us close with the infinite strength of his tenderness; but he is wise, he is loving, he knows that if he pours himself out into us with all his divine impulse he would kill us. He has to restrain himself with divine discretion so that in the fragile vessel of our flesh we can receive his divine influx.

Surely every time the Holy Spirit descends he expands our hearts, as he fortifies our weakness. Each day we are capable of receiving a tighter hug, a more burning kiss… But on earth we can never receive the entire influx of God.

Scripture says that man cannot see God and live (Ex 33:20); no one can receive the opulence of his love without dying. God must restrain himself. And so he restrained himself in order to pour himself out into the soul of the Virgin; he contained himself in order to caress her; he contained himself in order to embrace her; he contained himself in order to manifest to her the immensity of his tenderness.

But one day the Holy Spirit was not able, or rather refused, to restrain himself any more. Love is like this: a moment arrives when it goes through everything, when it destroys everything in its triumphal march. And that day the Holy Spirit did not restrain himself: he poured himself out without the least consideration into the soul of the Most Holy Virgin, and he flooded it with love, and, embracing it, he took up her life... The amphora was broken and exquisite perfume rose to the heavens in mysterious and perfumed spirals...

But I have not spoken of the complete mystery. I will not say that the Holy Spirit gathered the fragments of the broken amphora and marvelously put them back together; no, it was not put back together.

The almighty force of love transformed that broken amphora into a heavenly amphora, and again the body of the Virgin, beautiful, delicate, splendid, heavenly, came to be united with her spirit; the exquisite liqueur again occupied the transfigured amphora. And there in the bosom of God, Mary reigns on the throne of love and eternally sings the marvels of the Uncreated One...

II

THE life of the priest is also a continuous Pentecost. We know it by sweet experience, and would to God that we knew it better every day. We ascend to the altar, and everyday the stupendous wonder is carried out in our consecrated hands. Every day Jesus comes to our hearts. We find him everywhere, in the praise that leaps from our lips, in the souls that come close to us so that we might give them the Bread of God.

The priestly life is a continuous Pentecost. In the priesthood, we are receiving the Holy Spirit; and even before we received the holy anointing, before the hands of the bishop rested upon our heads, already the Holy Spirit was pouring himself out into us, already he was preparing the masterpiece of the priesthood in our heart.

But as in Mary, in the priesthood there are also floods, singular floods in which the abundance of the gifts of God resembles the waves of a river when it expands, when it gets rough, when it escapes its channel and extends over the flowering countryside.

The first influx of the Holy Spirit in priestly souls is purity. Not in a day, nor in a definite and determined instant, as it was on the day of the Immaculate Conception of Mary, no; those outpourings are hidden, are mysterious, but frequent.

We see in the bosom of a Christian home a boy, like the rest it seems. Certainly, his look has a marvelous cleanness, his smiles are innocent and delightfully celestial, but who can discover in the depths and in the heart of that boy the sign of predestination?

Whatever the doctrine that is professed about the vocation to the priestly order, nobody will deny that the Holy Spirit, who does all things by number, weight, and measure (Wis 11:20), who arranges all things with energy and gentleness (Wis 8:1), comes to us from a very young age to prepare our hearts, our souls, and our bodies for the great mystery.

That boy, that young man, when his eyes are opened to contemplate the scene of life, when he feels in his veins the abundance of his youthful blood, when he feels that his heart expands, when his spirit dreams of mysterious and mischievous things, who prevents him from feeling in those moments, like so many others, that which Scripture calls the fascination of vanity (Wis 4:12)? Why does that which he sees around him not dazzle his eyes? Why does the sound of earthly happiness not begin to disturb the silence of his heart? Why does he see the things of this earth as vain and yearn for inexpressible divine dreams? Who put in his heart that divine restlessness, which makes him desire something mysterious that he himself does not understand but that attracts his spirit, that divinely entrances his heart?

Neither knowledge, nor art, nor glory, nor love, nor all the beautiful things of the earth captivate that heart. He feels, it is true, the attraction of them all, but there is something, like a vague premonition, that says to him: "You are greater and you were born for greater things." And his eyes are lost in the distance, as his spirit examines in the mystery the secret of the divine restlessness that he has in his soul...

Little by little he continues clarifying the mystery. Perhaps in a radiant evening, in a quiet church, full of silence, between the spirals of incense, or upon hearing the harmonious notes of a church song, that young man looks at the Sacred Host and feels that it is transfigured before his eyes, and...there is the key to his life, the secret of his restlessness!

Jesus, the divine Jesus, calls him; and as in the Gospel stories, the young man listens to the divine word: *If you wish to be perfect, go, sell what you have and give to the poor...then come, follow me* (Matt 19:21). And the young man does not think, he does not reason it out, he does not analyze it, because the heart neither analyzes nor reasons it out. Under the impulse of divine inspiration, he leaves everything, and he goes in pursuit of the divine Jesus, of the mysterious Unknown who calls him, who carries him away with the fascination of his word and the immense charm of his love...

It would please me to describe the entire secret story of the priestly vocation; quite gladly I would run through those hidden and silent, but brilliant, years of the young man, of the priest; but it would be too extensive. What I do say is that in all of this there are mysteries: it is the Spirit of the Lord who descends into our souls and who continues creating priestly purity in us little by little.

Today arouses one of the affections that had been born in our poor hearts; another day a secret fiber breaks within him that leaves him bleeding; tomorrow, a sacrifice; after, a renunciation; later, a consolation, a sweetness, a new light, a new impulse...what can I predict?

Who can scrutinize the marvels of God in priestly souls?

But the Holy Spirit continues preparing in us little by little a purity similar to that of the Most Holy Virgin: that which a priest requires to exercise his divine functions in a holy manner.

When the individual work is concluded, the Spirit of the Lord returns to descend with a flood of fecundity upon the priestly soul. This influx has its day and its hour: the young man transfigured by love and by hope draws close to the bishop, who with the solemnity of his high dignity waits for him by the altar. The young man kneels, the bishop puts his consecrated hands upon the head of him who will be a priest, and silently, ineffably, lovingly, the Holy Spirit descends upon that young man.

What miracle has the Holy Spirit accomplished when the hands of the bishop settle upon the head of the young man? A miracle of fecundity. It is like the echo, the likeness, of the great mystery that took place in Bethlehem.

Perhaps there will be someone who is surprised that I have wrapped the priestly graces and those of the Most Holy Virgin together in this formula: *Spiritus Sanctus superveniet in te et virtus Altissimi obumbrabit tibi* (Luke 1:35). Perhaps there will be someone who thinks that I go beyond the sense of the text, that these words that signify the influx of the Holy Spirit in the solemn instant of the Incarnation do not merit to be applied to the influx of the Holy Spirit in priestly souls.

But it is not so. It is the same mystery: in the former in a real manner, in the latter in a mystical manner; but the mystical is real, the mystical is mysterious, it is secret, it escapes our eyes and our poor human judgment, but it is a reality. It is even in a certain sense, if you will allow me the expression, more real than the reality that we feel with our senses.

What is it that the Holy Spirit accomplishes in the soul of this our brother whom we came to accompany on the day of his glory and the joy of his heart? It was, I repeat, a mystery of fecundity.

On the credence table there is a white host, prepared with exquisite solicitude, chosen with immense love. There it is, very white, very pure, if you like, very beautiful, but it is nothing but material bread, it barely differs from that which we bring every day to our mouth except for being unleavened. In a few brief moments, our brother will ascend to the altar; he will take in his hands that most pure host, he will pronounce the mysterious words, and he will perform a stupendous wonder.

Oh! If we could see spiritual and divine things as we see the earthly, let us make no mistake—we would all faint from respect and from love! But the mysteries of God are veiled, and in the silence that will then reign, before our faith and our love, there will come about the wonder of Nazareth and of Bethlehem: the eternal wonder of Jesus. Jesus will appear on the altar, Jesus will appear in the hands of the priest, and the new priest without disturbance, without sacrilege will be able to say with his own lips the words that Mary was able to say, the words that the celestial Father says eternally: *Filius meus es Tu, ego hodie genui te. You are my Son; today I have begotten you* (Ps 2:7).

And this is not the only fecundity of the priest. In the restlessness of his first years, in the fervor of the most abundant grace of his ordination, our brother will go through those realms of God looking for souls because God has made him, like Peter and his companions, a fisher of men. He will go to them to satiate the thirst for God that all have in their souls but that many do not know, others despise, and very few esteem.

We shall not present him with riches, because he has left them for God; we shall not flatter him with glory, because he knows that the glory of this world is vain smoke; we shall not speak to him about earthly loves, nor of knowledge, nor of the wisdom of men, which he has definitively lost and discarded for God. Let us speak to him about souls, because in them he discovers a divine trace that corresponds to the mysterious desire that he carries in his heart.

And he will draw close to them with the purity of an angel, with the tenderness of a mother, with the skill of a teacher, and he will pour out upon them the graces of heaven, and he will communicate to them true life, life eternal. He will wash them of their stains, he will separate them from the things of the earth, and he will elevate their eyes and their hearts to heaven, where there is true peace, the only true happiness.

And our brother, at the same time that he received the mysterious power of making Christ appear on the altar, also received the mysterious, strange power of making Jesus appear in souls. He will go by the paths of this world as a divine sower, throwing the blessed seed upon the fecund furrow of souls.

I need to contain myself. Gladly I would speak forever about this most holy mystery, which is, for us priests, so personal, so intimate. It is said that, speaking of it, I discover the heart of God and our own hearts.

Is one able to say that because a new priest is going to celebrate his first Mass he has consummated his life?

One could say so, perhaps. Well, the years gone by with all their vicissitudes, their sacrifices, and even their miseries, are they not directed to this culminating point, to receive the priestly anointing and to offer the divine immolation?

It is like that in a certain sense. The priestly ordination is a glory, but in another sense it is nothing more than a seed, it is a beginning. Oh! If I could speak of the priestly life: a life of pains and of joys, pains of hell and joys of heaven; fecund life, life of silence, life of astonishing activity and of supreme seclusion; life on heaven and life on earth.

Oh, I could not in a few brief words say what the life of the priest is! But today's mystery invites me to speak to you about another mystery: that of the priestly death.

Yes, I know that in the world it is not tolerated to speak of death on the day of joy and happiness; and if, for example, in the middle of a wedding banquet someone spoke of the future death of the newly married, even though it was supposed that it would happen much later, that person would be taken very poorly. Why speak of death in the moment of the joy of love?

But for us Christians, and, above all, for us priests, death barely has the most subtle accent of sadness; for us, death is the door to happiness, death is our last Mass, death is our consummation; it is the final, definitive, magisterial touch that the divine craftsman puts on the masterpiece that he has accomplished in us.

The death of the priest! We should not die like all die, no. Unfortunately, at times we die as all die, and what is the most terrible, we die like sinners die; but no, that is not how we should die.

I will speak with naïveté, and I will say what I think in the depths of my heart. I see three types of death, the only three worthy of a priest.

I think that the priest can die of fecundity, pardon the expression. Have we ever seen how in the fall the trees are bent over and their branches are ripped off under the irresistible weight of their most abundant fruit? I think the priest should die like that, burdened under the abundance of his fecundity…

There is another way of dying worthy of the priest: as St. Ignatius of Antioch died, as the apostles died. When the venerable forefather thought about martyrdom, ah!, he rejoiced in the depths of his heart to see that his members were going to be made into pieces, that his flesh was going to be cruelly torn apart by the teeth of wild beasts, and that he was going to be made into immaculate bread. He said: "Now I begin to be a disciple of Christ, who lovingly let himself be ripped to pieces for me. Now I will be the perfect priest."[2]

After celebrating Mass every day, does it not seem logical that we die saying our final Mass, the Mass of our martyrdom, and that like St. Ignatius of Antioch, as the holy apostles, we mix our poor blood with the divine blood of Jesus?

There is another type of death for the priest: that of the Virgin Mary.

Ah, yes! During our priestly life, as during the life of Mary, the Holy Spirit descends without ceasing upon us, restraining himself in order not to destroy the fragile vessel of our poverty. But if we receive the heavenly treasures, if we are faithful to our priesthood, if we preserve unscathed the purity of our heart and of our body, if we guard in a miserly way the graces we receive on our ordination, the grace that we received by the imposition of the bishop's hands, if we are faithful servants that bring Jesus to every soul, whom we treat with the delicacy of our Lord, if we fulfill our holy, our august ministry...one day the Holy Spirit will not be able to bear (we say with the vehemence of our beautiful language) the exuberance of his love, and he will pour himself out into us in a most vehement manner, and under the divine oppression of his divine embrace, under the ardor of a mysterious caress of the Most High, we will feel that the amphora of our body is broken, and that our priestly spirit will lose itself in the august bosom of God...

CHAPTER 4

Mary and the Priest

AT A FIRST MASS

Et ex illa hora accepit eam discipulus in sua.
And from that hour the disciple took her into his home.
(JOHN 19:27)

NO matter how many times we have attended a first Mass, it always seems to us something new, interesting, and moving; as the dawn looks enchanting to us, such that every day we can enjoy its freshness and joy; as the spring always seems lovely, such that each year it passes over the earth spreading its warmth and perfume.

A first Mass strikes to the most intimate part of the heart. It is the mystery of the Upper Room that is renewed, and it always seems that, when a priest ascends to the altar for the first time, the transfigured face of Jesus in the Upper Room is contemplated, the host and the chalice are seen in his hands, and those unforgettable, solemn, divine words are heard: "Haec quotiescúmque fecéritis, in mei memóriam faciétis. Do this in memory of me."[1]

A first Mass produces in our soul the impression that the Church is immortal, that her priesthood is perpetual, and that this priesthood is responsible for preserving Christianity until the consummation of the ages.

We wane. Under the weight of the years, we feel our strength weaken, and we see that death draws near. Would to God that we might say like the Apostle: *Bonum certamen certavi, cursum consumavi, fidem servavi. I have competed well; I have finished the race; I have kept the faith* (2 Tim 4:7). But either way we die in peace.

We die, but the priesthood does not die. In our place come those who receive as a precious inheritance the treasure that we received from our elders, the one we receive from Jesus. Every day men in the prime of life, in the splendor of youth, come to be established as perpetuators of the sacrifice of Christ. And, in the midst of all the persecutions and vicissitudes, the Christian priest passes gloriously through the world, always renewing the supreme sacrifice of the cross.

And if we delve into this mystery, if we penetrate to its depths, we will glimpse all the grandeur of the work of Christ, all the fidelity of the Church, all the strength she has to resist the attacks and persecutions of her enemies.

That is why I want to speak to you all about the mystery of the priesthood, now that we are persecuted, that we are defamed, that some would like us to be erased from the face of the earth. It is necessary that the world understands what we are, because, although miserable and sinners, under this earthly covering a divine treasure is hidden.

But the mystery of the priesthood is a profound, inexhaustible mystery.

Could the marvels of the firmament ever be exhausted? The wise scrutinize the sky without ceasing; every day modern science invents devices more precise and of greater reach in order to discover the mysteries of the firmament; but they are inexhaustible, and for as many centuries as the human lineage lasts, it will not be enough to say the last word about the astral world.

The mysteries of Jesus and the priesthood are like the sky, for as much as they are scrutinized and studied in depth, they are never exhausted, because the divine is never exhausted. The priesthood is a mystery that is in an intimate relationship with all the Christian mysteries, and when we have to speak of the priesthood, we should examine and see which of so many marvels must be expounded to the faithful.

Now I do not hesitate in the selection. Holy Church celebrates today a feast of the Ever-Virgin Mary. I will speak, then, about what Mary is for the priest. It is something that the circumstances call for, it is something that my heart asks. I will try to reveal that treasure that we possess, that we have received from Jesus on Calvary: that Blessed Virgin, who is for us our strength, our consolation, our hope, our life, our love; that Blessed Virgin without whom the priesthood would be a burden too heavy for our weakness.

I

JESUS, before leaving this world, bequeathed his treasures to humanity as a precious inheritance. The treasures of Christ are ours, are everyone's, but these treasures were especially entrusted to priests. They are, if you will allow me to use this term from our ordinary life, the executors that possess the divine inheritance of Jesus, and they have the mission of distributing it justly to the rest, since all are his heirs.

And the treasures of Jesus are precious. Especially the Eucharist. And Jesus left it to his priests on the eve of his Passion. Who can recall the unforgettable scene of the Upper Room without being moved? On that night of eternal memory, before the astonished gaze of the disciples, Jesus carried out the Eucharistic mystery; and when he had finished breaking the bread of life, and had finished wetting his lips with the wine of salvation, the disciples heard these creative words: "Haec quotiescúmque fecéritis, in mei memóriam faciétis. As many times as you do this, do it in memory of me." It was his inheritance; Jesus left in our hands and in our hearts the treasure of the Eucharist.

After the resurrection, on the lovely banks of Lake Tiberias, the risen Jesus said to his disciples: *Go, therefore, and make disciples of all nations, baptizing them in the name of the Father, and of the Son, and of the Holy Spirit* (Matt 28:19). With the inheritance of his word is the inheritance of his sacraments, which he puts in the hands and in the hearts of his priests.

But Jesus left us another treasure, a treasure most dear to his heart. Who could not guess it? It is Mary! Jesus did not spare the priest that most precious treasure, and in the most solemn hour of his life, in the most tragic moments of his sacrifice, he gave us as an inheritance his own Mother. In the midst of the anguish of his agony, in the midst of the sadness of his death, Jesus turned his dying, but always gentle, eyes to the earth. At the foot of the cross, there is Mary and there is John, and a divine word resounds in the universe: *Behold, your mother. Behold, your son.* (John 19:26-27). The inheritance of Jesus is consummated. John was the representative of the priests, and in him we received the Most Blessed Virgin; she is ours, she is our treasure.

And after the Gospel had painted the scene I just recalled, it says: *From that hour the disciple took her into his home* (John 19:27). And from that hour, the solemn hour of the sacrifice of Jesus, Mary Most Holy is ours, she is our treasure.

Blessed be Jesus, who left us such a precious inheritance! We should be deeply grateful to him for having left us his words, his sacraments, and his Eucharist; but our gratitude for having left us Mary, how tender, loving, delightful!

What would have become of us without Mary? I think that the weight of human life is too great for a single soul to bear. That is why our Lord God formed tight bonds between us, and he wanted man to be eminently social, so that souls, not isolated but united to each other, might carry the greatness and the miseries typical of human existence. Neither for sorrows nor for joys does a single soul by itself suffice. When we suffer, we look for a heart that understands us, a soul that helps us to drink the chalice of bitterness. And likewise in the joys we also need relief, because the human soul has perhaps a greater capacity to suffer than to rejoice. When the happiness that our souls desire passes through us like lightning from the sky, we are not able to bear it alone; it is necessary that another soul help us to support its most sweet weight.

That is why our Lord wanted us to be born in the heart of a family. When we opened our eyes to the light of this world, we found the support of a father and the tenderness of a mother, we found brothers, and we found friends; we are not alone. When the moment set by God arrives, then a man looks for a companion so that she might help him to support the weight of life, so that the sorrows and the joys might be mutual.

And we priests, will we have to live alone, will we have to be isolated, carrying a weight more formidable than that of the faithful? Because if a single soul does not suffice to support the weight of ordinary life, much less will it be able to support the weight of priestly life. Jesus himself did not want to carry it alone, and that is why he wanted sweet Mary to be near to him, that between the two of them they would carry the weight of the joys and the sufferings of the thirty-three years of his mortal life.

There is always a tabernacle close to us, and in it is Jesus, the friend that does not forget us, that does not betray us, in whose heart we always find that which ours desires. We can think that Jesus would be enough for us; but he himself wanted—surely because he himself formed our hearts and knew their aspirations—Mary to be close to us together with him, because our heart needs the tenderness of a mother. And like this, with Jesus and with Mary, we are able to traverse the rough paths of the priestly life and carry the cross of Christ on our shoulders.

Funiculum triplex difficile rumpitur. A three-ply cord is not easily broken (Eccl 4:12). Jesus, Mary, and the priest form an indestructible three-stranded rope.

II

But it is sweet for us to contemplate more closely the good things that Mary does for the priest. Why does that most sweet Mother of ours serve us? What services does she render us? What do they have to do with us her priests?

What Mary does with us is exactly what she did with Jesus. Because we came to stand in for him, we remain in his place. For this reason, he did not say to St. John: "I entrust my Mother to you, take care of that treasure for me." No, rather he said to him: *Behold, your mother*. And then to Mary: *Behold, your son*. The only Son of Mary is Jesus. By saying to her, *Behold, your son*, he wanted her to understand that from now on this one will be your Jesus. And St. John is the representative of priests. It is as if Jesus had said to Mary: "Look, until now you have been my Mother, my confidant, my help; from now on, he replaces me, you will be for him what you have been for me, because he is your son, because you are his Mother."

And, indeed, Mary does with us what she did with Jesus.

We can reduce to three the services that she rendered to her divine Son, corresponding to the three stages of the life of Christ: the hidden life, which lasted the first thirty years; the three years of his public life; and the last days, the last hours of his sacrifice and of his agony. And in these three stages of the life of Jesus, the Most Holy Virgin had a most special role to play.

In the first thirty years of the hidden life, Mary was the confidant of Jesus, where he put all of his trust. Who could have listened to those sweet confidences? Who would have been able to understand the celestial mystery of that intimacy? How, excited before his Mother, could he not reveal to her his secrets, not tell her his plans? Mary was the first to whom he told the great secret of his heart: the secret of his Eucharist. To the Most Blessed Virgin he must have told the secret of his sacrifice; he must have confided to her the deep sorrows that lacerated his heart and the celestial joys that inundated his soul.

She was his sweet confidant. What would Jesus have done carrying in his heart so many secrets of love and of sorrow if he had not had a motherly breast, a most pure heart upon which to place his sacred mysteries?

Later, Mary was the one who inspired Jesus, so to speak, to begin his apostolic life in Cana of Galilee. His hour had not yet come, it was not yet time for him to be manifested to the world. But the Most Blessed Virgin says to him in a charming way, *They have no wine* (John 2:3), and although Jesus protested that his hour had not come, Mary understood that her words had a powerful effect over her Son, and she said to the servants: *Do whatever he tells you* (John 2:5). And Jesus performed his first miracle, he began his public life at the pleas of the Virgin Mary.

I think that in the midst of the weariness of his ministry, in the midst of that cold and indifferent atmosphere, in the midst of the follies of his enemies and even of his own disciples, Jesus must have looked, as a most sweet solace, as a longed for rest, as support and strength, to Mary, whom he must have seen from time to time and whose memory and love Jesus carried in the most intimate part of his soul.

Finally, Jesus traversed the final stage of his life: in Gethsemane he sweated blood, and after disgraces beyond telling and unspeakable pains, he went up the rugged ascent of Calvary. Near that blessed cross Mary was standing, full of strength and love, feeling in the depths of her heart the pains of her Son, her breast pierced by a mysterious sword, participating in his immolation, as she had participated in his public life, as she had been his confidant during the thirty years of his hidden life.

For priests, there are the same three stages: we have an interior life, a public life, and also we have our passion.

Our interior life is perhaps the most interesting of all: not only for the priest but for every person, the most important thing is not what appears on the outside but what there is within. Only God sees the true worth of man, when with his penetrating eyes he gazes into our interior. And in the priest, especially, what he says to the faithful should not be other than what overflows from the plentitude of his contemplation, the Angelic Doctor assures.[2]

The apostolic life, which is the priestly life, should be an overflow of the contemplative life. The priest should have a banquet within his soul, the banquet of light and of love, the banquet of his Mass, that of a constant communion with God. When the priest has nothing within, it is like a hollow nut, which has nothing more than the shell, something useless, something barren; he will only be able to speak and make noise, never will he be able to reach the depths of souls.

And in that interior life of the priest, Mary is our confidant. That life is composed, like all human life, of joys and sorrows. And precisely because we have been lifted up from the earth, our joys are more elevated, our sorrows are deeper, our secrets are torrents that overflow.

Because of this we need someone who understands us, who receives our secrets, who encourages us with her word, who wipes the sweat away from our brow and the tears from our eyes. We need a mother in whose lap we can rest when we feel tired, a mother of whose heart we are sure, to whom we can tell everything, the great and the small, the heavenly and the earthly, the graces of God and our deepest misery.

And for this, Jesus gave us Mary.

There are secrets—priestly secrets—that we cannot tell anyone, not even to our earthly mother who loves us so much and understands us so well. Only to her, only to Mary, only to her heart, can we entrust ourselves in order to rest.

For our interior life we have two treasures on the earth: the tabernacle and Mary. There is all of our life; there is where we learn and hear in secret what we sometimes say from the holy chair. The tabernacle is our Nazareth, it is the center of our life.

But we would not be able to enjoy the delights of Jesus, nor put ourselves in contact with him, if the Virgin Mary did not teach us to know him, to relate to him, and to love him.

Next, public life comes to us.

Ah, the priest cannot enclose himself within himself, because for him souls are everything! Our Lord put them in his hands, they are another treasure that he entrusted to him and that he has to preserve and increase with the sweat of his brow and with the blood of his heart. We cannot fortify ourselves in our egoism, because we are at the service of the faithful; we are their servants, and the faithful have the right to ask us for what we as priests should give to them. And our life, our joy, and all that we have belongs to them, because this is how Jesus wanted it, because he gave us souls not to enjoy them but to sacrifice ourselves for them.

And how arduous, how severe is the apostolic life! St. Paul said that we carry a spiritual treasure in fragile vessels. If we were angels, it would be very easy for us to carry that divine treasure in our soul. Furthermore, the priest is not a strange being: he has all the miseries and he has all the greatness of man. The great and the small alike make us suffer; the great and the small alike make excessively heavy the cross of our priestly life.

But we are not alone: with us is Mary, who never abandons us.

If we were able to see divine things as we are able to see earthly things, we would see that Mary is always near the true priest. She suggests to us what we say to the faithful when we preach. She enlightens us so that we can examine the abyss of the human conscience. She supports our weakness when we want to fall under the weight of exhaustion and suffering. She is the one who propels us towards the apostolic life, as she propelled Jesus in Cana of Galilee.

And in the midst of our difficulties, we can always flee to her. Mary is our support, our strength, our joy. And when worn out in the priestly ministry we need rest, the lap of Mary offers it to us sweetly. And when we feel that her blessed hand wipes away the sweat from our brow, the greatest pains are turned into heavenly joys.

For us, as for Jesus, our Calvary and our cross must come. We cannot stop following the Master because of the rugged ascent of Calvary.

And if we were offered another way, we would reject it without hesitating, since our love and our priestly honor demand that we go where he went, that our soles are torn where the blood of Jesus left his footprints, that our hands and our feet are nailed where his feet and hands were nailed.

That is our glory, that is our honor, and thanks to God we will never be without it. The same Jesus Christ said: *If the world hates you, realize that it hated me first... If they persecuted me, they will also persecute you* (John 15:18, 20). We have known this for twenty centuries, for twenty centuries our precious inheritance is persecution and martyrdom.

And even when the enemies of the Church do not persecute us, the priest always has secret Calvaries and very hidden crosses. We have to deal with all the needs of human life, and we have to deal with our own, the inner ones, the priestly ones. We make ours the afflictions of souls, as well as their joys. As a mother suffers all that her children suffer and always feels her heart torn when one of her children goes astray, so we feel the afflictions and the wandering of souls that have been commended to us. *Who*—says St. Paul—*is weak, and I am not weak? Who is led to sin, and I am not indignant?* (2 Cor 11:29).

We priests suffer for souls and we suffer for Jesus, for the beloved of our hearts, for the intimate friend of our lives. Every injury that is done to him hurts our souls, every blasphemy directed to him wounds our hearts.

Yes, the priest has to be on the cross, that is his place of honor, there where he received the inheritance of Mary in the priestly hour par excellence. The priest always has to be on the cross; but, at the foot of every priestly cross, Mary is always there, she who contemplates our sacrifice and fills our souls with heavenly consolation.

Ah! If from the height of the cross we saw nothing but emptiness, if our eyes contemplated nothing but the earth, if we heard nothing but the blasphemies of Calvary, we would not be able to bear the terrible fight. But from above on the cross, Mary is always seen nearby, very close to us. When the blood of our wounds runs and our pains are exacerbated and we believe we have arrived at the height of suffering, we lower our eyes and find some very loving eyes, very sweet eyes, eyes of a mother, the eyes of Mary, that comfort us and encourage us, and then we feel that our suffering is small and that we can participate still more in the sacrifice of our Lord.

And here we have what Mary is for the priest: our confidant in the interior life, our help in the apostolic life, our consolation at the foot of the cross.

More than anyone, you should consider it in the intimacy of your heart, priest, that, for the first time, you will celebrate the tremendous sacrifice.

St. John says: *And from that hour the disciple took her into his home.* That hour is this one. It is the hour of your first Mass, it is the hour of Calvary. You also—take her as your own; she has always been your treasure, you have always loved her with all your heart, but now in a special way she will be yours. Because now she is yours as a priest: yesterday the priests dispensed to you this treasure from heaven; now you possess it as your own. Value this very rich treasure that you have received from the hands of God, never separate yourself from Mary nor allow that by your fault a single tear fall from her most pure eyes.

She will be your confidant, she will be your help, she will be your love, she will be your Mother; in her lap you will rest quietly;

her hands will wipe away the sweat from your brow; her lips will lull you to sleep so that you can rest in her maternal arms; to her you will recount your sorrows and your joys; and in her heart you will live peacefully all the days of your life.

Mary will be your support and your strength in the apostolic life; do not take a step without her. Look how human life is too heavy for a soul to bear it alone. Do not carry the weight of your priestly life alone, since Jesus and Mary carry it with you, so that you all may form the three-stranded rope impossible to break.

And when Calvary comes for you, which has to come—you would not want to remain eternally on Tabor, knowing that Jesus, the beloved of your soul, is on Calvary—when the immolation and the bitterness come for you, think how close Mary is to that cross, and turn your eyes to her, and in her eyes you will find strength, consolation, and peace…

CHAPTER 5

Jesus, Friend of the Priest

AT THE TWENTY-FIFTH ANNIVERSARY OF A FIRST MASS

Jam non dicam vos servos, quia servus nescit quid faciat dominus ejus. Vos autem dixi amicos: quia omnia quaecumque audivi a Patre meo, nota feci vobis.
I no longer call you slaves, because a slave does not know what his master is doing. I have called you friends, because I have told you everything I have heard from my Father.
(John 15:15)

In the Scriptures, friendship is compared with wine, undoubtedly because friendship, like wine, makes one forget the sorrows of life and fills the heart with joy; but, above all, friendship, like wine, is made more exquisite and profound with time.

A new friend is like new wine. New wine is sparkling and fervent; with time its aroma becomes finer, its taste more exquisite; upon drinking it, it diffuses a smooth warmth in the body and a sweet joy in the soul. Old friendship is like aged wine. Time, which either destroys everything or withers it, neither destroys nor withers true friendship; rather, it refines it and makes it sweeter and more profound.

The priesthood, which contains many mysteries, is at its core the mystery of an intimate friendship. In our ordination we heard from the lips of the bishop, which is like hearing it from the lips of Jesus, the words: *I no longer call you slaves, because a slave does not know what his master is doing. I have called you friends, because I have told you everything I have heard from my Father* (John 15:15).[1] And these words are not empty, because they are divine. On that unforgettable day, we received the treasure of an intimate friendship with Jesus.

And because that friendship is true, solid, and divine, with time it loses neither its pleasure nor its sweetness; rather, like mature wine, it anoints our souls with its divine perfume and fills our hearts with its savor of eternal life, always ancient and always new, when the years have passed by and the soul has tasted all the joys and all the pains, the concealed delights and the deepest sorrows, of the priesthood.

The first Mass is sweet and unforgettable like the days of youth; it has the smooth tints of dawn, it has the rich perfumes of spring; it is the first fruit of a new friendship, the first priestly embrace with Jesus, the first caress of his new love, the first conversation filled with sweet intimacy and unspeakable charms; it has something of new wine, sparkling and fervent.

We guard in our souls its immortal memory, and after many years it feels as if it was yesterday when our hands were trembling out of respect elevating the Sacred Host, when our hearts were palpitating with love and our souls were shaking before the divine mystery.

After twenty-five years, our friendship with Jesus has been made more exquisite and profound. So many years treating him with sweet familiarity! How firm the experience of his goodness and his love! How intimate the conviction that he is faithful, of how he knows to forgive and to forget!

Time has taught us to know him and to love him; we have suffered setbacks and disillusions, and in the midst of the ruins of our affections and many hopes, he alone, Jesus, remains firm, every day greater, every day more beautiful, every day more loving. The words of the Church, repeated so many times, has now for us a clear and profound meaning: "For you alone are the holy one, you alone are the Lord, you alone are the Most High, Jesus Christ."[2]

Our hearts, purified by sorrow, have broken all the ties that held them to the earth and have adhered completely to the sweetest friend who filled our youth with joy. By an intimate and lengthy relationship with Jesus, we have recognized his concealed delights, his inexpressible finesse, his moving gentleness. Even our miseries that he has forgotten, our ingratitude that he has forgiven, have unveiled the bottomless mercy of his heart; and although we mourn them bitterly, we also bless them, because they have revealed to us the profound reality of those words of the psalms that we have repeated so many times without comprehending: *For he is good, for his mercy endures forever. Quoniam bonus, quoniam in aeternum misericordia ejus* (Ps 136:1).

With our eyes swollen with tears, with our spirits filled with memories, with our hearts saturated with deep emotions, we approach the altar of God after twenty-five years of the priesthood, to the God who fills with joy the eternal youth of our souls.

Is it not true, my brother, that upon celebrating today your magnificent anniversary you taste, in the profundities of your soul, the aged wine of friendship with Jesus, sweeter and more exquisite than on the unforgettable day of your first Mass?

All those present here accompany you in giving thanks to God for your twenty-five years of priesthood; and I, who united with you also by an old friendship rejoice with your joy and share in your holy emotions, want as a priest to remind you and to remind the faithful of the mystery of that intimacy with Jesus and to show the profound reality of those words that you heard, as we all heard, on that day of your ordination.

Do you remember them? The bishop had already made that mysterious imposition of hands upon your head, and your hands had already been anointed with the oil, you were already covered with the sacred vestments, and you had received the chalice and the host of the sacrifice; with the bishop, you had already made God descend from heaven onto the holy altar; and when filled with recollection you tasted the delight of your first priestly communion, the bishop, in the name of Jesus and with a supernatural solemnity, as if they had come from the Upper Room, pronounced these words: *I no longer call you slaves, because a slave does not know what his master is doing. I have called you friends, because I have told you everything I have heard from my Father.*

Jesus, then, has revealed to us the mystery of the priesthood by declaring the mystery of that new friendship.

Only to friends do we tell our secrets and only to those intimately close to us do we open our hearts to their depths. And to us priests Jesus revealed the profundities of his soul. *But I have called you friends, because I have told you everything I have heard from my Father.* Have we heard it? *Omnia, everything.* Although Jesus's soul is immense, everything is clear to the gaze of the priest; although what Jesus heard from the Father was something extraordinary, he told us everything in the incredible confidences of his friendship.

And I do not exaggerate, because the words of Jesus are most clear: *I have told you everything I have heard from my Father.*

Moreover, how can he reveal anything to us, if what he hears from the Father is infinite, if it is the unfathomable abyss of the wisdom of God?

The Father does not have more than one word, which is his Word; and Jesus, as God, is that infinite word; and as man, he heard that word with divine plentitude, because that substantial word filled the sacred humanity of Jesus with its divine treasures.

And that sovereign word is what Jesus revealed to us, revealing it to our souls; and he did not say it only one time and in passing, the way Moses saw the holy glory of God pass by on the mountain (Exod 33:22), but rather he gave us that word forever, since he gave his very self to us.

Jesus is ours, he is the gift of the Father to us: *For God so loved the world that he gave his only Son* (John 3:16). We carry in the fragile vessel of our nature that divine treasure of the only word of the Father.

We bear Jesus in our souls by faith. St. Paul teaches us: *Christum habitare per fidem in cordibus vestris* (Eph 3:17). We bear him more intimately by our love: *Whoever loves me will keep my word, and my Father will love him* (John 14:23). We possess him with all the riches of his sacred humanity and with the unfathomable abyss of his divinity in the Holy Eucharist; and in the mystery of Holy Communion, Jesus enters into the intimacy of our being, and in the fragility of our flesh we bear the secret of the Father, the glory of God, his only word, and we possess everything that Jesus heard from the Father.

Certainly these wonders are not exclusive to the priest. They can be for all Christians, and because of this we all enjoy the friendship of Jesus, which has an ineffable name in the Christian language: charity, which is a divine name, because like St. John told us, *God is love* (1 John 4:8,16).

But we priests have a new way, a singular and most secret way of possessing Jesus, a way of receiving the revelation of the only word of the Father.

The simple Christian faithful listen to that word, they possess Jesus, but they do not have any kind of power over him. When he comes down to earth, they adore him, they love him, they receive him, they intimately embrace him in their souls; but they cannot make him come down from the heavens. All their prayers full of faith, all their longings of love, all their cries of hope, all their roars of desire are not enough on their own to draw down Jesus, to rip him from heaven, to make him live among us and to imprison him in the tabernacle, to make him our treasure and our passion. They are friends of Jesus, but they are not his most intimate friends. To them he has not given the plentitude of his secret.

To us, yes. A thousand times we have witnessed the stupendous mystery, which we do not often sufficiently admire because it is already familiar to us, and in a few moments we will witness it again.

The holy altar is empty; the purity of the materials that cover it seems to say to us that it is waiting for the pure Victim, the holy Victim, the spotless Victim; but it is not there yet. Everything is prepared for the sacrifice: the wax burns, the incense slowly burns on the embers, the sacred canticles resound, the faithful kneel, the souls wait in loving silence; but as Isaac said upon ascending Mount Moriah: "Where is the sheep for the burnt offering?" (Gen 22:7).[3]

The priest, who ascended to the altar twenty-five years ago for the first time, ascends again, and in the midst of the silence of heaven and earth, he will pronounce some divine words, those which Jesus pronounced in the Upper Room, those which he taught us to say; and from the bosom of the Father Jesus will come into the hands of the priest; and in between the candles of the altar, in the middle of the perfumed spirals of incense, he will elevate Jesus, hidden by mysterious veils, but clear to faith and love; and the eternal Victim, the only pleasing Victim to the Father, will renew on that altar the mystery of his holy and fecund immolation.

Does it not seem to you that the mystery of the altar is like an image of the eternal mystery that is realized in the intimate life of God? *You are my Son; today I have begotten you* (Ps 2:7), says the Father; and in the splendors of holiness, from the bosom of the Father, comes forth his Word, whiteness of the eternal light, stainless mirror of the divine majesty, image of his goodness.

Like an echo of the eternal word, the mysterious words of the priest resound on the altar: "This is my body. This is the chalice of my blood." And upon the altar appears also the whiteness of the eternal light, veiled by the whiteness of the holy host, and the splendor of the Father, hidden under the accidents of the wine of salvation.

Is it not true that Jesus reveals to us priests the fullness of his ineffable secret? Is it not true that he gives to us the sacred privilege of knowing everything that he hears from his heavenly Father?

We are his intimate friends; he has given us his treasures; he has given us his very self in an ineffable way; and we, though poor passing creatures, are given a wonderful power over the eternal.

Not only on the altar are we priests able to realize the image of the eternal mystery of God. No, Jesus reveals to us the secret of the Father in its fullness.

If Jesus descends to the altar, if he lives hidden in the tabernacle, it is to enter into souls and live in them, because it is for them that the Word of God became flesh, it is for them that Jesus died on Calvary. Souls are the glory of God.

When Jesus does not live in them, souls resemble the immense and greatly sad chaos of the beginning of time; they are something great, but without light and without beauty, because Jesus is the clarity and the beauty and the bliss of souls. To the souls that do not have Jesus, one can apply those energized epithets with which Scripture characterizes the primitive material of the earth: *inanis et vacua* (Gen 1:2); they are something empty, unformed, desolate.

But when the Holy Spirit passes triumphantly over souls, like he passed over the waters at the beginning of time, when he puts Jesus into souls, these souls light up, they beautify, they transform, they become heaven, because like the author of the *Imitation* said: "Being with Jesus is a sweet paradise."[4]

But who will perform this miracle? Who will bring to desolate and empty souls the efficacy of the divine word, the ineffable fecundity of the Father? One word, an image of the Word of God, put order and harmony in the primitive chaos, for it is written: *Ipse dixit et facta sunt; ipse mandavit et creata sunt* (Ps 33:9; 148:5). The eternal word put something like an echo of his very self in the matter, and the universe emerged splendidly and beautifully, like a poem of love to the divine glory.

Who, I repeat, will say the efficacious word, the fecund word that carries to souls not an echo of the eternal word but rather this same word, the Word of God, that is not merely a canticle to the glory of God, but rather this same glory?

According to the ordinary economy of grace, the priest is the only one who can pronounce this sovereign word. In baptism it is the word that regenerates and in penance the word that forgives and cleanses. And when the priest pronounces those words of life, an unspeakable transformation occurs in souls.

Who can ever explain the mystery of the justification of the sinner? *Eratis enim aliquando tenebrae; nunc autem lux in Domino* (Eph 5:8). Before justification, souls were darkness; afterwards, they are light in the Lord. It seems to me that not even the contrast between the dark night and the splendid day is sufficient to make us glimpse this mysterious transformation because our nights always have some kind of light. If we were able to appreciate the grand contrast between the chaos of the beginning and the universe after the divine lips said, *Let there be light* (Gen 1:3), we would have an idea of what happens in the sinner who is justified.

As in the shining sunrise the shadows flee and the light spreads like a caress of love over the awakening earth, and with the light life and joy are spread everywhere, so it happens with souls when they are justified; they are bathed in divine light, the love of heaven vivifies them; grace divinizes souls to their foundations and the majesty of God thus fills his purified and holy temple.

And the priest performs this transformation with his efficacious word! If God would have communicated to us the secret of his creative word, he would have, in a certain sense, given us a lesser gift than communicating to us the secret of his word that justifies; for St. Thomas teaches that the justification of one sinner is a work greater than the creation of the world, and that the grace of one soul is a greater good than the natural good of the whole universe.[5]

Permit me to repeat the same question: is it not true that Jesus told us everything he heard from his Father?

But justification, as wonderful as it is, is nothing more than the beginning of the spiritual life: I would compare it with the appearance of light in the universe. And just as after that radiant appearance of light God completed the work of creation in the other five days and passed through the universe, filling everything with order, harmony, and beauty, as St. John of the Cross expressed it in this incomparable stanza:

> Pouring out a thousand graces,
> he passed these groves in haste;
> and having looked at them,
> with his image alone,
> clothed them in beauty[6];

until, having concluded his grand work, God saw that everything was good, and the heavens sang the glory of God, and the earth was filled with his majesty; likewise in souls after being justified, God pours out on them precious and innumerable graces and places in them another order, another harmony, another incomparable beauty, superior to those of creation, in such a way that, better than the heavens, souls sing the glory of God, and more than the earth they are filled with the majesty, the goodness, and the love of God.

Virtues flower, much like the countryside flowers in the springtime; the gifts of God luminously arise in the soul like the stars emerge from a clear sky; in the depths of the soul shines the image of the Most Holy Trinity, like the glory of the sky reflecting on the crystalline surface of a tranquil lake. And God himself lives in that pure soul, he fills it, he possesses it, and he divinizes it, like the sun bathes the little clouds that float in the sky with its vivid glow, illuminating it, penetrating it, seeming to transform it in light.

The marvelous lives of the saints make known to us to what a high degree this work of God attains in souls, those lives which are the most beautiful poems that have been sung on the earth, some of them sweet like a love song, others sublime like a deep tragedy.

There is no beauty in nature, no wonder of art, no discovery by modern science that can compare itself with the stupendous work that God accomplishes in souls when the holy seeds that they received in baptism develop and arrive at maturity.

And God, who accomplished the work of creation without the use of any creature as an instrument, has desired to use us his priests as ministers and dispensers of his mysteries. Just as on each of the days of creation only his voice resounded in the immensity, arranging the order and harmony of the universe, so to adorn and beautify that other universe, that of souls, small in extension but immensely greater due to their divine transcendence—who would believe it?—he desires that our voice, the poor voice of the priest, which has so many limitations and deficiencies, be the one that resounds in the most intimate recesses of souls in every stage of the spiritual life, each stage more beautiful, more solemn, more grandiose than the days of creation.

Before continuing, I need to publicly recognize our miseries—all of those that we have as creatures, those that are proper to our corrupt lineage, those that are the work of our personal malice. Like other men, we bear in our hearts the seeds of iniquity, and, in spite of the copious gifts that we have received from the hand of God, we have, perhaps, stained our priestly dignity with our faults.

I say this for the glory of God; I confess it so that by contrast the divine friendship of Jesus, his most rich gifts, his incredible graciousness, his infinite love, stand out all the more.

Though we are so fragile, so miserable, and even so sinful, Jesus has desired to associate us with his sublime work in souls. Our voice is that which makes in them those profound separations that grace demands, as the voice of God divided the waters in the dawn of time; our voice ignites those divine lights in souls that preside over their days and their nights, as the voice of God made the sun, the stars, and the moon shine in the heavens; and as that creating voice made all those plants that beautify the earth sprout, we, with our voice, make the rich variety of virtues in souls blossom.

We do more, since we transform souls into Jesus, we breathe on them to infuse into them the Holy Spirit as a breath of life, and we form souls in the image and likeness of God.

We can be the smallest and most miserable, but, nonetheless, we form the saints.

Our word is the one that has divine efficacy to sanctify; the public word that, like sowers, we scatter from this holy chair; the most intimate and most secret word that we speak into the ears of the faithful in the divine ministry of spiritual direction; the sacramental word that does what it says, as the word of God does; and the word of the father and the teacher that, having or not having the characteristics of eloquence, of wisdom, and of human prudence, has the unction of the Holy Spirit, the flash of light of the Eternal Word, and the divine fecundity of the heavenly Father.

Per stultitiam praedicationis voluit Deus salvos facere credentes. It was the will of God through the foolishness of the proclamation to save those who have faith, said St. Paul (1 Cor 1:21). And we preach always, whether it be in the midst of the most solemn of feasts or in the confessional.

And the mystery of our word is always the same, that which the Apostle expressed with fervent energy, *per stultitiam praedicationis,* through the folly of our preaching. He who desires to explain the power of our word according to human reason will fail. According to human reason, our public words, as well as our private words, are foolishness and insanity. Many others might be more eloquent, more artistic; but God has rejected those things, the wisdom of the wise, the prudence of the prudent.

The divine efficacy that hides in the depths of foolishness, in the folly of our preaching, do we know of what it consists? In that Jesus has confided to us in the excess of his exquisite friendship everything that he heard from his Father; in that we envelop in inexpert words, if you like, the only word of God, the eternal word, the fecund word, the word that penetrates like a two-edged sword as far as the division of the soul and the spirit (Heb 4:12), the word that never returns empty and unfruitful to the divine lips that eternally pronounce it.

We do not possess the eloquence of words, but rather the secret of the Word of God.

And so that the fullness of the secret of Jesus would be perfect, we not only communicate the Word of God wrapped in the fragile veil of human eloquence, but we also communicate it hidden under the whiteness of the Eucharistic veil, and with our consecrated hands we place on the lips and in the heart of men the Word made flesh, the Word made our Eucharist, to be the food of our souls.

Ah, yes! Jesus confided to us his secret, Jesus handed his treasure over to us. Jesus gave us himself in a way that was new, singular, ineffable. We have the divine prerogative to repeat like an echo the eternal word of the Father, the mysterious words that place Jesus on the altar, the sanctifying words that place Jesus in souls.

We are not servants, because Jesus does not hide from us the mysteries that he accomplishes on the earth; we are his friends, because everything that he heard from his Father he has revealed to us.

That is why the bishop spoke to us on the day of our ordination the most sweet words of the Upper Room.

Do they not still resound in your ears, my brother, as if the deeply missed bishop who ordained you pronounced them today? Do they not still resound bathed in the twilight of memory and anointed with their exquisite perfume? But, no, it was not only yesterday when you were told those words; Jesus has always told them to you, he still tells them to you. Do you not hear them in these moments, most clear, most sweet, most solemn, like a soft caress of love from your most faithful friend? And now you understand them better than you did twenty-five years ago; your spirit, now mature, has clearer light to penetrate them; your heart, purified by sorrow, opens wider to receive the loving confidence; your soul, shaken by the strong winds of life, has now that august serenity that helps us to listen to Jesus better.

Listen to them in the silence of your soul; listen to them coming from those divine lips that have not ceased to tell them to you for twenty-five years. You have felt, you have tasted in the whole of your priestly life the sweet, the most faithful friendship of Jesus; you have tasted it in those heavenly moments that every priest close to Jesus has; you have tasted it in the middle of the struggle, even in the depths of your misery, even in the disgracefulness of your ingratitude towards Jesus.

When you have returned to him after your failures, have you not found him always sweet, always merciful, always loving, always the same? Has he not told you the ineffable words of his eternal friendship, when, humble and contrite, you have thrown yourself into his sweet arms?

Ah! Jesus, the incomparable friend of our priestly life, he is most faithful, he knows how to forgive and knows how to forget, and, above all, he knows how to love as no one will ever love, as no one will ever be able to comprehend. His gifts are irrevocable and his friendship is eternal.

Surrender yourself without reserve to that divine friendship; open to him your heart and confide your secrets to him as he has confided his secrets to you; give him your priestly heart and your priestly life; be a true friend of Jesus as he has been your incomparable friend.

Be faithful unto death, so that when your eyes close to the light of this world and open to the splendor of eternity, you will hear from the lips of the judge the sweet priestly words, the words of friendship that you heard twenty-five years ago, and you will receive the supreme, the definitive, the eternal revelation of the secret of the priesthood of Jesus in the immense and loving bosom of the Father.

CHAPTER 6

The Epiphanies of Jesus to the Priest

AT THE TWENTY-FIFTH ANNIVERSARY OF A FIRST MASS

Mihi vivere Christus est.
For to me life is Christ.
(PHILIPPIANS 1:21)

THE true value of a man and the glory of his life is not in the words that flow from his lips, as eloquent as they may be, nor in the success of his undertakings, no matter how great we suppose them to be; the true value of a soul and a life is inside, in the words that a man says to himself in the silence of his intimate sanctuary, in the treasure that he carries hidden in the deep cavities of his soul, in something that others ignore, in something that the very person who bears it hidden in his own heart often ignores.

The artist creates beauty by sculpting it in marble or by making it resonate in a marvelous variety of colors, but his external work, even when it is a masterpiece, does not express the best and most exquisite ideals of the artist. This is hidden, because he bears it hidden in the folds of his spirit; it is the ideal that he has seen and that cannot be fully expressed; it is the inexpressible aesthetic illusion that is translated to the exterior, but that never discovers its finished plenitude.

The wise man illuminates with the light of truth the minds that surround him; but he carries the source of that light inside, the sun from which those rays emanate is hidden, in the same way that the daystar, before appearing in the east, illuminates the earth but our pupils cannot contemplate its radiant disk.

A hero, who goes down in history because of his great deeds, carries within himself the source of his heroism, the intimate strength from which his noble and glorious deeds emanate.

The true value of a man and of a life is within, and this law of our life is also realized in the supernatural order. Supernatural life is something hidden in the deepest part of ourselves: *Ecce enim regnum Dei intra vos est*, Jesus Christ said, *The kingdom of God is among you* (Luke 17:21). *Omnis gloria filiae regis ab intus, all glorious is the king's daughter as she enters*, it is said in the psalms (Ps 45:14).

Ah, we ourselves contemplate with admiration the lives of the saints! Their biographies reveal to us the marvels they performed on earth, in their writings we perceive the heavenly perfume of their virtues; but the glory of the saints is hidden in their hearts, and we will contemplate it only on that day in the exalted light of glory.

And since the priesthood is something sublime, exquisite, in the same supernatural order, the glory of the priesthood is also something interior. The best things of the priesthood are not the words full of unction that fall on souls; it is not the consolations that pour into wounded hearts; it is not the hand that extends to lift the fallen from the mire of sin or to guide souls to the summit of perfection, no. The most exquisite, the most beautiful, the holiest of things of priestly life is something intimate, it is something hidden that we bear in our soul. Perhaps we do not even know perfectly the secret of our priesthood.

While we live in the world, what we are does not appear; only at times and in solemn moments does lightning flash in the depths of our hearts, which reveals to us the divine treasure that we carry hidden within us.

For this reason, today I must discuss the priesthood because, full of jubilation and joy, we have come to accompany our brother who is celebrating twenty-five years of priestly life. I want to speak about that hidden, exquisite, divine source of our life.

I will not say anything about the priest who passes through the earth doing good in the likeness of the divine Master. I will not deal with his word that fills the world, nor with his action that makes him the salt of the earth. I only want to talk about the interior, hidden, intimate life of the priest, of that life that constitutes our glory, which is the most perfect and most excellent gift that we have received from our Lord God.

So that I can talk about those hidden and deep mysteries; so that I can touch my brother's heart by telling him about his memories, his realities, and his hopes; so that I can build your lives, making you all understand better what we priests are so that you all might surround us with veneration, esteem, and affection, it is necessary that we implore God's help, that we invoke the Holy Spirit—the only one who can fathom the mysteries of the priest's heart—and that we make an intercessor of the Blessed Virgin Mary.

St. Paul, who scrutinized all the mysteries with a profound gaze and who had the gift of finding adequate and beautiful words to express them, has a comprehensive and concise phrase to express the intimate life of the priest: *Mihi vivere Christus est. For to me life is Christ.* That secret that we priests bear in our souls, that life that constitutes our glory could not be expressed in fewer words and with greater precision and energy. The life of the priest is Jesus, Jesus who appears to our radiant and transfigured spirits and envelops them in the splendors of his light; Jesus, who stole our hearts and inflamed them with divine fire; Jesus, who like an exquisite perfume spreads in our being and in our lives, infusing them, pervading them, and transfiguring them...

The first contact we had with Jesus, his first appearance in our soul, was in the quiet days of our childhood. At that time, his figure appeared distant and mysterious, like the star of the Magi, but also radiant and attractive like that star.

We hardly knew in the first years of our lives who Jesus was, but we felt the powerful attraction that he exerts on simple hearts and pure souls. We already catch a glimpse of that Jesus who, throughout the centuries, continues to repeat his divine word: *Let the children come to me for the kingdom of heaven belongs to such as these* (Matt 19:14). And attracted by his light we ran to him, and our naive eyes searched for him, and our hearts began to love him, and our lives began to belong to him.

Our heart is our treasure, but this heart we must give so that it may grow; happiness consists in giving someone the gift of ourselves. And creatures surrounded us, and we felt their attraction. To whom would we give our hearts?

And in the midst of the ardor of our youth, Jesus returned to appear before our soul: beautiful, sweet, divine, and we do not hesitate—we judged all things on earth as nothing and we gave Jesus our hearts, completely and forever.

And one day we bowed our heads before the bishop, and he cut our hair, at the same time that we said with all the youthful expression of our souls: *Dominus pars haereditatis meae et calicis mei, tu es qui restitues haereditatem meam mihi. Lord, my allotted portion and my cup, you have made my destiny secure* (Ps 16:5). And from that unforgettable day Jesus entered our hearts; since then we bear him within. He is our life, he is our only life.

But the Jesus that we receive when we enter the clerical state, the Jesus of our first Mass, there is no doubt that he is, if you will allow me the expression, a limited Jesus. Later he will grow in our soul, we will know him better; but, in the meantime, it is the Jesus who called us, the Jesus to whom we gave our hearts, that Jesus of our youth whose charm does not repeat itself, for it is the charm of everything that begins, dim and rosy like the dawn, jubilant and fresh as the morning, perfumed and splendid as spring, ardent and smiling as youth...

We will never again feel those unforgettable and unique impressions that we felt when Jesus called us, when he opened his arms to us, when he smiled at us for the first time, when he asked for our hearts, when we gave them to him with all the generosity of our souls.

But although the Jesus that we knew and loved in the smiling days of our youth, in the first years of our priesthood is so beautiful, he is nothing more than a dawn that grows, that is always growing until it becomes the fullness of noon.

Priestly life, in what is most intimate and exquisite, is Jesus, who grows in the depths of our souls. He is first a dawn; then, a sunrise; later, a bright morning; and if we are faithful to the grace of our ordination, he will become the fullness of the midday sun.

St. Paul expressed this mystery with another formula also exquisite and profound: *Nos...gloriam Domini speculantes, in eamdem imaginem transformamur, a claritate in claritatem, tanquam a Domini spiritu. All of us, gazing...on the glory of the Lord, are being transformed into the same image from glory to glory* (2 Cor 3:18). That is the intimate life of the priest: to walk from glory to glory to come to know better each day the Jesus to whom we have given our hearts and lives; to walk from glory to glory so that our hearts grow from love to love, from fire to fire, until one day we are transformed into the divine image.

We could say, attending to the spirit of the liturgy in these days, that the priestly life is a constant epiphany, or rather a series of epiphanies. It is Jesus, who is manifesting himself more and more clearly, who is stealing our hearts more, who is possessing our life more, and to whom we give the symbolic gifts of gold, frankincense, and myrrh, which express the unique gift, the unspeakable gift of ourselves.

I distinguish in the priest four epiphanies, four manifestations of Jesus, each of which grows from glory to glory, until we reach the divine transformation.

The first epiphany of the priest is in the Gospel.

The Gospel reveals Jesus to us; those pages of the immortal book are full of him. Ah, if only we knew how to understand the Gospel deeply! Through the words and the teachings, the symbols and the figures, we see nothing more than the sublime, the august, the divine figure of Jesus.

The priest is constantly studying the Gospel, and the Gospel is constantly revealing Jesus to him. Every day the pages of the sacred book are clearer for us; every day the holy Gospel opens before our spirit vaster horizons; every day the words of Jesus have a deeper meaning for us, and, at the same time, every day Jesus fills our spirits and our lives more.

St. Paul teaches us that the only knowledge of the priest must be the knowledge of Jesus: *For I resolved*—he said to the faithful of Corinth—*For I resolved to know nothing while I was with you except Jesus Christ, and him crucified* (1 Cor 2:2). He is our knowledge, the only knowledge of the priest. If we learned other things in the classroom, if our ingenuity, if our experience has accumulated a lot of knowledge, ah, we must despise all these things! They are at most the pedestal, the poor pedestal of the only priestly knowledge, the knowledge of Jesus Christ, and of Jesus Christ crucified.

Everything we have learned, like everything we have taught, is of no use to us, it cannot be of use to us for anything other than to know Jesus better, so that the Gospel gives us its mysteries and through its simple pages—but full of light—we can contemplate the great and divine figure of the Christ.

And so it has happened to us. From glory to glory, the Gospel has revealed its secret to us; from glory to glory, each day the captivating person of Jesus Christ our Lord has appeared before us more precisely, more closely, more luminous, more sweetly.

The priest's first epiphany is an epiphany of light.

But there is another, I will not say more perfect, but more intimate: it is the epiphany of the tabernacle.

The priest and the Eucharist are absolutely united. Jesus made the priest for the Eucharist, and he made the Eucharist primarily for the priest. The day we disappeared, the Eucharist would disappear from the earth; and the day the Eucharist ended, the Catholic priest could not survive. We are united, our bonds with Jesus in the sacrament of love are very close; he is the faithful friend, the confidant who never abandons us, who always receives the intimate expressions of our hearts.

Let us not be fooled by appearances. Do we know what the best and happiest hours in the priest's life are? Will they be the moments in which, in the name of God, he announces the divine word and illuminates souls and moves hearts? Will the priest's best moments be those in which he dedicates himself to increasing grace and refining the purity of the soul? Will the sweetest moments for the priest be those in which he extends his consecrated hand to purify the sinner and tear him from the clutches of the devil and throw him into the arms of God? Is it not perhaps when, after painful efforts, the priest comes to contemplate a soul that has gone through all the stages of the spiritual life, and has reached the summit, and there found the Beloved of his heart, and has been united to him with indissoluble ties?

No; the best moments of the priest are those that he spends near the blessed tabernacle, with his close friend, with the inseparable companion of his life, with the one who is his strength, his consolation, and who has become his own life.

In the silence of the priestly soul, Jesus communicates, and he teaches us without the noise of words, and the emanations of love from his heart reach the depths of our poor hearts. How many times, like St. Peter, do we want to say at the foot of the tabernacle: *Bonum est nos hic esse! It is good that we are here* (Matt 17:4, Mark 9:5; Luke 9:33). How many times do we say to Jesus: "Lord, do not allow me to be separated from you;[1] let me live near your tabernacle, near this tent that I myself have raised for you, so that I may always live in the eternal Tabor of the Eucharist."

In that intimate contact of prayer, of love, of faith, of trust, of intimacy, Jesus is growing in our souls; every day he is more familiar to us; every day he is more intimate to us; the silence of the tabernacle is filled with divine words; close to the divine Eucharist we feel such an indescribable mysterious attraction, joy of beatitude, prelude of heaven.

The second epiphany of the priest is an epiphany of love and intimacy for the Eucharist.

But let us not think that the priest meets Jesus only in the Gospel or in the Eucharist: he finds him everywhere. The priest knows how much truth the expression of the Apostle contains: *Omnia et in omnibus Christus. Christ is all and in all* (Col 3:11).

Do we know what the priest's third epiphany is? It is souls. In souls we find Jesus. Ah! Perhaps many do not understand this thought, perhaps believing that souls are a burden for the priest; yes, they are indeed, in the way that Jesus is a burden. Legend has it that when the giant Christopher was carrying Jesus on his shoulders, he said to him: "Child, you weigh more than a world." This is how much Jesus weighs, this is how much souls weigh; but it is a very sweet burden, because when we carry the weight of souls on us, it is Jesus we carry, Jesus who weighs more than a world; but Jesus, who is sweeter than heaven.

We would not know Jesus well if we did not draw close to the depths of souls, because when we approach those abysses we discover what Jesus is for them, his goodness, his kindness, his love, his ineffable delicacy. Jesus is very sweet for each soul, he marvelously adapts to each one according to their mentality, their temperament, their attractions. He is a child with children, and an artist with artists, and wise with the wise, and simple with the simple. And we see him work in souls, and as we see him, we get to know him and know his way, his touch, his spirit, his goodness, his mercy.

So if we did not draw close to souls, Jesus would not reveal himself to us in all his greatness and in all the splendor of his goodness and mercy.

Even more: the souls themselves reflect Jesus to us. Each soul is a crystal of a lake in which the divine Sun is reflected. To see souls is to see Jesus; in them the divine features of Christ are contemplated, are touched.

For the priest, souls are the complement of the Gospel, and, I will dare to say it, they are the complement of the Eucharist; the epiphany in souls is the splendid epiphany that makes us know Jesus marvelously, that makes us discover his intimate way, his mercy, his love, his goodness, his greatness, his omnipotence.

I still have to talk about another epiphany, the most intimate: the epiphany of Jesus in our own hearts.

Ah, in our own hearts we bear him! He entered there the day that we gave him our souls, the day we told him: *Dominus pars haereditatis meae et calicis mei; Tu es qui restitues haereditatem meam mihi. Lord, my allotted portion and my cup, you have made my destiny secure.*

During the course of our priestly life, Jesus has been growing in us, and we have found him outside: in the Gospel, in the tabernacle, in the sanctuary of souls; but, above all, in our own hearts.

And in our hearts is our Jesus, the one who has fully adapted himself to our smallness, the one who understands us, the one who loves us, the one who considers our work and our sorrows, the one who knows the most intimate aspects of our secrets… It is our Jesus, the one who reveals himself in our own hearts and manifests to us what he does not manifest to us anywhere else.

To know how Jesus loves, we need to go inside ourselves; only then can we know all the delicacies and delights of his love.

Love is like that: you can form some concept of what love is studying other hearts, but to know perfectly the science of love, we need to enter our own heart. We learn what love is when we love; we understand that mystery the day we are loved.

And that Jesus who is within us is the Jesus who loves us, from whom we have received exquisite delicacies here, within our hearts.

But let us not believe that we know Jesus, more than anything else, by the consolations that he pours into our souls and by the lights with which he illumines our spirits. No, the intimate transfiguration, the one that Jesus does within our own hearts, is manifested to us not so much by consolation and light but by sorrow and humiliation.

Ah!, when we suffer, when we priests feel mortal sorrows in the interior of our hearts, then, through our suffering, the figure of Jesus is perfected.

I do not know why, but sorrow transforms swiftly and easily into light. Have we not seen that even worldly people, when shaken by sorrow, open their eyes? Have we not verified that the light of sorrow is the most splendid, the only one with which we come to understand certain mysteries of life? He who has not suffered, what does he know? "The one who has suffered," someone has said, "is like the one who knows many languages: he understands everyone, and is understood by everyone."[2] He who has suffered a lot has a great treasure in the depths of his heart.

When we suffer, the vanities that darkened the firmament of our souls like clouds dissipate, and Jesus appears radiant before our spirit.

To know Jesus fully, one must know the sorrowful Jesus; you have to look at him nailed to the cross, on the bloody peak of Calvary; but, to look at Jesus there, it is necessary that we participate in his sorrows, that we bear the stigmata of his Passion in our bodies and souls.

But I still want to talk about another mystery, perhaps stranger and more disconcerting than the mystery of sorrow: I want to talk about another epiphany of Jesus in the intimacy of our hearts. We not only see him through our consolations and through our sorrows, but, what is more, we look at him through our miseries. And for this reason, if we had no other reason to love and bless them, this would suffice for us.

Happy miseries that reveal Christ to us!

We all have them, and if someone said that he does not have them, he would be deceiving himself, and the truth would not be in him (1 John 1:8). We all carry within our being an inheritance of the curse that our first parents bequeathed to us; as the apostle St. Paul says, *we hold this treasure in earthen vessels* (2 Cor 4:7).

In priestly ordination the very fragile vessel was not transformed, but rather the priestly treasures were deposited in it.

We are full of miseries, I repeat it again: neither the grace of ordination nor the opulence of the gift of God that we have received have removed the coarse and fragile things from the vessels in which we receive heavenly treasures; and our priestly life, that life that is full of graces and gifts from God, is equally full of miseries. But those miseries have revealed Jesus to us in a most divine and delicate aspect.

He is the only one who understands our miseries and who does not depart from us when they appear; it could be said that our miseries attract him, it could be said that our miseries soften his heart.

Men, when they discover our defects, move away; they are to some extent right to do so, our defects are so repugnant! The only one who does not walk away because of our miseries is Jesus. Jesus knows how to forgive, Jesus knows how to forget, Jesus knows how to heal, Jesus knows how to transform!

How many times, like that poor Jew of whom the Gospel speaks (Luke 10:30), are we covered with wounds on the side of the path of life, and Jesus is the good Samaritan who approaches us with love, who pours wine and oil on our wounds, and who not only pays so that our wounds are cured, but he himself carries us in his blessed arms and places us on his shoulders and embraces us in his heart!

Ah! I thank Jesus for loving me, I thank him immensely for all the gifts with which he has filled me; but if I have to tell the truth, I thank Jesus above all for supporting me, for not withdrawing from me because of my miseries, but rather, on the contrary, drawing closer to me with the sweetest smile of his lips, with the most tender love of his heart... Blessed Jesus who knows how to put up with us and who is not frightened by our miseries!

That is why through them we discover the Jesus who is superior to all our defects, the Jesus who is not horrified by our sins, the Jesus who opens his arms to us and introduces us into his heart so that we may live in him and from him become like an anticipated heaven.

There are four epiphanies in priestly life: an epiphany of light in the Gospel, an epiphany of love in the tabernacle, an epiphany of fecundity in souls, and an unspeakable epiphany in the intimacy of our hearts.

Through our sorrows, through our miseries, we contemplate

Jesus, that Jesus who grows more radiant each day, each day more precise, each day more beautiful in our souls, that Jesus who stole our hearts, the one whom we are following each day more perfectly and who infuses our whole life with a divine perfume. That Jesus is the life of the priest: *Mihi vivere Christus est. For to me life is Christ.*

Twenty-five years of priestly life is the triumphant march of Jesus in the soul of the priest, the triumphant march of light, love, sorrow, humiliation, and hope.

Our brother has felt all these things in the intimacy of his soul; our brother has seen Jesus grow in his soul, from glory to glory, he has known these epiphanies; and he, in turn, like the mysterious gifts of the Magi, gave Jesus his heart from a young age.

By participating in his triumph, by helping him to give thanks to our Lord God for the benefits received in this quarter of a century, let us ask God's graces for him. Let us kneel in homage to God, let us kneel before the Virgin of Guadalupe, whose image he bears carved in his soul.

Mary, to your heavenly feet and under your blue mantle, our brother has come to celebrate twenty-five years of priestly life.

Mother! Mother! Keep giving Jesus as you have given him so far.

The Magi found Jesus in your arms, in your lap; all priests find Jesus in you and all priestly epiphanies appear in your lap and in your heart.

Lord, may Jesus grow in the soul of our brother; may your epiphanies be more splendid and more radiant every day; may Jesus fill him with his light and with his love and with his fecundity and with his sorrows; may Jesus fill him with all his graces; may he find Jesus in the sacred pages of the Gospel, in the heaven of the tabernacle, in the sanctuary of souls, in the intimacy of his heart; may our brother grow more and more so that, from glory to glory, he is transformed into his divine image as he approaches the ineffable, the eternal epiphany of heaven!

CHAPTER 7

The Mystery of Fidelity

AT THE TWENTY-FIFTH ANNIVERSARY OF A FIRST MASS

Vocabatur fidelis et verax.
He was called Faithful and True.
(Revelation 19:11)

Time appears to be one of the greatest enemies of our lineage: it destroys our works, disorients our designs, strips down our hopes. Under the slow but devastating and effective action of time, empires crumble, human institutions are destroyed, and our history changes course.

In a special way, it appears that time is the enemy of our heart. How time withers our illusions, how it dissipates our dreams, how it chills our affections and uproots them from our heart when we believe they are very deeply rooted!

When we love, we always dream of an immortal love; when we love, we never stop saying that we will always love... Ah! And one sad and embarrassing experience teaches us how inconstant our heart is, how fragile our affections: time comes and strips those we love of their charms, it produces in them inevitable decay, and with the garments that it takes from them, it appears also to take the affections of our hearts.

And time often does not even need to do that plundering in order to uproot love from our hearts; it is enough for time to pass, for it to smooth away what is human bit by bit, so that by the natural inconstancy of our hearts we stop loving today what we loved yesterday and stop thinking of love immortal.

That is why, when we manage to reach a victory over time, when one of our institutions, a work of our hands and, above all, a love of our hearts triumphs over time and survives in spite of the devastating action of time, we celebrate the event with rejoicing and admiration, and paraphrasing the words of the apostle St. Paul, we confront time and we say to it: Oh time! Where is your power? Where is your victory? (1 Cor 15:55).

This is the profound meaning of the anniversaries that we celebrate; each anniversary is a triumph over time, each anniversary is a victory of our hearts over the typical vicissitudes of human life.

Today we celebrate a very gratifying and transcendental anniversary. A brother of ours in the priesthood completes twenty-five years of priestly life, twenty-five years that in the eyes of God are like a fleeting moment—even in the course of human history twenty-five years are an instant—but that in our poor individual lives are a triumph over time. That any institution would last twenty-five years is already something notable; but that a noble affection would last twenty-five years in our hearts is a victory over time, is something that merits our rejoicing and our admiration.

And have we thought what twenty-five years of priestly life are? Ah! The opulent graces that God has poured out upon the priest do not stand out to me; only God knows the number and the quality and the nature of the priestly graces that he pours out upon a soul throughout twenty-five years. Neither does the countless number of sacrifices and efforts that a priest has to make during twenty-five years attract my spirit. For our inconstant hearts, for our poor nature so fragile, do we know what it is to have the care of souls for twenty-five years, what it is to be intimately united with Jesus Christ the High Priest?

But more than the graces received from heaven, more than the efforts that poor human nature makes in the priestly life, what calls my attention in these moments is the mystery of love and fidelity that twenty-five years of priestly life contain. They signify that Jesus, for twenty-five years, has loved the priest with a divine fidelity; they signify that the priest, for twenty-five years, has loved Jesus Christ the High Priest, with fidelity.

I think that, above all, the priesthood is a mystery of love and that a priestly jubilee is a mystery of fidelity: of fidelity on the part of Jesus, of fidelity on the part of the priest.

That is why within the innumerable names that Scripture gives to our Lord Jesus Christ, I have taken this name from Revelation, *He was called Faithful and True*, and I want, in the midst of this solemnity—of this solemnity that is for all, since the priest is for all—to speak of this mystery of fidelity and say how Jesus is faithful, admirably faithful, delightfully faithful, divinely faithful; I want to say how the priest also, although poor and paltry, is nevertheless faithful to our Lord Jesus Christ when for twenty-five years he has carried on his shoulders the heavenly, but immensely heavy, burden of the priesthood.

I

TWENTY-FIVE years ago the bishop put his anointed hands on the head of our brother, made the Holy Spirit descend upon him, and in him a mystery was accomplished, a divine mystery: his heart, his being were transformed.

God loved that heart so much that he wanted to deposit in it the ineffable treasures of the priesthood; on that day, which already appears distant, our brother received the mission of Jesus; since that day that man, as Scripture says, was lifted from the dust of the earth to be placed among the princes of the Church of God; since that day, that man, converted into another Christ, had the mission of carrying out on the earth exactly what Jesus Christ did twenty centuries ago during his mortal life.

The lips of the priest continue pronouncing throughout the centuries the words of eternal life that Jesus pronounced on Lake Tiberias; the hands of the priest continue bestowing the pardon that Jesus bestowed; the lips of the priest give testimony to the truth as Jesus came to give it; the priest continues igniting on the earth the sacred fire that Jesus brought from heaven; like Jesus Christ the priest can say: *I came so that they might have life and have it more abundantly* (John 10:10). His mission is the same mission as Jesus's mission.

Twenty-five years ago our brother received the powers of Jesus. He had said: He who would be my disciple *will do the works that I do, and will do greater ones than these* (John 14:12). We priests extend our hands and pronounce a mysterious word, and souls are purified; sinners arrive at our feet covered with offenses, and we say to them the words that Jesus Christ has ordered us to say to them, and with the precious Blood of the Lamb we cleanse those soiled souls. Every day we say mysterious words on the altar, and by the divinely omnipotent efficacy of those words, God descends from heaven. Jesus Christ descends into our hands and a marvelous miracle is accomplished. In those consecrated hands are all the powers of Jesus; what the priest forgives, Jesus forgives; what the priest retains, Jesus retains.

The priest has in his hands the treasures of God; he is the minister of Christ and the dispenser of the divine gifts that he shares and diffuses into souls.

The treasures of Jesus are two—the Eucharist and souls—and Jesus put the Eucharist and souls into the hands of the priest on the day of his ordination. Since that day, he has a tabernacle, he also has some souls that Christ has entrusted to him; he has received the treasures of Jesus.

But all these things of which I have spoken appear to me very little in comparison with what I am about to say.

The priest receives the mission of Jesus, the powers of Jesus, the treasures of Jesus; but though these things are very great, mission, powers, and treasures, there is a greater thing, sweeter, more divine, that the priest receives on the day of his priestly ordination, that our brother received twenty-five years ago. Can we guess what it is? It is the heart of Jesus. On the day of our priestly ordination, Jesus not only gives us his powers, his mission, and his treasures: he gives us his heart, the richest gift, the most heavenly gift, the most divine gift.

That is why within the solemnity of the priestly ordination, when the priest has just finished receiving his first priestly communion, the bishop, in the name of Jesus Christ, says to him—sweet mystery!—*I no longer call you slaves, because a slave does not know what his master is doing. I have called you friends, because I have told you everything I have heard from my Father* (John 15:15).[1] As if he said "It would be very little to give you my mission, my treasures, and my powers; I give to you the greatest thing that I have, the most exquisite, the most profound, the holiest thing: I give you my heart." And from that day, the priest is an owner of the most Sacred Heart of Jesus.

Ah!, we are all owners of the heart of Christ, because he gives it to us all; but the priest is in a singular way the owner of that divine heart; he knows all its secrets, hears all its beats, can take from it all its treasures, and, above all, the priest knows that Jesus loves him in a special way. The divine heart is his treasure, it is his riches and his gift.

Now, all this that the priest receives from Jesus Christ on the day of his ordination, all this that our brother received twenty-five years ago, he still has without diminishment, without change, without vicissitudes; the mission that he now has is that of twenty-five years ago; his powers are unscathed: twenty-five years have not diminished his powers, have not changed his mission.

But what I want to inculcate in souls, what I want to say in these solemn moments, is that the love of Jesus has not changed, that Jesus loves him as he did twenty-five years ago: because Jesus is called faithful, because his fidelity is indestructible, is divine.

The apostle St. Paul says to us that *the gifts and the call of God are irrevocable* (Rom 11:29). When we give, many times we repent of having given, we give until a certain moment, we give as long as certain conditions are realized: our gifts are full of repentance. However, the gifts of Jesus are without repentance: what he gives, he gives always; the love of Jesus is a most faithful love.

So that we might be able to understand how far the fidelity of God reaches, I am going to reveal a secret taken from Scripture: Do we believe that the predilection that God had for the Jewish people has disappeared? We deceive ourselves. No, there is the epistle in which St. Paul teaches us that that predilection of God is suspended, but not derogated. In the end times, the predilection of God will return, and the Jewish people will always be his chosen people.

Is such fidelity of God to his promise believable? The promises that he made to Abraham, to Isaac, and to Jacob are valid. Heaven and earth will pass away, but the words of God will not remain unfulfilled (Matt 24:35).

And that most faithful God gave us his heart, he gave us his love the day of our priestly ordination. Twenty-five years are not sufficient to diminish the love that God has for his priests; nor are fifty years, nor a century, nor a millennium capable of changing the love of God, because his love, like his gifts, are without repentance.

Right now he loves our brother like he loved him twenty-five years ago. I do not say that he loves him more, because when one loves with an infinite love he cannot love with greater intensity, but the graces that our brother has received throughout twenty-five years are the proof of that love so intense; they are speaking to us of that fidelity of our Lord Jesus Christ.

I understand that my words are clumsy, that I cannot even pluck the flower of this mystery, that I am not managing to explain how I see in the intimacy of my heart that fidelity of Jesus that surpasses all fidelities.

When the decay of men starts, when we grow old, when our faculties decline, when bit by bit the years wear away the vigor and lushness of our youth, we feel that an emptiness is forming around us. People forget us precisely when they should think of us, when we need support and love; such is the poor human heart!

Jesus is not like that. As time passes, his tenderness becomes fine and delicate, his love is like a full-bodied wine, which becomes more exquisite with time. Each day that passes Jesus loves us more; what does it matter that our head becomes white, what does it matter that our body degenerates, what does it matter that we see all our hopes wither if there is a heart that loves us with a love that does not change, with a love that overcomes all vicissitudes, with a love without repentance?

Nor are our faults, nor our negligences, nor our defects sufficient to diminish even the love of our Lord. Ah, if our Lord changed when we change! We poor things are so fragile, so inconstant! If our Lord would stop loving us because of our negligence and our ungratefulness, what would become of us, who are filled with ungratefulness and negligence?

Ah, no! But Jesus is so obliging, so merciful, and above all he knows how to forgive so delicately, knows how to forget completely, that, despite our ingratitude, he loves us. When we fall, his kind hand lifts us up; when we sully ourselves, his most sweet hand cleans us; when we go far from him, he is the Good Shepherd who goes in pursuit of the lost sheep in order to bring it back to the fold (Luke 15:4).

Jesus is faithful even with the ungrateful, Jesus is faithful even with the miserable, that is why when speaking about Jesus we do not need to look at our history and contemplate our interior: it is enough for us to look into his eyes, to divine the greatness of his heart, that we might know that he is most faithful, that he loves us, despite all the vicissitudes of life and all the inconstancies of the human heart.

Truly, his name is faithful...

II

BUT twenty-five years of the priesthood are not only a wonder of fidelity on the part of Jesus; they are also a wonder of fidelity on the part of the priest.

Twenty-five years ago, our brother heard in the intimacy of his heart a question that Jesus asked him, the same one that he asked St. Peter on the banks of Lake Tiberias in a radiant morning: *Digilis me plus his? Do you love me more than these?* To this lovely question of Jesus St. Peter answered: *Yes, Lord, you know that I love you* (John 21:15-16).

Observing a due proportion, Jesus asks all of us priests this question in the intimacy of our souls so that he can bestow on us the supreme dignity of the priesthood.

Do you love me more than these? Do we know what this question means? All of us Christians love Jesus, at least we all should love him, because St. Paul already said: *If anyone does not love the Lord, let him be accursed* (1 Cor 16:22). But Jesus wants the priest to love him in a special way, more than lay people, more than religious; the priest should love Jesus in a special way.

What does that singularity mean? What are the characteristics that priestly love has?

The priest has to love Jesus in an exclusive way. The simple faithful love our Lord and must love him, but the love of Jesus and whatever other noble and legitimate love can live side-by-side in their hearts. The simple Christian, the simple faithful, can, while loving Jesus Christ, form a home on earth, can devote his heart to his wife and his children without those legitimate and noble loves coming to disturb the peace of the love for Jesus.

We cannot. Jesus tells us: *Do you love me more than these?* In our heart no other affection fits than the love for Jesus and those that are directly derived from that divine affection. The day that our brother received the clerical vestiture he said to the Lord: "My riches are you, my glory is you, my love is you." *Lord, my allotted portion and my cup, you have made my destiny secure* (Ps 16:4).

And the day that he received the ordination to the subdiaconate, he affirmed still more his surrender and took a new step along this path; that day he renounced forever the more noble and legitimate affections of the heart and he consecrated his whole, entire heart to Jesus so that heart might be Jesus's, so that he would love no one else.

Ah! *Do you love me more than these?* This question means: these can love me and my creatures; you cannot; your love must be exclusive, your heart must be only for me, with all its beats and all its vital energy; this heart must be uniquely mine.

But it still has another meaning that I see clearly and palpably: on the day of our priestly ordination we surrender ourselves to Jesus so that he might make use of us. Our life is his, our thoughts are his, our words are his; our actions, work, time, and sacrifices are his; we do not live for ourselves; we live for him and we live for souls, but we live for souls because we live for Jesus Christ.

Because he has said: *whatever you did for one of these least brothers of mine, you did for me* (Matt 25:40). We ourselves do not have enterprises, we do not have treasures, we do not have glory to which to aspire. We only have one thing: *Jesus*. Jesus is our richness, Jesus is our love, Jesus is our life, as the apostle St. Paul said very well: *For to me life is Christ* (Phil 1:21).

And this singular love that the priest swears to Jesus Christ on the day of his ordination, and that could be expressed with the lovely formula of St. Peter, *Yes, Lord, you know that I love you*, that love that the priest swears the day of his ordination becomes fidelity when the priest has the good fortune of remaining always in that love.

Twenty-five years have not cooled the love in the heart of our brother that he swore to Jesus Christ on the day of his ordination; he still loves him, he loves him much more now. Also, after twenty-five years of the priesthood, he can repeat to our Lord the words of St. Peter: *Yes, Lord, you know that I love you.* And this phrase, if it is not more sincere, is richer than the one he said twenty-five years ago, because already for a quarter of a century he has proved the sincerity and the depth of his love.

For twenty-five years our brother has been faithful to Jesus; his heart has been for him, for Jesus; his life has been for him, for Jesus; and he has worked and has suffered for him. Now, with the security of twenty-five years of apostolic works, our brother can repeat the phrase of St. Peter: *Yes, Lord, you know that I love you.*

I am not unaware that in our priestly life there are many shortcomings and miseries; they are surely in the life of our brother. As the apostle St. Paul said, *we hold this treasure in earthen vessels* (2 Cor 4:7); the treasures of the priesthood that we have in this poor heart are so inconstant. Like the Latin poet, we can say: "I am human, and nothing human is foreign to me."[2]

We priests have all the grandures and all the defects of human nature; therefore, our fidelity is not like the fidelity of God, so pure, indestructible, perfect. Ah, no! Our fidelity is a poor fidelity; it is a fidelity that has deficiencies, that has stains. And, nevertheless, I think that it is something glorious that a poor creature like us is faithful; that it is something admirable that, in spite of all the vicissitudes of time and of all the ruses of the devil and of the temptations of the world, we, full of miseries, would preserve intact the love of God and be faithful to him.

How much I could say about this, if I did not fear exhausting your attention! We, I repeat it again, have all the human frailties, we live in a corrupt world, we feel the attraction of the things of earth; and, nevertheless, when for twenty-five years in spite of all those obstacles we preserve our heart and our life for God, ah, how are we not to be faithful, how is our fidelity not truly glorious?

God is faithful in a divine way, we faithful in a human way, but he and we are faithful; and I dare to apply to the priest the words of Scripture that refer to the Word of God. The priest also can be called *faithful and true* like Jesus; in his way, the priest is faithful, our brother has been faithful.

After twenty-five years, he preserves the same old priestly attitude; now, as a quarter of a century ago, he says to Jesus, *Yes, Lord, you know that I love you*, and the heart and the life of our brother is totally for Jesus. He will have had deficiencies and miseries because, after all, he has a fragile nature; but in the midst of those deficiencies, his heart, his body, his life, and his being belong to Jesus. He loves him as he did twenty-five years ago, he loves him more than he did twenty-five years ago, and the works and efforts of that very long period are an evident proof of his love and his fidelity.

Have we begun to glimpse what twenty-five years of priestly life mean? It is a mystery of profound fidelity; it is a mystery of fidelity on the part of Jesus for the priest; it is a mystery of fidelity of the priest for Jesus.

When we see that these twenty-five years, that took the charms and the freshness of the youthfulness of our brother, that have changed the face of our country and our world, that these twenty-five years that have made so much destruction on the earth have not been able to uproot the love of the heart of Jesus and of the heart of the priest, we feel joy and admiration, and paraphrasing the words of the apostle St. Paul, we say to time: Oh time! Where is your triumph?

I have concluded saying what I proposed, but I have another intimate, sweet word to say to Jesus in these most solemn moments:

Jesus, sweet Jesus, High Priest and Prince of priests; Jesus, you who are rightly called in Revelation by this most just name of Faithful! Oh Lord, I have not been able to translate your inexpressible fidelity of which my soul catches a glimpse!

Ah! I know that you are faithful like no one has been faithful, like no one can be, that your gifts are without repentance, and that your love has, oh faithful Jesus!, oh sweet Jesus!, what my clumsy words have not been able to express. Make it felt in the depths of souls, tell them that you are the most faithful, divinely faithful. You never forget, you always forgive, you tolerate, but, above all, you love, you envelop us with your tenderness, which rises above time, above that terrible enemy that is time!

Lord, but is what I have expressed about the intimate sentiments of your heart when I have spoked of our fidelity, of the fidelity of the priest, true?

Many will think that we are unfaithful because we are miserable; Lord, many will think that we are unfaithful because sometimes our eyes see the fascination of vanity and our hearts appear to want to withdraw from your gaze.

Ah, but you who are human, profoundly human; you who know what we suffer and fight; you who fathom the intimacy of our heart; you who are very merciful; you who have the sweetest patience, ah, Lord!, you see our deficiencies with eyes of love, and, in spite of them, you proclaim us to be faithful—is it not true?—when, in spite of our deficiencies, we preserve for you our hearts and our souls.

Lord, our brother, who celebrates twenty-five years of being a priest, has been faithful; if you will permit me a word from everyday language, he has been haphazardly faithful, Lord, but he has been faithful; his heart and his life have belonged to you always.

Lord, corroborate, perfect, enlarge this mystery of fidelity. I am not telling you to be more faithful than your priests, because you cannot do so! Continue being faithful, Jesus, continue loving us with tenderness, continue loving us with predilection, continue pouring into our hearts the treasures of divine love!

And make it, oh Lord!, so that we are more faithful each day, that each day we separate ourselves more from this world, that each day we love you more than the laity, that we love you more than religious, that we love you in a singular way, with an exclusive love, with a total love, with a selfless love, with a most faithful love, so that, Lord, whenever our life ends you can say to each one of your priests: *Good and faithful servant...share your master's joy!* (Matt 25:23). Amen.

CHAPTER 8

St. Francis of Assisi and the Priesthood

AT THE TWENTY-FIFTH ANNIVERSARY OF THE FIRST MASS OF A FRANCISCAN PRIEST

Non enim iudicavi me scire aliquid inter vos,
nisi Jesus Christum, et hunc crucifixum.
For I resolved to know nothing while I was with you
except Jesus Christ, and him crucified.
(1 CORINTHIANS 2:2)

ST. FRANCIS of Assisi is a remarkable saint. His soul and his life are saturated with poetry; his heart encloses a volcano of love; he bears in his body the stigmata of the body of Christ; he is a saint profoundly human and at the same time marvelously divine; he feels vibrating in his heart all the fibers of the heart of man and appears to feel the impulses of the heart of God. Being poor, small, and ignorant according to the world, he has had a decisive influence on human history. For seven centuries his word has resounded on the earth; for seven centuries his figure, sweet and heavenly, has shone in the midst of all the vicissitudes of history; for seven centuries he has fed an immense multitude of souls with his doctrine and his life.

But he appears to me specially remarkable, because without being a priest he is the father of an immense, of a distinguished, priestly family.

Out of humility, without a doubt, and because it suited the

loving and providential designs of God, he was not a priest; and, nevertheless, his doctrine, his example, and above all his spirit are eminently priestly and more than sufficient to form a priest in an admirable way. Furthermore, that doctrine and that spirit of St. Francis adds certain extraordinary and exquisite characteristics to the life of the priest.

And today since we come to accompany our brother, who is not only a priest but a Franciscan priest, and since he comes to give thanks to God for his twenty-five years of priestly life, I want to expound, taking advantage of this occasion, the Franciscan spirit and how the one who follows it can perfectly and marvelously realize the ideal of the priest.

The apostle St. Paul said that he did not want to know anything else but Christ, and him crucified. These words express the entire priestly spirit. The priest is a man who should have knowledge of only one thing, the knowledge of Jesus crucified.

But this divine knowledge is multiple, complex, profound. To have the knowledge of Jesus crucified means to have the knowledge of creatures, to have the knowledge of the divine, and to have the knowledge of sorrow.

St. Francis of Assisi marvelously possessed the knowledge of these three things, and, therefore, very few are able to say like him: *I resolved to know nothing while I was with you except Jesus Christ, and him crucified.*

He had the knowledge of creatures that produced in his heart that detachment, that heavenly poverty, that is like the pedestal of his glory. He had the clear and profound knowledge of Jesus that converted his heart into a volcano of love. And he had the deep knowledge of sorrow; that is why his heart was bursting with what he himself called "the perfect joy."[1]

You could say that St. Francis of Assisi is a man who, knowing creatures, detached himself completely from them; he is a man who, knowing Jesus, loved him with his entire heart; he is a man who, embracing Jesus, discovered the deep meaning of sorrow and tasted the perfect joy.

That is why it has always seemed to me that one of the best paintings—I do not say from the artistic point of view, but rather from the symbolic point of view—for representing the spirit of St. Francis of Assisi is that one in which the saint appears trampling the world with his foot and holding within his wounded arms Jesus crucified.

Now then: this noble knowledge that is founded in that knowledge of Jesus crucified, of which the apostle St. Paul speaks to us, is precisely that which we priests need. For us, the human and profane sciences, as brilliant as they may be, are not our own; at times they get in the way, at times we find the secret of utilizing them, but as a king utilizes the plebeians for his royal retinue. Our knowledge is the knowledge of Jesus crucified, and that knowledge, if we analyze it, includes the knowledge of the three things that I have just named: the knowledge of detachment, the knowledge of love, and the knowledge of perfect joy.

Perhaps one might think that I call detachment knowledge due to the need to accommodate myself to the text of Sacred Scripture that has served as my epigraph; but no, in order to love poverty one needs knowledge. You do not love what you do not know; you do not love passionately unless you know with profundity. In order to love poverty, to be married to her, it is necessary to have that knowledge, that knowledge of the Holy Spirit, that makes us understand in an ineffable way the vanity of the things of the earth.

Let us not believe that when St. Francis and his sons despised the things of this world, they always did it with heroic strength, no; they have done it with a logical movement of their spirit. They despise them because they have discovered that they are contemptible, because they have a celestial knowledge that makes them understand that divine detachment.

There is still more: every Christian should have that knowledge. Do we not remember what Jesus Christ taught us in the holy Gospel? *Which of you wishing to construct a tower does not first sit down and calculate the cost to see if there is enough for its completion? Otherwise, after laying the foundation and finding himself unable to finish the work the onlookers should laugh at him and say, "This one began to build but did not have the resources to finish." Or what king marching into battle would not first sit down and decide whether with ten thousand troops he can successfully oppose another king advancing upon him with twenty thousand troops? But if not, while he is still far away, he will send a delegation to ask for peace terms* (Luke 14:28-32).

After these two comparisons, in an unexpected manner, Jesus Christ says to us: *In the same way, everyone of you who does not renounce all his possessions cannot be my disciple* (Luke 14:33). At first glance, what do the tower and the money, the soldiers and the war, have to do with detachment? But if we enter more deeply into the words of the Gospel, we will find this perfectly true doctrine: to fight one needs soldiers and to build one needs money. Likewise, to be a Christian you need detachment.

That is why the same Jesus said in the Sermon on the Mount: *Blessed are the poor in spirit, for theirs is the kingdom of heaven* (Matt 5:3).

If the Christian must be detached, with greater reason must also the priest, as a consequence of the doctrine of Jesus.

Two of the disciples of John the Baptist who followed Jesus, attracted by the sweetness of his voice, by the eloquence of his words, and by the power of his miracles, asked him: *Teacher, where are you staying?* (John 1:38) Jesus Christ answered them: *Foxes have dens and birds of the sky have nests, but the Son of Man has nowhere to rest his head* (Luke 9:58). As if he wanted to say: Do you want to be my disciples? Do you want to accompany me in the apostolic work that I want to carry out? Do you want to be my collaborators? I do not even have a place to lay my head. The secret of my knowledge is poverty; that of my greatness, my detachment.

One day Jesus sent his apostles to carry out an apostolic mission as preparation for his future ministry (Mark 6:7-8). He sent them two by two and gave them precise instructions, not to enumerate the human means that they must use but, on the contrary, to prohibit them from carrying money, provisions, and a change of clothes. For the apostolic mission, money and provisions are a nuisance. The apostle, the priest, must have the holy liberty of the poor; and when we worry about provisions and clothing, then our ministry loses efficacy because it loses detachment. Blessed the priest who does not want to carry provisions or money! Blessed the priest who is going to fulfill his mission without thinking about the material resources of this world!

And where do you go to learn this divine knowledge of detachment? Ah! We know it very well: Francis of Assisi is the great master. He even threw his own clothes at the feet of his father, in front of the bishop of Assisi; and, poor and naked, he went to be married to Lady Poverty in St. Mary of the Angels, in the Porziuncola, in that Fraciscan monument anointed with the exquisite, with the lovely memories of the little poor one of Assisi.

His doctrine is the doctrine of poverty. He teaches us with his word and with his example how in the priestly life it is indispensable that our hearts be empty.

There is still more: Francis of Assisi possessed the secret of making detachment sweet, of making it beautiful, of making it practical. We consider poverty as something very repugnant, as something dirty, as something full of misfortunes; but when with his magic hand Francis touches poverty, then we see it as something of heaven: it is a ray of light, it is a spark of God, it is something that steals our hearts. Do we not believe that it is a most solid foundation for the priesthood to carry in our heart that spirit of detachment?

But the spirit of Francis is not only the spirit of poverty. Poverty is nothing more than the way, poverty is the antechamber, it is the atrium of what truly comes to constitute the Franciscan spirit. This spirit is love, a love that, due to its unique characteristics, is traditionally called *seraphic love*, because among the blessed spirits those who love with greater intensity are the seraphs.

Ah! The priest needs to love much; even more so: the priest needs only one thing—to love!

And this doctrine is not mine. We have received it from the very lips of Jesus Christ, when in order to constitute St. Peter as supreme head of the whole Church and to put in his hands all his treasures, he only demanded of him one thing, he only asked him one question, but he did it three times: *Simon, son of John, do you love me?... Do you love me more than these?* (John 21:15–17), as if he wanted to say, in a most eloquent way, that in order to shepherd the lambs, to continue the apostolic work, to be a priest, you only need one thing—to love Christ.

And truly the priest is a prodigious work of love. Some think and consider the priest as a professional who knows his art, who works by his own knowledge. No, we are not professionals.

At times the priest is thought to be an office worker of God, who is disposed to hear all, to give them all advice. No, the priest is not an office worker; he only devotes himself to loving.

The Christian people call us with the sweetest name of father, and truly we are, because it is proper for a father to love. He is the man who has his heart full of love and who does all that he does for his children because he loves them. Such is the priest, the father of souls.

The priest needs to love. He who does not love is not apt for the priesthood, he is not capable of aspiring to the divine paternity. Analogously, Jesus Christ asks us this question before our ordination: *Do you love me more than these?* And until we say with all the sincerity of our souls, *Yes, Lord, you know that I love you*, until then our hands are not anointed and the priestly spirit does not descend upon our soul.

Where do you learn the knowledge of love? How do we make it such that our heart is surrendered to make Jesus Christ be all for us and that for him we live and for him we die?

There is a marvelous school of love in the Church: the school of St. Francis of Assisi. Ah! He knew the marvelous divine knowledge. In his heart there was an immense love, an impassioned love, a most tender love. What characteristics does Francis's love have? It is divine and human at the same time, as human as a love that cries, a love that becomes small…our hearts tremble with tenderness when we see him in that distant night of Christmas arranging with his own hands the Nativity scene, embracing with his arms the image of the Child Jesus, with a heart full of emotion and eyes full of tears…

It is a human love, a love that cries, a love that is moved; but at the same time, it is a love that becomes entranced, that passes the nights savoring this word: my God and my all.

It is a human love that sings, that feels; but at the same time it is a divine love that in this world receives the sacred wounds and savors joys and sorrows that it cannot express in the language of man.

In order to learn how to love, there is nothing like the school of Francis.

Jesus would like for all priests to learn in that school, to love Jesus like Francis loved him, in a most tender and passionate way, at the same time divine and human; for in Jesus is concentrated all our affections, since he is the delight of heaven and earth.

But the divine knowledge of Jesus is not complete when creatures are despised nor when Jesus is passionately loved. Jesus Christ, before all and above all, is Victim and Priest. Jesus Christ appears in diverse ways on earth, but the most sublime way was on the cross. That is why a great French orator said with much justice: "There is nothing greater in the universe than Jesus Christ; nothing greater in Jesus Christ than his sacrifice."[2] Jesus Christ crucified is the ultimate word of wisdom and of power and of love. That is why St. Paul not only said that Jesus was the only knowledge, but Jesus crucified. We, who immolate him every day on the altar; we, who live from his sacrifice, because the supreme reason of the priest for existing is the divine mystery of Calvary and of the cross; we, who every day share with souls the fruits of the sacrifice of Calvary and of the altar, should not preach anything other than Jesus Christ, and him crucified.

We live from Calvary, we live from the cross, and we should for the same reason understand Jesus Christ crucified. But this does not simply mean that we are filled with compassion when considering his cruel sorrow. To understand Jesus Christ crucified, it is not enough that we feel torrents of divine love, but rather it is necessary to know and participate in the unfathomable mystery of his sorrow.

Priests should penetrate those depths, not only because we have to teach the doctrine and the spirit of Jesus Christ, which is only known in sorrow; not only because we have to say that the cross is the symbol of the Christian, not a hollow symbol, not a cold symbol, but a living symbol; but rather we should know the depths of the sorrow of Jesus because we have to bear in our souls and in our bodies the marks of the sacrifice.

The priest is not always a martyr in the ordinary sense of this word, but he is a martyr because he has to suffer that martyrdom, unknown and slow, which is the priestly life, because in it he has to renounce all things, even legitimate affections of our hearts; he has to live devoted to souls, sacrificing our time, our tastes; he has to be the target of the enemies of God and bear in his heart those intimate sorrows that Jesus Christ tends to share with his friends.

All this is proper to the priest. The priest has to be a martyr, and therefore he has to know sorrow thoroughly.

And do we know when love is thoroughly known? When from it joy springs up. Knowledge of creatures produces detachment; knowledge of God produces love; knowledge of the cross and of sorrow produces joy.

All the saints have told it to us in one way or another. Do we not remember the words that St. Thérèse of the Child Jesus said, that contemporary of ours who in full youth lost her petals like a rose: "I have found happiness and joy, but only in sorrow?"[3]

Paradox, worldly people will say; mystery, we say.

But for the sons of Francis, it is a doctrine that is very familiar to them. It is enough to remember that delightful parable of perfect joy, which we have savored so many times, in which Francis declares that in suffering for the blessed Christ, who suffered so much for us, is the secret of perfect joy.

This is the deepest knowledge you can have of sorrow—when from it sprouts celestial joy. The other joys are imperfect, passing, ephemeral; this one is not; it is solid, it is immortal, it is the perfect joy.

The priest should have the knowledge of sorrow, should possess the secret of perfect joy, because only thus can he completely fulfill his priestly ministry.

Is the Franciscan spirit not adequate for priestly life and work?

The priest who is pervaded with the spirit of St. Francis fulfills his priestly duties perfectly.

The twenty-five years of priestly life of our brother are pervaded with the priestly spirit and are full of the Franciscan perfumes—the perfume of poverty, the perfume of love, the perfume of sorrow—and those three perfumes form the celestial salve with which he anoints the head of Jesus and is filled with consolation.

Let us then give thanks to our Lord God for the gifts that he has poured out upon his Franciscan and priestly soul. Let us ask him to continue pouring out his graces intensely upon him, so that he might always fulfill his priestly ministry.

But what better hands than those with the stigmata of St. Francis to elevate our thanks toward heaven on the occasion of the priestly jubilee of our brother, who is one of his sons who is known to have engraved in his heart all the symbolism of his doctrine and of his spirit?

Oh Father St. Francis, without being a priest yourself, you are the father of this distinguished family of priests, and a father not by an artificial coincidence, but because your sons have come forth from your truly priestly heart, even if you have not received the priesthood!

May the thanksgivings of our brother arrive in heaven by your hands and by the immaculate hands of the Virgin Mary, enriched with the thanksgivings of all those of us who love him. Present them before the throne of God so that he sends him a torrent of the most abundant graces so that he becomes a perfect Franciscan and a priest according to the heart of God.

CHAPTER 9

Divine Friendship

AT THE FIFTIETH ANNIVERSARY OF A FIRST MASS

Jam non dicam vos servos, vos autem dixi amicos; quia omnia quaecumque audivi a Patre meo nota feci vobis.
I no longer call you slaves, because a slave does not know what his master is doing. I have called you friends, because I have told you everything I have heard from my Father.
(John 15:15)

Holy Church has the prerogative of perceiving with a marvelous intuition the depths of the mysteries of Jesus and of expressing what she contemplates in a simple ceremony, in a rapid and comprehensive phrase, like the words I just cited and that Jesus Christ our Lord pronounced in the Upper Room on the night of the ineffable mysteries.

The Church has picked these words and has made them the golden ring that connects the two principal parts of the rite of priestly ordination. The bishop has already imposed his august hands on the head of the ordained; he has dressed him with the priestly vestments; he has anointed his hands with the holy oil. Then, the bishop and the new priest celebrate the Mass together, forming one single heart, one single soul, saying in unison the mysterious words of the Eucharist. And when the sacrifice has been consummated by communion, when the new priest feels in the depths of his soul the unutterable delight of his first priestly communion, Holy Church makes the bishop say in a solemn manner—and wrapping it, so to speak, in the folds of that mysterious and divine chant of the Alleluia—the sweet phrase that Jesus Christ pronounced in the Upper Room: *I no longer call you servants; I have called you my friends, because I have made known to you all that I received from the Father.*[1]

And when the accents of the Alleluia cease, the second part of the ordination begins, brief but bursting with profundity and beauty. The bishop returns to impose his hands on the new priest so that he receives the Holy Spirit. He takes between his hands the hands of the new priest so that he can promise obedience and reverence, and then he seals the sacred ritual with a kiss of peace.

I think that the golden ring with which the two obvious parts, so to speak, of the priestly ordination are connected, I think that the phrase of the Holy Gospel that Holy Church places in a magnificent setting and repeats to our ears the day on which, full of respect and love, we just received holy ordination, expresses the depths of the mystery of the priesthood in what is most intimate.

Ah, yes! To be a priest is to be a friend of Jesus, intimate friend and favored friend. The phrase from the Gospel is extended to all Christians, because all are friends of Jesus. But we are friends in a singular way. The words of Jesus in the mouth of the bishop on the day of our priestly ordination have a new meaning, a divine one. They speak to us of an exquisite intimacy, of an ineffable friendship. The intimate depths of our priesthood is there, it is a very close and singular friendship with our Lord Jesus Christ.

And I want to talk about that friendship today, because we came to accompany a brother of ours who, in the joy of his heart, comes to give thanks to God for fifty years of priesthood.

What are fifty years of priesthood? They are fifty years of friendship with Jesus, of intimate friendship, of priestly friendship.

And the friendship of Jesus is not like the poor human friendship that time often withers, that is subject to all the vicissitudes of life, no; Jesus is the faithful friend, he is a friend forever; the Book of

Revelation teaches it to us, his name is faithful and true (Rev 19:11); he is the faithful friend that does not abandon, that knows how to pardon, that knows how to hold close those whom he loves. And that priestly friendship is a friendship that is always growing, like the resplendent dawn, whose light keeps growing without ceasing, until it reaches the fullness of midday, according to the saying from Sacred Scripture (Prov 4:18).

I want to talk about that friendship of Jesus with the priest. Ah, I feel the difficulty of plunging my poor pupils into the profundity of the mystery; it is so deep, it is so beautiful, that I feel something like a kind of spiritual humility. Because the mystery about which I am going to speak is an intimate mystery, one of those that is guarded in the sacred amphora of our hearts, one of those that does not emerge to the exterior, one of those that is felt in the silence of seclusion.

But I am sure that what I am going to say will find an echo in the heart of a priest fortunate to have lived fifty years of priesthood; I am sure that what I am going to say will also carry a ray of light and of love to the hearts of the faithful that they might better understand the priest, so that they might love him with all their soul, so that they might protect him with their love, with their respect, and with their prayers, so that there might be established more intimately than ever that very close union that should exist between the priest and the faithful, since all are one in Christ Jesus, the Supreme Priest, who in a burst of love and of mercy has wanted to make us participants of his priesthood.

Scripture says that God is love (1 John 4:8,16). And he is indescribable love who in his perfect unity, in his ineffable simplicity, encloses fullness and richness. Our love, our poor love, the poor affections of our heart, imitate that infinite love, but it is impossible that our love can take in its fullness; each one of our affections, as it receives a spark of that infinite love, and likewise all the human affections, have their own characteristics: nuptial love is burning, a father's love is generous, and maternal love is gentle and delicate.

Friendship is characterized by trust and is fed by secrets; because of this our Lord Jesus Christ, when on the night of the Last Supper he declared the secret of his soul saying that he was our friend, characterized that divine affection of his heart with this unmistakable quality: *I have called you friends,* because I have made known to you all the secrets of my heart, *because I have told you everything I have heard from my Father.*

It is not one of many reasons for his friendship: it is the typically characteristic and specific quality. He is our friend because he has given us the secret of his soul. I think that one cannot better characterize friendship than by saying that the friend pours out his heart into the heart of his friend; and our Lord Jesus Christ pours out his soul into our soul, he makes known to us the secrets of his heart.

But, will this saying of Jesus Christ prove to be divine hyperbole? Is he, perchance, able to deposit in the smallness of our spirits the treasures of light that he received from the heart of the Father? Are our narrow hearts able to receive from the loving lips of Jesus all that he heard from the Father? Heaven and earth will pass away, but the words of Jesus will never pass away (Matt 24:35); if we do not manage to understand them, what does that matter! Our ignorance does not limit his power, does not put up fences to his love.

He has said it to us: we have received all the secrets of his soul, and those secrets should be like the precious seed that is hidden in our hearts, and that develops little by little, like the grain of wheat that falls on the earth, and later emerges as a tender shoot that turns into a firm stem, and produces leaves, flowers, and fruits.

We have the secrets of Jesus substantially in our soul. But God, who knows how to adapt himself to our smallness, who knows how to accommodate himself to his creatures, makes it such that they develop according to the laws of human psychology, which needs time, in such a way that each passing instant is able to bring a development to that blessed seed that has germinated in our hearts.

And time is in charge of developing the secrets of Jesus Christ little by little, in such a way that the profound and vivid word of the apostle St. Paul is fulfilled: *Nos...gloriam Domini speculantes in eamden imaginem transformamur a claritate in claritatem* (2 Cor 3:18). The friendship of Jesus is a marvel of light, and that marvel of light does not shine from one moment to another in all its splendor; rather, we continue contemplating the divine glory, we are continually transformed little by little into the same image, but from glory to glory.

Would we be able to contemplate that marvelous development in fifty years of priesthood? Through what fullness of light, what marvels of splendor would the priest pass through in order to arrive at fifty years of his priesthood? What transformation would happen in his soul when he has contemplated the glory of God for half a century?

Let us examine it with respect and with love.

I have the audacity to peek into the heart of Jesus and to discover his divine secrets.

The first secret that he tells to his priests is the personal secret of each one of us. The first thing that Jesus has said to me is the mystery of my destiny, I would almost say that mystery of my predestination. It seems incredible, but we are a mystery to ourselves. Scripture makes us understand it: *Nondum apparuit quid erimus. What we shall be has not yet been revealed* (1 John 3:2). I would dare to say: it has not yet even appeared what we are; it is so difficult to penetrate the profundities of our souls!

And Jesus tells us what we are, what we will be; he tells us our own word, the secret of our destiny, the secret of our mission.

One day, in the splendid dreams of our youth, we received the first revelation of ourselves: with astonished eyes, with beating hearts, with souls in an attitude of adoration, we listened to the words of Jesus, which he said to us as to his apostles on the shore of Lake Tiberias: *Come after me, and I will make you fishers of men* (Matt 4:19; Mark 1:17).

And, like the apostles, we left the nets, we left our parents in order to go in pursuit of the Divine Unknown who called us. We believed in our naïveté that we had found the solution to all our problems: I already know my destiny, I already know my mission—I will be a priest.

But, with this first word of light and love, did what we were going to be appear? No. St. Thérèse of the Child Jesus, the most refined observer of spiritual things, teaches us that our Lord God does not tell us in one moment all that he has to tell us; little by little, with a divine slowness, he lifts for us the veils that cover our own souls and our own destiny. Ah! During our life we continue little by little learning what we are and what we should be, and the supreme revelation of ourselves is not realized on the earth but in eternity, when man receives, as Scripture says, that *new name, which no one knows except the one who receives it* (Rev 2:17).

In our priestly life, little by little our mission was specified. Not all priests have the same mission. St. Paul made us understand: *Numquid omnes apostoli? Numquid omnes prophetae? Numquid omnes doctores? Are all apostles? Are all prophets? Are all teachers?...Do all have gifts of healing?* (1 Cor 12:29-30). No, the Holy Spirit spreads his gifts as he wants; among those same apostles that were formed in the most holy heart of Jesus there is a notable variety, I would almost say an opposition that is felt in their destinies: St. John, the sweet one, the contemplative, how distinct he is from Peter, the active, the burning one. On the shore of Lake Tiberias, our Lord made note of the diversity and even the opposition when he said to St. Peter: *What if I want him to remain until I come? What concern is it of yours? You follow me* (John 21:22). Those two apostles, such friends, so united, go distinct ways, have distinct appearances, have received a distinct mission. One's mission is mysterious. What did Jesus mean by these mysterious words: *What if I want him to remain until I come? What concern is it of yours?* We do not know, but we understand that that word is distinct from the other that he said to St. Peter: *You follow me.*

Little by little he reveals what we are; our Lord tells us the secret of ourselves. And when one arrives at the summit of life, when one arrives like our brother at fifty years of priesthood, I will not say that one comprehends the new and divine name that we will receive in eternity, but, yes, one knows enough to feel the serenity of the heights, to observe the tranquility on the summit, and to contemplate in that region to which the noises of the earth do not arrive the path traveled, and to foresee with great assurance the path that we have yet to travel.

Blessed serenity of the summits, full of light because the years have made Jesus reveal to us little by little all that he heard from the Father about our destiny and about our predestination!

But the priest does not only know the secret of his own soul; he knows the secret of many souls. Ah! Precious secret! Let us not think that the intimate mystery of souls consists in the application of prescribed formulas, of ready-made spiritual medicines that are taken with the hand and are given to each according to their needs. This would be a very paltry and inexact way of conceiving of the ministry of souls; no, every soul is a revelation.

If we are faithful, Jesus tells us his secret about each soul, because each soul is unique. "There is hardly a soul," says St. John of the Cross, "that in the middle of its journey seems like another."[2] Every soul has its own appearance, its own mission, and its own resources. And he who dedicates himself to the ministry of souls needs to receive from God the secret of each one of them.

At the same time, one gradually penetrates the secrets of Jesus; substantially he has told us everything, but the imperfection of our spirit requires that little by little we begin to understand the secrets of light of Jesus Christ, and a whole life is not sufficient to exhaust those ineffable treasures.

Each soul is a revelation; and we do not only learn in it what God wants of it, but through souls we understand Jesus. Ah! There is no Gospel similar to the gospel of souls, there is no way of knowing Jesus Christ comparable with this way.

When we have drawn close to souls many times, when we have probed their depths, when we have received the revelation from God about them, then we know in a better way who Jesus is, his goodness, his love, his mercy, his justice, his sanctity, the divine things, the proceedings that he employs with souls, the sweetness that he pours into them.

I do not know if I exaggerate, but I have to say what I feel and what I think. It has been said that if the Gospel had been lost, one would be able to remake it with the writings of the holy Fathers; but I think that if the Gospel and the writings of the holy Fathers were lost, one would be able to remake it substantially with souls. Whoever knows them, whoever has received the revelation of them, would be able to express all the words of the holy Gospel and describe the heart of Jesus Christ, just as in the immortal book that was shown to us.

How can we not be the intimate friends of Jesus if he reveals the secrets of souls to us?

Let us think about the richness of light that our brother will carry in his spirit after fifty years of probing the depths of souls; fifty years of intimate ministry of souls is like a half century of probing the spaces of the firmament. Let us imagine an exceptional astronomer who possessed marvelous apparatuses, who had extraordinary knowledge, and who had spent his life contemplating the heavens: what marvels of light would he not have contemplated? The firmament of souls is more splendid, is more beautiful, is greater than that which our eyes contemplate in the calm nights; it has stars more numerous, more beautiful, more splendid; it sings the glory of God in a more sonorous way.

What will our brother have learned in a half century of probing the depths of numerous souls, chosen by God, loved by him? Let us respect his intimate secret, and let us proclaim to the face of the earth that priests are the friends of Jesus, because we have received the secrets of his soul.

Although these treasures are so rich, they are not the most opulent that the priest has. Jesus has revealed to us other secrets, greater, more profound, more beautiful, because he has revealed to us the secret of his own heart.

The earthly friend has given us evidence of his friendship when he speaks to us about his projects, about his hopes, about his sorrows; but the supreme manifestation of his friendship is when he speaks to us about himself, when he tells us his intimate secrets, when he pours out his heart into our heart. And Jesus Christ has done this: he has revealed to us all of his secrets, he has told us who he is, he has uncovered his indescribable origin in the bosom of the Father, he has told us how he was born from that infinite bosom into the splendors of sanctity, and he has spoken to us about his profound self-emptying upon coming to this earth, and of the throbbings of love and of sorrow of his most holy heart, and he has told us the secret of his sorrow and the secret of his fecundity and the secret of his joy.

Do we doubt it? Does the insidious objection again rise in our spirit? Are these just divine hyperboles? Is Jesus actually able to pour out his heart into our poor human hearts? Would we be able to hear all that he heard from the Father? If he heard it from the infinite Father, no one would be able to understand it, except he who is God!

But there is a phrase from the apostle St. Paul that helps us decipher the divine mystery; the Apostle says that *faith is the substance of things to be hoped for* (Heb 11:1[3]). Do we understand the beautiful and profound word? He who possesses faith has substantially what the blessed possess in heaven, the substance of what we hope for. Ah! We hope to contemplate God face to face, we hope to be bathed in the splendors of his light, we hope to look into the divine abyss. So, we have the substance of what we hope for.

Whoever has in his hands a grain of wheat can say that he has many ears that will sprout from it, and he who has a handful of seeds can say that he has in his hand the opulent future harvest. We have faith—the divine seed of eternal life—in our hearts, so we already possess heaven. But, ah! the comparison is insufficient; the grain is not the ripe corn, but the origin of it; and what we possess by faith is the same substance, not the seed, the substance of the things we hope for.

In order to explain my thought I will say: all the knowledge of St. Thomas Aquinas is contained in that seed of life that we learned from childhood. The contemplation of the greatest mystics does not surpass that picture; what they know, we know; only they know it in a way so profound, so clear, so beautiful, and we know it in a way so imperfect, so enigmatic, so covered in shadows. But the object of our knowledge is the same: we have—I enjoy repeating it—the substance of the things we hope for, the substance of what St. Thomas Aquinas knew, the substance of what John of the Cross and Teresa of Avila contemplated. We have, by our faith, the substance of all those divine things.

Ah! Jesus has revealed to us all that he heard from the Father: divine revelation, the opulent, the marvelous explosion of light that Jesus contemplated in the bosom of the Father, we have here, Jesus Christ gave it to us enveloped in the sacred shadows of faith.

But if all Christians possess the substance of the things we hope for, priests possess them in a singular manner, in a divine manner; for us, those secrets of Jesus are clearer, they are more beautiful, they are more harmonious. Did Jesus Christ not say to his apostles: *Knowledge of the mysteries of the kingdom of God has been granted to you; but to the rest, they are made known through parables* (Luke 8:10)?

Because Jesus Christ, before ascending to heaven, made a request of us, a transcendent and glorious request: *Go…teaching them to observe all that I have commanded you* (Matt 28:19-20). What a gigantic and glorious undertaking, yet terrible! To teach everyone, to teach everything. Can our littleness realize the divine undertaking?

But one cannot teach except what one knows. If God commands me to teach all things, it is because he wants to teach me all things; if he says to go throughout the world to preach the mysteries of the kingdom of heaven, it is because he plans, in secret, in the silence of the tabernacle, to communicate to me the divine treasures of his light.

And so it is: by the grace of our ordination, by the graces of this state, we receive torrents of light in order to know the mysteries of the faith and power to teach them to our brothers. Similar to the apostle St. Peter, we have been confirmed, and we have the duty of confirming our brothers in the truth.

When the priest has received from God as a special mission to teach the great mysteries of Jesus Christ, when he has filled his life with a half century of theological teaching, ah! imagine the treasure of light that he will carry in his soul. There are the secrets of Jesus, there are the treasures of heaven. Truly, Jesus is his friend, because he has revealed to him the secrets of his heart, because he has told him all that he heard from his Father.

But there remains for me to say a mysterious and most secret word.

Up to this point one could follow the parallel between human friendship and divine: to our friends we say what we think about them, we explain to them our affections and our projects; but human intimacy stops there. We can give all, communicate to our friends all that is ours, but we are not able to give to them the gift of ourselves.

The substantial secret of our hearts and of our souls is that we are powerless to do it. We say that we give ourselves, that we make a gift of ourselves, but this is something of a hyperbole, it is a manner of speaking. We give our hearts and our souls because we give all that comes from our hearts and our souls; but to give the heart itself, to give the soul itself, to take our heart, to put in another heart, to pull out our soul and to fuse it with another soul so that the other soul, without needing words, discovers what ours has inside, who we are and what we think, is impossible.

But what is impossible for men, is possible for Jesus.

Ah! The ultimate, the profound, the divine secret of Jesus is a substantial secret; he not only makes us know his affections, but he gives us his heart, and he has given us his soul: we have it within ourselves.

Blessed be Jesus, who is able to fully satisfy the desires of his heart! We cannot; we inevitably have to stop ourselves before the limit of our littleness and of our own fragility. He does not; he has given himself to us without limits, he gives himself to us in the Holy Eucharist, he enters within our own hearts.

And if I have to say all that I feel, the Eucharist does not even satisfy me. It is a sacrament, it is a means; what fills my soul is the fruit of the sacrament, the reality of the sacrament, as the theologians say. Because communion is something fleeting; it is, we could say, something imperfect; what is perfect, what is divine, what is immortal is what communion leaves here within. It leaves me Jesus, it leaves me God, whom nothing and no one can snatch from me; not angels, nor demons, nor the heights, nor the depths are capable of taking away that God whom I carry in my soul and who is the definitive and profound secret of our Lord Jesus Christ (Rom 8:38-39).

Do we see how Jesus Christ can say, "I have given you everything I have received from my Father"? What was it that he received from the Father? He received his being: he is the word of the Father, the wisdom of the Father; he received from the Father the substance of life. And that substance and that wisdom and that word he gives to us.

Ah! I do not only have faith, I have God within my heart, I have Jesus within my soul; what Jesus received from the Father, his substantial secret, I have in the depths of my heart.

And to have Jesus in one's soul for fifty years, and to possess him every day more and more closely, to become familiar with him, to divine his thoughts, to feel the beating of his heart within our own hearts, to live with him for a half century in an intimate communion, in close familiarity, ah! It must not be my stammering lips that express the divine, the ineffable mystery!

Do we see it? Jesus has revealed to us the secrets of his heart. He is our friend, because he has told us all that he received from his heavenly Father.

Fifty years of priesthood are fifty years of intimacy and light; fifty years of priesthood can only be expressed by those words of the apostle St. Paul: *Nos...autem gloriam Domini speculantes, in eamdem imaginem transformatur a claritate in claritatem. All of us, gazing...on the glory of the Lord, are being transformed into the same image from glory to glory* (2 Cor 3:18).

I have said all that I had to say. I do not dare to speak to my brother because my words perhaps would wound his sensitive heart; I will speak to Jesus, to the Supreme Priest, and I will speak to him with all my heart and with all my soul:

Jesus, Eternal Priest, Supreme Priest, who on the night of your Passion declared to us the ineffable mystery of your intimacy, of your divine friendship!

Lord, I, united with my brothers present here, give you thanks because you revealed to our brother the secrets of your heart, because you filled his heart with light, because you have told him all that you heard from your heavenly Father.

Oh, Jesus! Guard in his heart the divine treasures. Ah! Do not only guard them, make them grow, make him know you better and know souls better. Make it so that every day he sinks more deeply into the mysteries of the kingdom of heaven and, above all, that he be united intimately and closely with you, that every day his clear and pure soul be filled with light, the light of your heart, the light of heaven.

Be his friend, his intimate friend, the friend that consoles him, that strengthens him, that elevates him, that sanctifies him; elevate him, sanctify him, and purify him with the light of your face, with the splendid light of your divine heart.

Oh Jesus, fulfill, consummate in him your priestly work, let nothing stop the emanation of your light, so that he knows on earth your secrets deeply and copiously, so that there in heaven, upon receiving the new name that no one knows except he who has received it, he might sink into the abyss of light where he can be eternally happy with the contemplation of your divine essence. Amen.

CHAPTER 10

The Image of the Father

AT THE TWENTY-FIFTH ANNIVERSARY OF THE EPISCOPAL ORDINATION OF MAXIMINO RUIZ Y FLORES†

Qui vidit me vidit et Patrem.
Whoever has seen me has seen the Father.
(John 14:9)

All the gifts of God are truly inexpressible; there is something hidden in them, something mysterious that disconcerts our spirit. God put within them the splendor of the infinite, and the infinite always dazzles our poor human understanding.

That is why Jesus Christ said to the Samaritan at the edge of the well of Jacob: *Si scires donum Dei! If you knew the gift of God...* (John 4:10). Who can fully know it on earth? Who can know that gift, at once unique and manifold, heavenly and human, who is our Lord Jesus Christ?

And the more excellent and perfect the gift of God, the more intimate and complete Jesus Christ gives himself to us, the more incomprehensible and mysterious is the gift of God. Now, the priesthood is a marvelous communication of Jesus Christ to our misery; it

† Original: This chapter is taken from the sermon that His Excellency the Archbishop of Mexico City preached at the episcopal jubilee of His Excellency Don Maximino Ruiz, titular Bishop of Derbe and Vicar General of the Archdiocese of Mexico City, on September 8, 1938, in the Basilica of Tepeyac.

is a most high gift, a perfect gift. That is why if all the gifts of God are inexpressible, even more so is the priesthood inexpressible.

St. John Baptist Vianney, who knew this divine gift with an experiential light, dared to say: "What the priesthood is no one will ever know on earth; we will only know in heaven. Because if we knew it in this world, we would die, not out of fear, but out of love."[1]

And in a more perfect way the fullness of the priesthood that God in his mercy and in his love has bestowed upon his bishops is truly inexpressible. If the priesthood is a mystery, the fullness of the priesthood has to be a greater one because, if you will allow me the expression, it is a more divine one.

That is why today we have come to give thanks to our Lord God for the twenty-five years of episcopal life that one illustrious prelate has received from the hands of God; we have come to accompany him in his righteous joy and in his immense gratitude. We have the closest ties with him, because he has spent many years in this diocese sacrificing to do good, because he has many holy ties with us. For us he is a brother, for many a father, for all a friend, perhaps with that exquisite friendship, similar to full-bodied and aged wine.

But because we cannot thank him whom we do not know, nor can we feel in our souls the whole weight of the gratitude when the magnitude of the gift received does not appear clearly to our eyes, it is necessary that we focus the gaze of our spirits on that inexpressible gift of the fullness of the priesthood for which we have to give thanks to our Lord God.

Our venerable brother has scrutinized the divine mystery many times; but perhaps my words, if God blesses them, will touch the most intimate fibers of his soul.

As for the faithful, what I am going to say will not only serve you so that with all your soul you can appreciate the inexpressible gift of the priesthood, but also so that respect and veneration for the bishops can grow in your souls; because, despite the magnitude of our miseries, we carry the riches of heaven in a fragile vessel. How the faithful should not be stopped by our human deficiencies! The precious pearl is not worth less because someone sets it in crude metal; rather, the crudeness of the setting will make the splendid iridescence of the set pearl stand out.

All the greatness and beauty of creatures depends on God putting in them a reflection of his divine countenance.

Even in the natural order, if there is beauty in the mysterious firmament, in the mysterious ocean, in the gentle countrysides, in the shady forests, it is because when God passed by them, according to the expression of St. John of the Cross, he went leaving a glimmer of his beauty in all the works of his hands:

> and having looked at them,
> with his image alone,
> clothed them in beauty.[2]

If this is true—and it is—when treating material creatures, how much more is it when treating souls.

Souls are worth what is divine in them: their greatness consists in their capacity for God. They can compare themselves to crystals. A crystal is nothing other than a capacity for light; its nature, its beauty, consists in seeing itself inundated with rays of the sun. In the same way, the greatness of a soul consists in receiving a glimmer of the divine: and the greater the capacity of the soul and the brighter the light that God puts in it, the greater and so much more beautiful and holier the soul is.

On the day of our baptism, our Lord poured out divine gifts into us. St. Peter describes them with magisterial words: *Per quem maxima et pretiosa nobis promissa donavit: ut per haec efficiamini divinae naturae consortes. Through these, he has bestowed on us the precious and very great promises, so that through them you may come to share in the divine nature* (2 Pet 1:4).

The Christian, who participates in the nature of God, is able to exclaim with the holy audacity of the apostle St. Paul: *Ipsius enim et genus sumus. We are the offspring of God* (Acts 17:29).

We bear in our souls something divine, and through that divine thing that is in us, we are able to enter into such intimate relationships with the three Persons of the Most Holy Trinity.

The apostle St. John helps us to glimpse the mystery: *Quod vidimus et audivimus, annuntiamus vobis, ut et vos societatem habeatis nobiscum, et societas nostra sit cum Patri, et cum Filio ejus Jesu Christo. What we have seen and heard we proclaim now to you, so that you too may have fellowship with us; for our fellowship is with the Father and with his Son, Jesus Christ* (1 John 1:3).

Indeed, the Christian has an intimate relationship with the heavenly Father: he is his adopted son. *See what love the Father has bestowed on us*, says the same apostle, *that we may be called the children of God. Yet so we are* (1 John 3:1).

With Jesus Christ I was going to say that we are brothers; no, more than brothers, we are one with him; we are incorporated into him, *for you are all one in Christ Jesus*, affirms St. Paul (Gal 3:28).

And the Holy Spirit has poured himself out into our hearts (Rom 5:5). On the day of our baptism he has made our souls his temple, and he has united himself to us in such a way that he is the soul of our soul and the life of our life.

Ah! If only we knew what it means to be a Christian! If only we knew the riches of our vocation!

But the priest has a new union, a more intimate relationship with the three divine Persons, because he has received from them a new and opulent infusion of the divine.

The priest, according to the Christian tradition, is another Christ, "sacerdos, alter Christus," because he is singularly united to Jesus, because he participates in something exquisite, profound, transcendental of Christ our Lord, which is his priesthood.

The priesthood of Jesus is related to all his titles and linked with all his prerogatives; because he is Priest, he is Redeemer, Master, Sanctifier, King. And we participate in that divine priesthood by the character that priestly ordination imprints on our souls.

And by participating in this priesthood, by having an intimate relationship with Jesus Christ, we have a new and very close relationship with the heavenly Father. He looks at us like he looks at Jesus Christ. I think—pardon my daring—that the priesthood participates in those words that the heavenly Father directed to Jesus Christ on the mount of the Transfiguration: *This is my beloved son. Listen to him* (Mark 9:7). Is the priesthood not a transfiguration, a transfiguration of our misery that he fills with heavenly light?

And the Holy Spirit, like the luminous cloud of which the Gospel speaks, envelops our priestly glory.

But if the priesthood places us in such close relationships with the Father, the Son, and the Holy Spirit, it is indubitable that the fullness of the priesthood carries these same relationships to their fullness of intimacy and perfection.

Indeed, the bishop has very singular ties with the heavenly Father. It has rightly been said that the episcopal order is the order of the Father, just like the presbyterate is the order of the Son, and the diaconate is the order of the Holy Spirit. The bishop is the image of the Father.

I have just said that the whole Christian tradition in a legendary sentence has expressed the priestly glory saying: "Sacerdos, alter Christus. The priest is another Christ." And truly he is. He has the same mission as Jesus, his same powers; he performs the same wonders that Jesus performed, gives the testimony of the truth as Jesus gave it, and comes as Jesus does so that souls *might have life and have it more abundantly* (John 10:10).

But if the priest is another Christ, I dare to say that the bishop is another heavenly Father. And I am not opposing one thing to another; but rather, if we are the image of the Father, it is because we are the image of Jesus Christ.

Do we not remember that when Philip told Jesus Christ, *Show us the Father*, Jesus Christ responded to him: *Have I been with you for so long a time and you still do not know me, Philip? Whoever has seen me has seen the Father.* So the bishop is the image of the Father because he is the most perfect image of Jesus Christ. The shadow of the Father appears to be cast over those who have received the fullness of the priesthood.

The bishop participates in the majesty of the Father, and that is why the Church surrounds him with honors. His powers are immense. In his heart throbs that robust and sweetest tenderness that exists in the heart of the Father.

The bishop is a priest that has reached the plenitude of fecundity. The Father possesses the plenitude of fecundity because he is the principle of all being, *of whom all paternity in heaven and earth is named*, says Scripture (Eph 3:15[3]). From his plenitude he begot the Son in the splendors of sanctity; and in loving each other the Father and the Son spirated, in an ineffable way, by way of love, the Holy Spirit. And the bishop participates in that fecundity.

The priest surely is fecund also! He speaks, and his word is the word of God that penetrates even to the depths of souls; he extends his consecrated hand and pronounces the mysterious words, and the blood of Jesus Christ cleanses the souls of sinners; he pours out water onto the head of those he baptizes and gives them life; and if all these things were not enough, his omnipotent voice makes our Lord Jesus Christ descend. When he celebrates the Holy Mass, when he pronounces the sacramental words over the host and the wine, it appears that he says, like an echo of the word of the Father: *Tu es Filius meus; ego hodie genui te. You are my son; today I have begotten you* (Ps 2:7).

But no matter how fecund every priest is, he who can give the life of grace and holiness, nevertheless, the simple priest cannot communicate the gift of fecundity to other souls, that divine fecundity of consecrating other priests who continue the glorious chain that in the course of the centuries communicates divine life to souls.

If there were no bishops, the priesthood, the Eucharist, and the other sacraments, and the entire Church would end on earth, because only the bishop has the perfect gift of fecundity. He not only gives life but is also able to consecrate priests that, in turn, can give life to souls.

The youthful man who has received from God the gaze of love and the ineffable call approaches us. Trembling with respect and emotion, he prostrates himself before us, and we place our consecrated hands on him, we anoint his youthful hands, we pronounce over him the sacramental words, and that youthful man rises converted into a father, and his word can make Jesus Christ descend from heaven, and his consecrated hands can console, purify, bless, sanctify...

In priestly ordination there is a simple and symbolic ceremony. After the first priestly communion, the new priest kneels before the bishop; the latter takes into his hands the hands of the new priest, and he makes him promise obedience and reverence to him and to his successors; and after, tenderly, and in holy way, he gives him a kiss on the cheek, saying to him: "Peace be with you."

I think that the kiss is like a symbol of that other ineffable and infinite kiss that the Father and the Son give each other in the mystery of their divine life... The Father begets the Son in the splendors of sanctity; and when he has begotten him, which is always, the two unite in one substantial kiss of love, which is the Holy Spirit. When the bishop, after having made another Christ of the youthful man he has just ordained, gives him that kiss on the cheek, who does not see in this kiss of time an allusion, distant but so beautiful, of the kiss of eternity?

When we speak of those mysteries so elevated, our stammering lips cannot but speak labored words: these mysteries are inexpressible, we will only know them fully in heaven. But it is very sweet for our heart to say what we can, like a kid with stammering lips is accustomed to saying to his father the word of love that he bears in the intimacy of his heart!

The bishop has a more intimate union with Jesus Christ than the simple priest.

Without a doubt a simple priest receives the highest part of the priesthood, which is the full power over the real Body of Christ. Any priest, just like the bishop, just like the pope, can consecrate and bring about the eucharistic mystery, the greatest wonder of the priesthood. In this sense, priests have nothing to envy of bishops nor of the Supreme Pontiff: the consecrating word has in them all the same efficacy.

It is not so with respect to the mystical body of Christ, in which, as St. Thomas teaches, the bishop has greater power than simple priests.[4] The bishop has special powers over souls.

Preaching, which is his divine sustenance, belongs by right to the bishop, as the Pontifical says: "Oportet episcopum praedicare. It is proper to the bishop to preach."[5] If priests preach, it is only as sent by the bishops and in their name.

We bishops have, with respect to the truth of Jesus Christ, with respect to his sacred doctrine, a special authority, as the same

Pontifical assures; and from here is born a special union with the spokesman of his saving doctrine.

Without a doubt, priests administer the sacraments; but there are sacraments in which only the bishop can prepare the matter, like Extreme Unction: only the bishop can consecrate the oil with which the priest anoints the sick.[6] And, in general, St. Thomas gives this rule: "It is proper to the bishop to arrange and do all that is directed to perfecting the souls of others."[7] It would take too long to explicate the meaning of these words; it is enough to deduce from what has been said that the union of the bishop with Christ is closer than that of simple priests; in a more special way he is another Christ, because he has received the plenitude of the priesthood.

He also has a close relationship with the Holy Spirit. It is proper to the bishop to give the Holy Spirit. By means of the bishop, God wanted to continue giving the Spirit Paraclete to the world.

Without a doubt, the priest also gives him, but in a different way. Because the Holy Spirit and grace are so intimately bound together, it is impossible that the Holy Spirit would remain in a soul without grace, as it is impossible that the Holy Spirit would cease to dwell in a soul that is in grace. This is how the priest gives the Holy Spirit, because he gives grace by means of the sacraments.

The bishop gives the Holy Spirit directly. There are two sacraments whose proper effect is to fill with the Holy Spirit and whose administration is reserved to the bishop: Confirmation and Holy Orders.

Confirmation is the sacrament of the Holy Spirit; through it, the divine Spirit is poured out upon souls. Because of this, they receive the grace and the fortitude to confess and defend the faith.

The sacrament of Holy Orders also has as its proper effect the infusion of the Holy Spirit. To the deacon, to the priest, and to the bishop they say, although in a different way: "Accipe Spiritum Sanctum. Receive the Holy Spirit."

And since he can only give what is his own, it means that the bishop possesses the Holy Spirit in a special way, that he carries him in his heart and as a most fecund fount of virtue that he pours out everywhere.

Can it not be deduced from all that has been said that the bishop has special relationships with the Father, with the Son, and with the Holy Spirit?

If there were time, we would draw out the innumerable consequences of this holy doctrine.

If we are representatives of the Father, we must have that exquisite and constant providence that the heavenly Father has over all his creatures, that providence that Christ expounded, saying: *Are not two sparrows sold for a small coin? Yet not one of them falls to the ground without your Father's knowledge. Even all the hairs of your head are counted* (Matt 10:29-30).

If we are the image of Jesus Christ, we must participate in that divine immolation with which he offered himself for the salvation of the world.

If we give the Holy Spirit to souls, we must bear him in our hearts, he who is love par excellence, love supreme, before whom all the loves of earth pale…

But I must conclude by inviting all to pray for our venerable brother, on this day of jubilation and glory for his soul.

Oh Jesus, High Priest and Prince of Pastors, in the inscrutable designs of your love and your providence you chose to elevate our brother to the plenitude of the priesthood; you desired him to be the shadow of the Father, a continuer of your redeeming work and a divine instrument so that the Holy Spirit would continue infusing himself in souls!

Thank you for these twenty-five years of episcopal life! If he carries any darkness in his soul, if there is any deficiency in his life—how could he not have some since our nature is fragile and miserable!—cover them, Lord, with your mercy and your love, and continue pouring into his heart heavenly blessings.

Perfect in him the image of the Father, transform him more perfectly into you, unite him more closely with the Holy Spirit, so that, bringing about your saving work on the earth, when he appears before you, the Prince of Pastors, you will crown him with a diadem of immortal glory.

CHAPTER 11

The Supreme Fatherhood

AT THE TWENTY-FIFTH ANNIVERSARY OF THE NAMING OF LEOPOLDO RUIZ AS ARCHBISHOP OF MICHOACÁN†

Nam si decem milia pedagogorum habeatis in Christo,
sed non multos patres.
Even if you should have countless guides to Christ,
yet you do not have many fathers.
(1 CORINTHIANS 4:15)

JESUS came to the world to bring us life. He himself said to us: *Ego veni ut vitam habeant, et abundantius habeant. I came so that they might have life and have it more abundantly* (John 10:10). His words are *spirit and life* (John 6:63), life in the fire of love that he spread in hearts and in which he desires that the whole world burn. Life lessons are his examples and the poem of life is the marvelous succession of his mysteries. And life is, above all, the effusion in souls of that *new creation* (2 Cor 5:17) that makes us *share in the divine nature, ut per haec efficiamini divinae consortes naturae*, as the apostle St. Peter said (2 Pet 1:4).

† ORIGINAL: This is a collection of fragments from the sermon at the Mass for the twenty-fifth anniversary of His Excellency, the Most Reverend Don Leopoldo Ruiz in the [Arch]diocese of Michoacán [now Morelia], preached on January 12, 1937 in the Cathedral of Morelia.

EDITOR'S NOTE: For more on the life of Ruiz, see note at beginning of Chapter 16.

The life that Jesus brought us is so rich that it is worth more than all created works; so beautiful that deep down it is beatitude; so high that it is a participation in the life itself of God; so lasting that it is life eternal.

Jesus, without a doubt, could have given us the gift of life by himself without using intermediaries or instruments, as he rules all the movements of our hearts by his Spirit, as he himself wanted to be the divine food of our souls. We men are such crude instruments of the divine action! Such is our fragility that we have the sad privilege of hindering the works of God!

But he wanted to use our smallness in order to bring about his wonders, so he gave us the honor of taking us as instruments, he bestowed on us the glory of participating in his divine fecundity. There is nothing more human than this design of love, since it is proper to our nature to use sensible things in order to ascend to the invisible and divine ones; and at the same time there is nothing more divine than putting in our fragile vessels the treasures of heaven.

If he would have given us life in a direct and immediate way, souls would live in an isolated pride, like stars that shine to each other from enormous distances, without any more bond than their coexistence in time and space. But the admirable purpose of the divine will to make use of us as instruments of his action and to vest us with his august fecundity established among souls intimate and sweet bonds; we are not isolated, there is in us a unity and harmony, we form one living and wonderful body: *so we, though many, are one body in Christ,* as St. Paul said with glorious boldness (Rom 12:5).

Not only did he give us the right to call ourselves children of God, but he also gave some privileged men the right to claim the divine name of father, and at the marvelous impulse of "the highest wisdom, of the divine omnipotence, and of the first love,"[1] spiritual fatherhood appeared on the earth, which is a mystery of love, fecundity, and sacrifice.

Let us briefly delve into the depths of this mystery.

This divine fatherhood is a mystery of love.

All noble fatherhood comes from love. How insignificant is the fatherhood that does not spring up from the heart! What ignoble fatherhood that is born of flesh and blood and not of the immortal spark that God himself put in our souls!

But even if human fatherhood were not a work of love, spiritual fatherhood still would be, which is a likeness of the eternal fatherhood of God, which is love. By an infinite love, the Father generates his Word in the splendors of holiness; by an incomprehensible love, Jesus gave us life, suffering death in an excess of love.

On a radiant spring morning, Jesus revealed to us the mystery of spiritual fatherhood on the ruddy banks of Lake Tiberias. In order to put souls in the hands, or rather in the heart, of Peter, to vest him with the plenitude of fatherhood, he asked him the sweetest question three times: *Do you love me more than these?* (John 21:15). The divine Master knew that to love him is to love souls and that the singular love that he asked of the apostle would be in the heart of Peter a volcano of zeal and paternal love.

To all us priests Jesus asks the delightful question, because we all bear in our souls the mystery of that love, which is not like the love of other souls but rather has extraordinary characteristics, divine glimmers, because it is the love of the Father: pure, selfless, fecund.

Love so disinterested that it inspired in the Apostle that triumphal phrase: *Ego libentissime impendam et superimpendar ipse pro animabus vestris, licet plus vos diligens, minus diligar. I will most gladly spend and be utterly spent for your sakes. If I love you more, am I to be loved less?* (2 Cor 12:15).

Love that gives life: is it not proper to love to give life? Like Jesus, we give life by the mystery of our words, by the administration of the sacraments, by the intimate direction of souls.

Selfless love that, like Christ, nails itself to the cross to make souls happy and suffers death to give life.

But the love of the bishop is not simply the love that burns in the soul of every priest. The bishop must love more than all of them, in a way more sublime than them. *Diliges me plus his? Do you love me more than these* (the priests)*?* Jesus says to the one whom he raises to the plenitude of the priesthood.

Every priest loves souls, but he is not by reason of his priesthood consecrated forever for them. Today he has the care of some; tomorrow, of others; it may well be that he is not able to receive or accept the care of souls lest he neglect his essential duties.

Not the bishop; by his office he is consecrated totally and perpetually to the love and service of the souls whom God has entrusted to him. The ring that he wears on his hand is a symbol of the loving fidelity that he must keep to the Church, to whom he is intimately and perpetually betrothed.

That is why St. Thomas says that the episcopate is a state, something the simple priesthood is not.[2]

And this unique love in the heart of a bishop embraces all his activity, all his life, and all his self-denial, and he puts it all at the service of souls who need to be nourished by the Lord.

Many priestly hearts will love us; but there is one who singularly loves us, who has for us the heart of a father: it is our bishop. *Even if you should have countless guides to Christ, yet you do not have many fathers, for I became your father in Christ Jesus through the gospel.*

And because the love of the bishop is unique, his fecundity is as well. You could say that fecundity is the proper function of love, and that, therefore, the characteristics of the former make known the characteristics of the latter.

Ah! Yes, all love is fecund and the priest is divinely fecund. I have already told you that all our ministries are reduced to giving life to souls.

But the fecundity of the bishop is singular, because he is absolute, universal, and unique in his diocese.

He is able to give life in all the varied and rich forms established by Jesus. In his consecration, it was said to him without limitation, "Accipe Spiritum Sanctum. Receive the Holy Spirit," and since this divine Spirit contains the plenitude of life, the bishop receives the plenitude of the priesthood.

Priests give life because they are fathers, but they cannot engender other fathers, they cannot communicate to souls the power to transmit to others the life that they receive. However, the bishop really can engender sons and daughters and create fathers; the opulent torrent of his life is not confined to narrow channels but rather expands majestically in space and time. If he did not exist, life on earth would be extinguished and the kingdom of Christ would not be able to subsist, of which the Church says there will be no end: "cuius regni non erit finis."[3]

But the most admirable thing about episcopal fecundity is that it extends to his whole Church and influences quietly and efficaciously all the souls that have been entrusted to him, just as the head silently exercises its vital influence in all the activities of man without any of them escaping its vivifying impulse.

Many give us life by feeding our souls with the doctrine of Jesus, but no one preaches without the episcopal mission.[4] Many forgive our sins, but all receive the jurisdiction from our father. Many vivify us by means of the divine sacraments, but no one can administer them without his good pleasure. His light illumines us, his norms govern us, and with his supernatural prudence, his pastoral solicitude, and his fatherly charity he is, as St. Peter said, one of *the examples to the flock* (1 Pet 5:3), who imprints on his Church his intimate physiognomy.

Truly, we can have—it is necessary to repeat it—many teachers, many guides, many consolers in Christ but not many fathers, because only one communicates life unceasingly to us by a universal and unique influx.

How admirable is the disposition of Jesus in his Church to reproduce in each diocese the mystery of the richest and most fecund unity that is like the seal of his secular and divine work! One faith, one life, one father!

But precisely because the bishop's fecundity is unique, his martyrdom is singular.

Jesus taught us that sacrifice is an indispensable condition of fecundity when he told us: *Nisi granum frumenti cadens in terra mortuum fuerit, ipsum solum manet; si autem mortuum fuerit multum fructum affert. Unless a grain of wheat falls to the ground and dies, it remains just a grain of wheat; but if it dies, it produces much fruit* (John 12:24).

And this essential law of fecundity applies to the fatherhood of the spirit in all its mysterious plenitude.

When Jesus, after the triple confession of love of the apostle St. Peter, entrusted to him on the shores of Lake Tiberias his lambs and sheep, he added in a solemn and mysterious way: *When you were younger, you used to dress yourself... but when you grow old... someone else will dress you and lead you where you do not want to go* (John 21:18). And so that no doubt remains about the profound meaning of this prophecy, which is at the same time a lesson about the apostolate, the evangelist teaches us that with these words Jesus announced to St. Peter the death that he would have to suffer, the martyrdom that awaited him.

And the link between the apostolate and martyrdom is not a fortuitous or individual coincidence. In the first centuries of the Church, bishop and martyr were synonymous, and in current times they are as well: we know only too well.

And for the divine likeness to be realized it is not necessary that a solemn martyrdom comes to seal the fecund life of pastors. There are most secret martyrdoms that only God knows: sorrows deep as they are cruel that are hidden underneath his chest adorned with the pastoral cross.

A father carries in his heart all the sorrows and weaknesses of his children. *Quis in vobis infirmetur et ego non infirmor? Quis scandalizatur et ego non uror?*—St. Paul would say—*Who is weak, and I am not weak? Who is led to sin, and I am not indignant?* (2 Cor 11:29).

This living and constant solicitude for souls is a martyrdom, the likeness of the one that Jesus carried in his heart all the days of his mortal life. All priestly hearts suffer it; but in the episcoal heart it is broader, deeper, more bitter, because his solicitude encompasses an enormous expanse, because his duties are more pressing, because by being the principle of unity and the font of life in his local Church, all the pains and waywardness of the souls entrusted to him flow back to him with all their responsibility and sorrow.

And his martyrdom is not only a passive reflux, so to speak, of what souls suffer; the duties of his august fatherhood impose on him constant, and at times heroic, sufferings. His consecration to souls is not purely theoretical and sentimental, for his consecration he must sacrifice his time, his pleasures, his activity, and even his life.

Every priest is obliged in certain circumstances to heroic sacrifices, but that obligation is neither constant nor essential, since he can cease caring for souls. The bishop is perpetually consecrated to souls, and faced with the demands of his pastoral charge, he must sacrifice even his life. Jesus said as much: *Bonus pastor animam suam dat pro ovibus suis. A good shepherd lays down his life for the sheep* (John 10:11). The mercenary can flee before the snares of the wolf, because he is not the shepherd nor does he bear in his heart the divine interest for souls. The shepherd never flees, and he heroically stands between the cruel wolf and the souls he loves.

Is not the bishop the target of the persecutions of the enemies of God? Can he not say, like no one else, what the Apostle said: *Non est nobis colluctatio adversus carnem et sanguinem sed adversus principes et potestates, adversus mundi rectores tenebrarum harum, contra spiritualia nequitiae in caelestibus. For our struggle is not with flesh and blood but with the principalities, with the powers, with the world rulers of this present darkness, with the evil spirits in the heavens* (Eph 6:12).

In the sacred mist of the mystery, one glimpses the mysteriousness of spiritual fatherhood: it is a glorious projection of the august fatherhood of Jesus. Like him, the bishop appears crowned with a triple halo, with the triple majesty of a unique love, of full fecundity, of an intimate martyrdom; his pastoral ring is the emblem of his most faithful love; his mitre makes him stand out among his priests, not because of the splendor of his glory, but rather because of the plenitude of his fecundity, and the shining cross that adorns his chest symbolizes the intimate martyrdom that is hidden in his heart...

CHAPTER 12

The Triple Word of Priestly Love

AT THE FIFTIETH AND TWENTY-FIFTH PRIESTLY ANNIVERSARIES OF ARCHBISHOP LEOPOLDO RUIZ AND BISHOP LUIS ALTAMIRANO†

Dicit ei iterum: Simon Joannis, diligis me?
Ait illi: etiam Domine, tu scis quia amo te.
He then said to him a second time, "Simon,
son of John, do you love me?" He said to him,
"Yes, Lord, you know that I love you."
(John 21:16)

By a happy coincidence, we are able to celebrate in the same solemnity and with the same joy two distinguished anniversaries: the pastor of the Archdiocese of Michoacán completes a half-century of priestly life, bursting with fruits, infused with the perfume of the episcopal virtues, and decorated with the most meritorious works; and his worthy coadjutor completes also twenty-five years of priestly life, already rich in virtues and merits, and richer still in hopes.

We are right to rejoice in the Lord, and our holy, our most righteous joy cannot be enclosed within the limits of the archdiocese. It

† Original: From the sermon at the gold and silver priestly jubilees, respectively, of Their Excellencies Don Leopoldo Ruiz and Don Luis Altamirano, on March 19, 1938.

Editor's Note: Leopoldo Ruiz y Flóres was archbishop of Morelia in 1938. For more on his life, see note at beginning of Chapter 16. Luis María Altamirano y Bulnes was coadjutor bishop to Ruiz and succeeded him.

has overflowed throughout the glorious province of Michoacán, and bursting its limits, has found an echo in all the confines of the Mexican Republic, because everywhere there are souls that accompany us in spirit on this solemnity; even more, the Supreme Pontiff, the father of us all, in whose immense heart fits all our joys and all our sorrows, from his august throne has sent congratulations and wishes to the two prelates, congratulations and wishes that are those of Jesus Christ in person.

I must, nevertheless, confess that in the midst of the joy that expands my heart I have heard in the depths of my soul a dissonant voice that appears to mar my joy: the voice of reason, of that poor human reason that formulates objections and does not resolve them, that plants problems and does not ascertain how to untie them. That voice has said to me: Why celebrate those anniversaries? Is it not celebrating our defeat? What are the years that we have lived on earth but a part of our heart and our life? Those years have withered our illusions, undone our projects, torn apart our hearts, withdrawn us from those whom we loved, made us feel our weakness, placed in our lives an aftertaste of bitterness and melancholy; why then celebrate our defeats?

But another voice that comes from heaven, the voice of faith that explains everything, that illumines everything, that idealizes everything, has given me the full and vigorous answer for that voice of poor human reason. We carry, certainly, celestial treasures in fragile vessels, and the human covering undoes itself; but the divine that it contains is immortal. What time snatches from us is the human, but it cannot snatch from us the divine; rather it increases and enlarges it.

I think that just as the chrysalis, enclosed in its prison transforms bit by bit into a butterfly, and when the prison crumbles, the triumphant butterfly unfolds its wings and soars towards the heights, so it also happens in human life: we carry within something divine enclosed in the fragile prison of our human nature; within, the divine grows bit by bit and outside the human crumbles, until the day arrives in which the prison is broken and the butterfly penetrates the most pure regions of eternity.

The divine appears and grows in us through the human, which is undone. What is more, precisely our defeats, which time inflicts on us, feed the divine and make it grow in our souls. That is why, after twenty-five and fifty years of having lived on earth, we can discover with a certain bitterness what time snatches from us of what belongs to our humanity; but we have to confess also in the jubilation of our hearts what time has increased in us, which is the divine; and when we see these things in the splendors of faith, we can throw the triumphal challenge in the face of time, and, paraphrasing St. Paul, say to it: Oh time! Where is your victory? (1 Cor 15:55).

I come precisely to sing the victory that is achieved over time, the victory that these two prelates have obtained over that time that devastates all that is human...

I

THE priestly life is something marvelous: it is composed of light and of love, of fecundity, of sacrifice, and of hope. But if from among all these multiple and very rich elements that compose it we should want to determine which is the first, the principle, the one that serves as the key to this wonder of God, I do not hesitate to affirm that the heart of the priestly life is love...the love of which Jesus spoke to Peter in a splendid spring morning on the ruddy shores of Lake Tiberias: *Simon, son of John, do you love me?* And Peter answered him: *Yes, Lord, you know that I love you.*

That immortal dialogue expresses in divine and poetic form the mystery of the priesthood. Its loves are those two that are found, that are connected, that are fused in one single love: the love of

Jesus for the priest and the love of the priest for Jesus. That dialogue is repeated in an ineffable manner each time that a priest is ordained, each time that a priest celebrates his first Mass: *Do you love me more than these?* Jesus says to us; and we, on that day of the joy of our hearts, we say to him like Peter: *Yes, Lord, you know that I love you.*

But that word of love that we say to Jesus on the day of our first Mass has special characteristics: it has the freshness, the coloring, the perfume of the spring.

Many times we will repeat to Jesus the same word, but none of them will have the charm of that unforgettable one. We will say many Masses in our life, but none will have the sweet, ineffable, mysterious appeal of our first Mass, because that Mass had the clarity of dawn, the perfume of spring, the ardor of youth. There will be others that are holier, more opulent, but none so enchanting as that one, in which we said to Jesus the first word of love, the echo that made the crystalline surface of the Lake of Tiberias shake.

That first word, the word of our first Mass, has, in my judgment, these characteristics: it is ardent, in it we put all the tenderness of our heart and all the ardor of our youth; it is certain, we said it with full confidence, because we did not even suspect that we could be unfaithful nor that our hearts could have deficiencies; that is why we pronounced that word with generous but naive security. We did not yet have works to offer to Jesus nor fruits to give him, but we offered to him in that first Mass the immensity of our desires and the nobility of our generosity. We did not know precisely which works and which sufferings to expect; but our heart, in one providential and delightful ignorance, extended in its enthusiasm over all the works and all the sacrifices to offer them to the Lord in one sonorous word of love.

II

YEARS pass... In our priestly life we have many works to endure, many sorrows to suffer; we accumulate merits mixed with deficiencies; we have success, we commit errors...because that is how all human life is, and even in a certain sense the very life of the saints.

And then, when our life has reached its maturity, when we have reached the summit of twenty-five years of priestly life, the immortal dialogue of love returns to resound in the intimacy of our soul, and Jesus tells us again: *Simon, son of John, do you love me?* And we tell him again the word of love: *Etiam, Domine; tu scis quia amo te. Yes, Lord, you know that I love you.*

With very just reason Fr. Lacordaire said: "Love only has one word, and always being said, is never repeated."[1] What we say to Jesus on the day of our first priestly jubilee is what we told him on the day of our first Mass: the word of love, the only one that the heart of the priest can express. It is the same, and we do not repeat it, because each time that mysterious word is said it has a new richness, a new meaning, a new splendor.

That second word of love that we say to Jesus after twenty-five years of troubles and of sufferings, of triumphs and of defeats, has another meaning; it is no longer the secure and confident word of youth, but rather we pronounce it like Peter on the shores of Lake Tiberias, remembering his denials and his infidelity, but feeling at the same time in his heart the sincerity of his love. Thus, we no longer say that resounding and robust yes, sure of itself, that we said in the days of our happily ignorant youth; this second yes has a kind of distrust of ourselves and a taste of humility and of repentance. Life has revealed the magnitude of our fragility, and we know that we can fall and be unfaithful.

But above all the doubts that have arisen in our hearts, our sincere love, which is not able to refuse itself, dominates, and between fear and hope of being faithful, we say to Jesus again: *Yes, Lord, you know that I love you.*

That second word of love is more solid, more profound. In the first we could not offer to God something other than the immensity of our desires and the nobility of our generosity. At twenty-five years of the priesthood, we have left behind the spring with its perfumes and its splendid clarities, and the summer, ardent and fecund, and we began to live the fall of life and to be filled with the mature fruits that make us feel the weight of our own fecundity.

Then the word of love that we say to Jesus does not only express good desires but also signifies the fruits of our ministry and the sacrifices of our priestly life. "Lord," we say to him, "I have been faithful to you; twenty-five years have not been able to squelch the sincerity of my love."

Undoubtedly, for God twenty-five years are not much, since Scripture affirms that *a thousand years in your eyes are merely a day gone by* (Ps 90:4); but for us fragile creatures, flowers of a day, for us amassed in inconstancy, a quarter of a century is a great part of our life. In a quarter of a century, how many hearts change, how many spirits go wrong, how many events are carried out in history! And if we, for twenty-five years, have entirely and faithfully preserved the tenderness of our first Mass, we can say to Jesus: "Lord, I have been faithful to your love… Time has changed many things in me and around me: my eyes, those naive eyes of a kid, have been opened to the rough realities of life; my arms have exerted themselves nonstop in the fight; my feet have become fatigued proclaiming peace, proclaiming the good; my heart has suffered much, has loved much… But in the midst of so many vicissitudes, the love of my first Mass is here unscathed, the love of my first Mass is here most pure, rather, more rooted and more profound… Lord, after twenty-five years of priesthood, you know it, I love you…"

I cannot deny that in twenty-five years of priesthood we have to lament countless deficiencies and fragilities: why deny them if we are human? But it appears to me that those miseries are not against our priestly fidelity; rather they increase it and make it more meritorious...

Ah! If we were angels, if like those superior spirits our minds were fixed immovably in the truth and our will in the good, what would be so strange about being faithful for twenty-five years? But that upon concluding a quarter of a century of priestly life, despite our fragility and misery, our deficiencies and falls, we can still say to our Lord, *You know that I love you*, is this fidelity not more meritorious and glorious, and all the more meritorious and glorious the more fragile and miserable we are?

III

YEARS pass... Some fortunate priests, blessed especially by God, come to celebrate fifty years of priestly life.

In that evening of life that has some kind of mysterious melancholy—a melancholy that I ignore if it happens to be the footprint that earthly life or the premonition of the heavenly life has left on my soul—in that evening, sweet and glorious, Jesus returns to ask the immortal question: *Do you love me?* And again the priest, laden with merits and sufferings, turns to say to him in the intimacy of his heart: *Yes, Lord, you know that I love you.*

Can we guess what is profound and divine about that last word of love? It is the word of consummation!

Fall is coming to an end; in the garden the trees break off loaded with fruits; already one begins to feel the cold of winter, and everything announces that the sad and austere time draws near... And as the farmer joyfully contemplates his orchard full of fruit and, in the warmth of his home, accumulates the opulent harvest in his barns, so does the priest who has reached fifty years of ministry. He is at the end of fall, and winter draws near; he feels the joy of the fecundity and the yearning of heaven, and in the midst of that sweet melancholy that overwhelms his heart, he utters in a new, profound, and very rich way the word of love: *Domine, tu omnia scis; tu scis quia amo te! Lord, you know everything; you know that I love you.*

What characteristics does the word of consummation have?

It is a word of wisdom, because when one has lived for a long time and in a holy manner on earth, his spirit rises, the prison of his body crumbles, and the chrysalis is transformed into a butterfly. In the last stage of the priestly life, the life of wisdom appears to envelop with its magnificent halo the entire being of the priest. He no longer has the ardor and the naïveté of the first years, nor even the spirit of fighting that characterizes the maturity of our life. It appears that everything has been converted into light for him: he sees everything, he knows everything; he lives in a superior atmosphere, from which he contemplates the splendid greatness of human things, in a watchtower from where he marvelously glimpses divine things...

The second characteristic of this last stage of priestly life is perfect peace. When life is complete, peace fills the heart, as if God desired the transition between the anxieties of the earth and the happiness of heaven not to be so abrupt and sudden; and that is why he fills and saturates and preserves our souls with the peace of heaven, and tasting that definitive peace is how the priest repeats to Jesus: *You know that I love you.*

That word of fifty years has, finally, another characteristic: it is a word saturated with myrrh. What the spouse of the Song of Songs says—*Manus meae destiliaverunt myrrham. My hands dripping myrrh* (5:5)—can also be affirmed of the hands of the priest who completes his life in a holy way. His hands distilled myrrh, because in the priestly life, more than in any human life, it is necessary to suffer.

Ah, yes! Suffering, because only suffering purifies and expiates; suffering, because only suffering is fecund; suffering, because Jesus suffered, the Supreme Pastor, the Prince of priests, and it would give us shame to go crowned with flowers behind him who for us desired to be crowned with thorns...

And in the last years of priestly life the sufferings increase. Why? Because our priesthood becomes polished, because our resemblance to Jesus is accentuated, because the maturity of the soul is perfect, because it is necessary to prepare us for eternity. And then the hands of the priest distill myrrh, while in his heart a most pure tenderness overflows, while his shoulders yield under the weight of fecundity, while the word of consummation vibrates in his soul: *Lord, you know that I love you!*

Oh! Who will be able to declare to us what that word of love with which life is consumed means, when God is pleased to prolong it during a half-century of the priesthood?

IV

I have spoken of the fidelity of the priest; but, how can I finish without saying one word about the fidelity of Jesus?

On the Lake of Tiberias, Jesus asked the priest if he loves him; but, who does not see that at the bottom of this question there is a most sweet declaration of love? Because to ask someone if they love us is like confessing our love for them.

And thus it is, truly. On the shores of Tiberias, Jesus confessed to Peter his love: *Do you love me more than these?* It was like saying: "I love you in a singular way."

So the word of love that the priest says to Jesus in his first Mass is not an isolated word, but responds to another deeper and more sonorous one, a word of love of Jesus.

On the day of our first Mass Jesus told us that he loved us, and we remember it still with delight... He was a splendid and most beautiful Jesus; he was the Jesus of Tabor, transfigured and luminous.

On that day we did not suspect anything of sufferings and of the cross; or if we suspected it, that premonition stayed relegated to last place, and we only thought about rejoicing in his love.

Years pass...and we arrive at the maturity of life. Will Jesus continue loving us? There are so many hearts that loved us before and have stopped loving us: some because they stopped beating, others because they were inconstant...will Jesus be inconstant too? The magnitude of our deficiencies, the weight of our ingratitudes, will they rob Jesus of the love he gave us on the day of our ordination?

Revelation tells us that the name of Jesus is *Faithful and True* (Rev 19:11); no one matches, no one knows, no one suspects the fidelity of Jesus: it is a divine fidelity that is above all human fidelities.

God is still faithful to the Jewish people; God still carries the chosen people in his heart; and the day will come, like the Scriptures have predicted, in which God will remember the predilection with which he has loved Israel, and he will seat them on his lap, and will caress and console them like a mother caresses her favorite son. Ah, no one can match God in his fidelity!

How then would he not be faithful to his priests? We know it by the sweetest experience... When we arrive at the plenitude of life and we look around us, we find so many voids: loved ones who distanced themselves from us, tortures that tore our hearts, ingratitudes, disdains, illusions that withered, projects that were undone... But in the midst of all the vicissitudes and above all the ruins, there is something that does not change, that does not move, that does not pass, but rather each day increases and reveals itself better: the fidelity of Jesus. Oh, he is always the Jesus of our first Mass; the Jesus of our priestly youth, of whom we say each morning when we ascend the steps of the altar, "Introíbo ad altáre Dei, ad Deum qui laetíficat juventútem meam. I will ascend to the altar of God, to God who gives joy to my youth;"[2] the Jesus who, despite all our defects, always loves and forgives us!

But he is no longer the Jesus of Tabor: the radiant vision has disappeared. He is the Jesus who works, who travels around the villages, who enters into the synagogues, who preaches from the boat of Peter, the fecund Jesus who passes throughout the earth doing good.

We feel Jesus in the midst of our apostolic fatigues and our priestly works; that is why we know that we are not alone, that we do not live abandoned. Jesus sustains us when we become weak, he lifts us up when we fall, he wipes off the sweat from our faces when we work, he hides us when we are persecuted, he propels us to do good to souls, he feeds us, offering us himself as our reward. And each year that passes we understand better how much Jesus loves us and how profound and divine his fidelity is.

And in the evening of life, at fifty years of priesthood, oh most beloved father, you who celebrate in these moments such a magnificent anniversary, only you would be able to tell us how faithful Jesus is, how he has never abandoned you in a half-century of priestly life, how he has been your strength and your fecundity and your reward; how the word of the psalm has come true in you, *qui laetíficat juventútem meam*, filling with joy the ever renewed youth of your soul!

In the last stages of priestly life, the fidelity of Jesus is revealed more fully: it is not the Jesus of Tabor, nor is it still the Jesus of Tiberias... It is the Jesus of the unforgettable night, the Jesus of the Upper Room and of Gethsemane, most tender and transfigured by sorrow!

Is it not true that the supreme fidelity of Jesus is in communicating to his priest the intimate secrets of his heart? Love, as time passes, is made like wine, more exquisite, more full-bodied; first it has superficial manifestations, then deeper ones, and lastly the most profound ones. The supreme fidelity of Jesus is in his opening his heart fully to us, depositing in our hearts the secrets of his. And the secrets of his heart, we already know, are tenderness and sacrifice, and the night of the Upper Room and of Gethsemane were the supreme revelation of his divine heart.

That is why that word of St. John—*He loved his own in the world and he loved them to the end* (John 13:1)—shows the fidelity of Jesus, who goes to the extreme of tenderness and to the extreme of sacrifice.

When Jesus loves a priestly soul for a half-century, the immortal dialogue of love through the years between the two is established. But upon arriving at the evening of life, Jesus opens his heart and deposits in the heart of the priest a double secret: the secret of his tenderness and the secret of his sorrow.

So the priestly life is an Upper Room and a Gethsemane: an Upper Room where tenderness overflows and a Gethsemane where the soul is intoxicated with divine sorrow...

CHAPTER 13

The Apostle of Unity

THE MOST ILLUSTRIOUS JOSÉ ANTONIO PLANCARTE Y LABASTIDA, ABBOT OF GUADALUPE†

Ego in eis et tu in me ut sint consummati in unum.
I in them and you in me,
that they may be brought to perfection as one.
(John 17:23)

In 1862, in Rome, in the grandiose Basilica of St. Peter, with all the opulence of the liturgy, with all the glory of the pontifical court, His Holiness Pius IX canonized St. Felipe de Jesús, the first Mexican martyr.

At that most happy solemnity was a young compatriot of ours, hardly initiated into the clerical state, a youth who carried in his soul

† José Antonio Plancarte y Labastida (1840–1898) was declared Venerable by Pope Francis in January 2020. In 1862, Plancarte attended the canonization of St. Felipe de Jesús, the patron saint of Mexico City, and he also began his studies for the priesthood in Rome. He was ordained in 1865. As a priest, he would help 60 young men go to Rome to study, thus solidifying a connection between the Church in Rome and Mexico. In Jacona, Michoacán, he founded a parochial school for girls in 1867 and also the Institute of the Sisters of Mary Immaculate of Guadalupe in 1878. The congregation was charged with the education of girls and women. He founded the National Expiatory Church St. Felipe de Jesús in Mexico City, which was constructed between 1886 and 1897. He prepared the Basilica of Our Lady of Guadalupe for the coronation of the image in 1895, the year in which he was also named abbot of the Basilica. As abbot, he is buried in the Crypt of the Abbots at the Basilica. For more information, see antonioplancarte.org.

a most noble passion: the love of his homeland. And upon witnessing the grandiose ceremony, when in the name of Jesus Christ and with the power of the apostles Peter and Paul the pope declared that a man is a saint and that he should be raised to the altars, he felt in his soul an ineffable impression.

Could it be that the light of heaven bathed his soul with divine splendors in those moments? Could it be that a spark of love fell from the heights that set fire to his most noble heart? Could it be that the soul of the first Mexican martyr was poured into the great soul of that young compatriot of ours?

The prelate who received from that youth this intimate confidence thought that in those moments St. Felipe de Jesús had identified himself with that youth in an ineffable way, that he had given him a message of love and of hope for the Mexican homeland, that he had sown in his heart a precious seed that would produce flowers and fruits in the future.

That young man was Don Antonio Plancarte y Labastida, abbot of Guadalupe, the excellent man whose centenary we have just commemorated.

I do not know if the opinion of the prelate to whom I am referring is accurate, but I am sure that if it was not in that place and in those moments, in any case Fr. Plancarte received from God a providential mission concerning the Mexican nation. It is very difficult to point out a place and a time for the divine motions; ordinarily the action of God over souls is like a heavenly dew that falls on them bit by bit and penetrates them until it makes them fully fecund.

On this blessed occasion in which we come to render a tribute of love to the illustrious man who accomplished grandiose works in our homeland, I want to say simply that Fr. Plancarte received from God a mission about our homeland and happily completed it.

What was that mission? I think that it is not an illusion of our patriotism, that it is not that most noble blindness that love puts in our souls so that we always see what we love as great and beautiful. I am sure that Mexico has received from God singular prerogatives: it has a splendidly divine sky, dreamlike panoramas, lofty mountains, mysterious lakes, shady forests, flowery countrysides; its bountiful soil surrenders opulent crops to the one who cultivates it; in the heart of its soil it possesses fantastic riches that have still not been completely tapped; and in the vast land of our nation, lulled to sleep by the gigantic murmur of two oceans, there is a multitude of souls who, however poor and ignorant they are thought to be, bear in their hearts prodigious aptitudes for science, for art, for all that is grand, for all that is noble.

And, above all, God poured out supernatural and divine gifts on Mexico with marvelous abundance. The Mexican people—history attests to it—has an indomitable faith, a tender, ardent, unique faith, very noble feelings, and, above all, it has a treasure more beautiful than its countrysides and its forests, more splendid than its firmament, richer than the core of its soil—who has not guessed it? Our treasure is a very sweet Virgin that smiles to us from the glorious hill; it is the sweet Virgin of Guadalupe, symbol of the divine predilection, figure of our destiny, very happy center of our hearts, vessel of our hopes, love of our loves.

What could our country have needed seventy-eight years ago? What could it have needed during this period of time for God to raise up an excellent man that would come to us to give us what we lacked?

I only want to answer this question. One thing is still missing: unity, harmony. The day that we find the secret of unity, we will have found the secret of happiness. United Mexico will be a great, prosperous, happy people.

But as soon as we were born into independence, the enemy, like in the Gospel parable (Matt 13:25), sowed discord together with wheat, and during this little more than a century of having autonomy, our history has been made up of constant battles. We have lost our time in futile battles, and, what is still more deplorable, there is not only in us those just and legitimate—although lamentable—divisions of those who think in a distinct way and are separated by an abyss, but rather even in our same camp it appears that our constant activity has as its purpose and path to divide us perpetually. Ah! The day in which Mexico finds the secret of unity, that day will ring for us the hour of prosperity, the hour of happiness.

Fr. Plancarte came to cooperate in a very efficacious manner in the realization of that unity. Of course, he did not complete it nor was he able to complete it; the unity and harmony of peoples is a work of many years, many times the work of centuries. Bit by bit souls are harmonized, bit by bit hearts are connected, and it is the work of titans, it is the work of giants, to bring about what can be called with one phrase of our Lord: the consummation of unity.

I think that the Most Holy Mary of Guadalupe, in the perennial prayer of her united hands, in the interminable roar of her maternal heart, is repeating the phrase that Jesus said on the night of the Last Supper: *That they may be brought to perfection as one.*

To begin to accomplish the wonder of our national harmony, God, in his mercy and in his love, sent us an excellent man, whose mission was this: the unity and harmony of the Mexican people.

The first unity that is needed for our happiness is the one that unites us to God; in it is the foundation of all the other unities. That is why Jesus Christ, on the night of his Passion, said to his heavenly Father: *I in them and you in me, that they may be brought to perfection as one.*

Ah! God is always united to us, God is always united to the Mexican people; yes, our people, our nation, arose from a very sweet gaze of the divine eyes, from a loving beat of his infinite heart; and to justify my assertion, it is enough for me evoke the wonder of Tepeyac, that wonder of which a pope dared to say: *Non fecit taliter omni nationi. He has not done this for any other nation* (Ps 147:20).[1] It would be enough to see the glorious image rise on the hill of Tepeyac so that we can be sure that God is with us and loves us.

But our links of union with God have loosened because of our sins. For people, just as for souls, sin is the great evil. Does Scripture not say: *Justice exalts a nation, but sin is a people's disgrace* (Prov 14:34)? Sin does miserable things to people, and we have many sins, individual sins and national sins; I do not count them because I do not want to obfuscate the brightness of this day with bitter memories.

So that our union with God is made closer, so that the Mexican people might be united with the Lord, so that the word of Jesus is carried out—*I in them and you in me*—it is indispensable that sin is erased, that it is ruled, that its disastrous influence is at least diminished.

In order to erase sin, we individuals need a divine sacrament; in order to erase national sins, there is only one resource: expiation.

The nations of Europe are giving us a grandiose, stupendous example of this truth. Very noble nations debate among themselves in great anguish. Why? Because of the will of a leader? Because of the caprice of those who govern the nations? No; because of the providential law of expiation. There were in them sins to pay and our Lord God, bringing together in one ineffable beam of light his mercy and his justice, cast over the peoples terrible vicissitudes.

But there not only exists the expiation that God sends; there also exists the one that we lovingly offer; and Fr. Plancarte, with deep gaze, with brilliant intuition, understood that Mexico needed expiation. And he wanted the expiation in our homeland to be constant, for it to have its place, and he raised up such a beautiful church so that under its vaults cries that beg for mercy would rise to heaven, so that under its vaults prayer and sacrifice and, above all, the Holy Eucharist would constantly be expiating the sins that we have committed against the Lord.

Perhaps we have not understood perfectly the great thought of Fr. Plancarte; perhaps we have not given to our national expiatory church the importance that we should. We have forgotten that for our good and for our happiness we have two national churches: Tepeyac and San Felipe—Tepeyac, the church of love; San Felipe, the church of expiation. And in the doctrine of our Lord Jesus Christ one needs to unite expiation and love so that peace springs up, so that happiness comes.

It was the first unity that Fr. Plancarte brought about; he united us to God with new bonds; he thought that, if the sins of Mexico were expiated, nothing else would be needed in order for the entire love of God to be poured out upon us, so that the hearts of children would be marvelously bound together with the infinite heart of the Father.

But after the unity, the union with God, another unity is needed on earth.

Jesus Christ was concealed on earth from our earthly eyes; but the eyes of our faith, the illumined eyes of our hearts, discover him constantly. Not only does Jesus live in the Holy Eucharist, he lives also in the pope; the pope is his vicar, the pope is the rock on which the Church is built, the pope is Jesus, who teaches, who rules, who consoles, who gives life.

Thanks be to God, Mexico has always been faithful to the Holy Father; but the great distance that separates us from Rome and, more still, the pernicious influence of a doctrine that in another time was en vogue, regalism, already a long time ago loosened the bonds that united the Church of Mexico with the Church of Rome, which is the pillar of truth, the center of unity, the most pure spring of life.

There was a time in which even in the ecclesiastical institutions regalism was taught, that pernicious error in which the rights of the Supreme Pontiff were reduced to please the sovereign, and so, with the plausible pretext of preserving our traditions and the traditions of our motherland, in our laws and in our doctrine—thanks be to God, not in the essentials—we have distanced ourselves a bit from Rome, have made greater the distance that separates Rome from Mexico.

Fr. Plancarte understood this. Great men have incredible intuitions; ordinarily, in their time people do not understand their ideas nor their tendencies, because most men do not know how to see far off; even more so, they do not know how to see the depth of present problems.

Fr. Plancarte wanted this unity to be established in Mexico, this very close activity with the Holy Apostolic See; and, only God knows at what cost of so many sacrifices and so much constancy, he formed a small group of youth and sent them to the Pontifical Latin American College, so that they could go to drink doctrine, the perfectly Christian spirit from the purest fountains of Rome; so that they could go to hear close up the immense beatings of the heart of the pope; so that they could come to bring Mexico a message of renewal and hope.

That group of young men became a group of distinguished prelates; many have died, others live still. And although that group of young men was very small, the first impetus was given.

Fr. Plancarte died, but his work did not; and after those young men a glorious caravan of the best seminarians from the Republic has followed, who are going to drink from the crystalline fountains, who are going to warm their hearts with the love of the pope, and who come to bring Mexico the spirit of the Holy Apostolic See.

And we are all witnesses that the work of Fr. Plancarte has been accomplished. Our liturgy, our law, and above all our spirit are each day more perfectly Roman; and even those of us who did not have the good fortune to go to drink from those purest fonts have participated in that great transformation and have cooperated to bring it about.

The second unity created by Fr. Plancarte was our very close union with the Holy Father.

Ah! If you will permit my heart some freedom, I will say that in these last days those bonds have been strengthened in an indescribable way; in the times of our sadnesses, of our sorrows, God aroused in the immense heart of Pope Pius XI a singular predilection for Mexico, and he directed gazes at us that arrived at the depths of the soul, and imparted blessings and consolations to us, and poured out his immense pontifical heart into the very hearts of the suffering Mexicans.[2]

Currently, a monument that stands in the Vatican gives testimony that two glorious hills have been united forever: the hill of the Vatican and the hill of Tepeyac.

But it was not enough to unite the people of Mexico to God and unite them strongly to the Vicar of Jesus Christ on earth. There was another undertaking, apparently more difficult: uniting all Mexicans among themselves.

But should we not all be united? Our divisions appear to be a lie. If we are weak, do we not need to shake hands and form a compact group in order to conserve strength? Our history, nevertheless, proves how difficult a thing it is to unite Mexicans.

What man, what ideal, what flag is there that can unite everyone? I think that our lack of unity is not the fault of nobility; it is the fruit of our ignorance or perhaps of our passions. We need and have always needed a center of unity, something where all our eyes can converge, where all our hearts can beat in unison, where all our lips form one single praise, one single canticle of love.

Ah! Thanks be to God, we have that center of unity, perhaps unlike any other nation! The phrase of Benedict XIV returns to my lips: *Non fecit taliter omni nationi.*

Fr. Plancarte understood it like that. And one day, one unforgettable day, one glorious day among those of our history, October 12,

1895, all the Mexican homeland was moved in a unique way.[3] On that day the oceans intoned a new canticle, the flowers of our countryside spread more exquisite perfumes, and even the stars of our sky emitted more splendid rays... A people moved, a people kneeling, put on the forehead of our august Mother, of our incomparable Queen, a crown of love and of hope.

And I already said a bit ago: that crown was, certainly, the work of a people, but it was also the work of a man. Fr. Plancarte traveled around the Republic, spoke like only he knew how to speak; his voice of fire penetrated into souls, moved spirits, arrived, so to speak, like a two-edged sword even unto the depths of the national soul (Heb 4:12). And that day was a canticle, was a nuptial song, was an epic that ascended to heaven, and on that day the wonder of our unity and our harmony was brought about in our homeland.

We know very well that a new era of love for the Most Holy Virgin of Guadalupe, a new era of union, originates from that event. In spite of what the appearances of our vicissitudes might show us, everyday we feel more united. And when the storm came and it appeared that it was going to rob the treasure of our faith from us, our enemies failed; they had destroyed many things, perhaps, but the faith, our Catholic faith, had come out unscathed and more secure, because the glorious image of Guadalupe stood more secure and more solid than ever on the blessed hill!

Is nothing lacking in the providential mission of Fr. Plancarte?

Great men have a vast gaze. Fr. Plancarte not only saw the present, he thought about the future, he wanted the past and the future to be founded in an ineffable unity. And it is natural that if he had thought about an expiation and Rome and Guadalupe, he also would have thought about the new generations, would have thought about childhood. To think about childhood is to think about the future, it is to connect the future with the past, it is to bring about the unity proper to a nation that is destined to live for centuries.

I think that his purpose was broader. The circumstances of his life made him focus on female childhood, and I believe he was right.[4] If I have to say what I feel, I want to pay a tribute of admiration in these moments to the Mexican woman, one of the greatest treasures that we have in our country and in our history. The Mexican woman, sweet, pure, pious, who loves her home, who surrounds her husband with tenderness, who knows how to pour out precious teachings into the hearts of her sons!

Ah! I do not need to cite the names of the heroines of our history; I think that the majority of Christian Mexican women are true heroines—the more hidden they are, the more meritorious.[5]

Is it not true that one of the secrets of the preservation of our faith, of the characteristics of our piety, of the noble sentiments of our heart, depends on the Mexican woman?

Our mothers forged our hearts; they deposited in our spirits our first ideas, which were luminous because they came from a pure heart; they sowed in our hearts the noblest sentiments, because they came from a Christian and pious heart. We can all give testimony to this truth. If there is something noble in us, something holy in our hearts, we owe it to our mothers, whose sweet memory moves our hearts.

In Mexico, men often go astray, but because of the impulse of passion, because of the unhealthy sources of errors; but for all, for almost all at least, there comes a moment, it is the moment of sorrow, or the moment of the tortures of life, or the majestic moment of death; and in those supremely difficult situations, the Mexican always has close to himself a mother, a sister, a wife, or a daughter, who, among caresses and kisses of tenderness, talks to him about God, and they remind him of the cheerful days of their youth and point out to them the holy Christian hopes in the distance.

And the wonder is almost always brought about, and with tears, all the more precious as they are more masculine: the poor Mexican changes, abhors what he loved yesterday, and prostrates himself before Jesus Christ and before the Most Holy Virgin Mary, led by the sweetest but irresistible pressure of a Mexican woman.

Fr. Plancarte understood this; that is why he set his eyes and his heart on female education. And so that in the course of the years and centuries there would be no lack of those who would unite in a tight Catholic bundle the female children who would later form homes, he drew from his immense heart, from his tender heart, a new spiritual family, which seems to fill our Republic and has even spread abroad.[6]

And he formed this spiritual family in his image and likeness, and infused into it his spirit, and made it profoundly Mexican so that it would yield to the exigencies of our situation, so that it might know how to speak to children, so that two great loves would spread everywhere: the love for Jesus Christ and the love for the Mexican homeland.

And he wanted them to have as a name the name of that Virgin, of that glorious image that constitutes our unity and our glory; he wanted them to bear the gloriously, the profoundly Mexican name of Guadalupe on their chests and hearts.

Fr. Plancarte brought about four marvelous unities. His mission was complete.

I could reminiscent of the holy books—say of him that he appeared in our land like fire, and that his word burned like a flash of lighting, that he placated the ire of the Lord and reconciled the heart of the Father with his children, that on the hill of the Vatican he contemplated the glory of God and on the hill of Tepeyac he gazed upon the love and the tenderness of the ever-Virgin Mary.

And I could conclude by saying what the Scriptures say of the Prophet Elijah: *Blessed are they that saw you, and were honored with your friendship* (Sir 48:11[7]).

But before finishing, I want to say that the life of Fr. Plancarte was not only the completion of a mission: it also contained a precious and interesting lesson for us.

Do we desire the greatness and the prosperity of our homeland? Fr. Plancarte has shown us the paths, the path of unity, the path of harmony. United to God, united to the Vicar of Jesus Christ, united to the Most Holy Virgin of Guadalupe, united not only to the past generations, but also to the generations of the future, we will bring about the miracle of a great homeland, of a prosperous homeland, of a happy homeland.

Ah! I repeat the prayer of Jesus in the Upper Room like an echo, which I am sure is the prayer that is hidden in the mystery of the joined hands of the Virgin of Guadalupe, in the mystery of her most tender maternal heart: that we might all be one, that we might find the secret of unity and of harmony, so that, all united in God, with the pope, with the Virgin of Guadalupe, and united among us, we can bring about the supreme longing of our soul: a great Mexico, a prosperous Mexico, a happy Mexico!

CHAPTER 14

An Undying Love for the Father

FUNERAL ORATION FOR THE VERY REVEREND FR. FÉLIX OF JESUS ROUGIER†

Ut cognoscat mundus quia diligo Patrem, et sicut, mandatum dedit mihi Pater sic facio: surgite, eamus hinc. But the world must know that I love the Father and that I do just as the Father has commanded me. Get up, let us go.
(JOHN 14:31)

WE find ourselves once more before the mystery of death. A thousand times we have stumbled into it; it is familiar to us, and, nevertheless, we never come to understand it fully.

A man who lived many years and did much good, who knew how to love and was able to be loved, who attracted innumerable souls to himself and infused his spirit into them, who spread words of life and brought about fecund works, fell, conquered by the fatal blow of death.

† Félix de Jesús Rougier, M.Sp.S., (1859–1938) was declared Venerable in 2000 by Pope John Paul II. Through his interaction with Blessed Concepción (Conchita) Cabrera de Armida in 1903, he was inspired to found the Missionaries of the Holy Spirit as one of the branches of the Works of the Cross, a religious family of institutes inspired by Blessed Conchita. He also founded the Daughters of the Holy Spirit (1924), the Guadalupan Missionaries of the Holy Spirit (1930), and the Oblate Sisters of Jesus the Priest (1937). He is buried in the National Expiatory Church of St. Felipe de Jesús in Mexico City, which is entrusted to the Missionaries of the Holy Spirit.

It is true that for his years and for his virtues he seemed ripe to leave the earth; but, oh! how he leaves in a sad orphanhood many souls for whom he was the principle of unity and the center of life. Founder and father of a congregation barely born, should he not still live because his very meritorious work still needed his warmth and his influence? Fecund trunk who fed with his life many lush but young branches. Why did he die? Will those blooming branches break off when the push of spring ceases, when the desolate winter arrives, when the devastating gale roars?

Ah! Death always disconcerts the human spirit. It wounds without knowing where, it tears out without worrying about the catastrophe that it produces. Blind, deaf, implacable, it does not look at our tears, nor does it hear our cries... It dissipates our hopes, as the clouds of fall dissipate; it dissolves our dreams, as the foam that crowns the waves of the ocean dissolves; and over the ruins of greatness and of glory and of human happiness, it flaunts its victorious chariot and brings about its work of destruction and of extermination.

Stipendium peccati mors (Rom 6:23), St. Paul said. Death, the fruit of sin, preserves in its unequaled bitterness the characteristics of the wicked tree that produced it.

But did not the mysterious hand of God put a drop of sweetness in the corrosive absinthe of death? When Jesus wrapped himself in it on the bloody summit, when on the blessed cross death and life fought in a gigantic struggle, did his miraculous hand not put a seed of life, a glimmer of love, a reflection of immortality, in defeated death?

On the eve of his Passion, Jesus said a divine word that appears to tear apart the veils that cover the mysteries of death. He had just brought about the wonder of the Eucharist, just taken from his loving heart the mystery of the priesthood; never had he spoken to his disciples as on that unforgettable night, when his soul overflowed upon them in a torrent of light, of tenderness, of intimacy, and of hope. But suddenly the heavenly love affair is broken. *Surgite, eamus!*

Get up, let us go! he told them, holding back the torrent of his intimate outpourings. Where are you going? To death. The prince of darkness comes. But, ah, yes! The prince of darkness does not find anything in him. In us he does at least find the mysterious mark of his ancient possession; but in Jesus? Why does he not stay forever in the Upper Room, which is the dwelling of light and of love and of peace? Why Gethsemane? Why Calvary?

Hear this: *But the world must know that I love the Father... Get up, let us go.*

The supreme explanation of the mystery of death is love. The divine passion for his Father that he carried in his soul explains the sorrows and ignominies of his Passion, explains his most sacred death.

And his love, like exquisite perfume, spread throughout the world when the alabaster of his heart was broken, and souls were anointed with the divine fragrance, and love can place in death its majesty and its sweetness.

Such is the thought that I want to propose for your consideration. With the help of God, I will evoke the sweet spiritual figure of the Very Reverend Fr. Félix Rougier, founder of the Missionaries of the Holy Spirit, and when we have contemplated him, when we penetrate into the secret of his soul, I hope that we will glimpse the mystery of death and place on the agonizing lips of the Reverend Father the same words of Jesus: *But the world must know that I love the Father... Get up, let us go.*

To know a man interiorly, one has to discover his spiritual physiognomy, just like to know him exteriorly it is necessary to look at his face.

And the physiognomy of souls is what is highest and most beautiful in them, what rises to the heavens, what communicates with God, what is bathed in the light of the divine face, which, according to the sacred text, seals souls.

The soul of Fr. Félix was bathed in that light; he had God on his lips and he had him in the illumined eyes of his heart.

What those eyes see in the divine splendor marks the physiognomy of a soul.

There are souls who see nothing: they are blind, and their face has no expression. There are souls who sink their pupils in the ocean of light, and from glory to glory they come to be transformed into that same divine image (2 Cor 3:18).

And that light has in each soul its proper nuance: for some it is the candor of purity; for others it is the reddish flame of love; for still others it is the purple of sacrifice; and, lastly, for some it is the heavenly brightness of hope.

What did the eyes of Fr. Félix see in the divine light? They saw, without doubt, many things. As a master of the spirit, he was familiar with divine things. He saw the glory of Mary and wrote a most pious book;[1] he glimpsed eternal love and ardently propagated the devotion to the Holy Spirit; he sat in the shadow of the cross and savored its fruits and said admirable things about it.

But not one of those rays of light imprinted in his soul the characteristic seal. His eyes were drowned in the mystery, and they glimpsed the majesty of the Father, and the shadow of the Father was projected onto him, and his devotion par excellence was his devotion to the Father—the same devotion of Jesus, the one that filled the soul of the Master, the one that made his most holy heart beat in an ineffable way, the one that disturbed his divine serenity. How much Fr. Félix wrote about this rare and profound devotion! How he was moved when he would speak of the Father!

Tell me, all of you who were his children and received his intimate secrets, did he not exhort you a thousand times to love the Father? Was this love not the holy obsession of his simple and pious soul? Did you not observe that his face was illumined and his eyes shone bright when he spoke of the Father? Still in his last hours, when, surrounded by his children he said goodbye to them and left them his blessing and his testament, the word that flowed spontaneously and ardently from his soul was to engrave in his children devotion to the Father.

This devotion of Fr. Félix is the key to his life and the secret of his death. It made of him an image of the Father, faint and distant without a doubt, but an image at last.

By that prodigious power of love that assimilates those who love him, devotion to the Father put in the soul and in the life of Fr. Félix vigorous traits of the Divine Beloved.

Many, very many, called him father, and he truly was, not only because of the glory of his priesthood and the prerogative of being a founder, but also because of his intimate physiognomy, shaped by his love for the Father.

When I think of the priest for whom we have come to pray and I reconstruct in my soul his unforgettable figure, what impresses and captivates me before all reasoning and all analysis is his goodness, the goodness that shone in his sweet gaze, that spread in his almost childlike smile, that vibrated in his smooth and calm word, that overflowed into his actions, his dealings, and his works.

Still I feel tempted to think that there was something in his goodness that was excessive; but, can there be excess in the goodness that is the gentle emanation of love that has no measure?

It is easy to feel goodness, but difficult to speak about it; it is experienced, but our spirit is unable to define it or explain it. It is the gift of self, disinterested and generous; it is the love that spreads with the smoothness and with the strength of a perfume; it is something ineffable that attracts with sweetness, that penetrates into the depths of souls and makes us think of God.

Because God is by his essence infinite goodness; but this divine prerogative we attribute to the Father, who gives himself and diffuses himself, filling everything and expecting nothing, who communicates his infinite richness to the Son and the Holy Spirit, and, without going out of himself, creates the universe and places in it the reflection of his sovereign beauty.

I think that Fr. Félix received in his pure soul a glimmer of that ineffable goodness; that is why he gave himself without measure, that is why he irresistibly attracted people. People can discuss his works and assess his virtues, but they cannot doubt his goodness, which the shadow of the Father cast in his soul and in his life.

But there is still something more characteristic of the Father: fecundity. Principle of all that proceeds in the uncreated and in the created, *of whom all paternity in heaven and earth is named. A quo omnis paternitas in caelo et in terra nominatur*, said St. Paul (Eph 3:15[2]).

From his infinite bosom he engenders the Word in the splendors of sanctity; from the mutual love of the Father and of the Son emanates, like an infinite kiss, the Holy Spirit; and to the Father is attributed the colossal and wonderful work of creation, who put in every star a radiance, in every flower a perfume, in every fruit a vital principle, and in every soul a glimmer of his divine light.

The souls who love him and who carry in their bosom a likeness of his paternity are especially fecund.

Fr. Félix was marvelously fecund in this way; he founded the Missionaries of the Holy Spirit, who are flourishing and spreading the aroma of love and pouring out into the world the precious fruits of the cross; he exercised an efficacious and indisputable influence in all the Works of the Cross, and in their shadow and by the fusion of his spirit he brought forth many religious congregations: the Daughters of the Holy Spirit, the Guadalupan Catechists, the Missionaries of Jesus the Priest, the Oblates of Jesus the Priest, and even left seeds of other spiritual families that in due time will become religious congregations, without counting the innumerable souls, the institutes already formed, who received the influence of his charity and of his spirit.

Time will tell the magnitude and the solidity of his work; but as far as we can probe the future, Fr. Félix appears to us like those ancient patriarchs whose descendants are numerous and immortal. It would seem that he died overwhelmed under the weight of his fecundity, like those prolific trees that break apart in the fall under the opulence of their fruits.

But no, it was not fecundity that was the secret of his death; we need to go deeper still into the abyss of his love for the Father to discover the mystery of his death.

It is not only the likeness to the Father that is the fruit of the devotion to the first person of the Most Holy Trinity. There is another unexpected and precious fruit whose plenitude appears in Jesus, the first, the supreme, the ineffable devotee of the Father.

In the divine heart of Jesus there is a gigantic, impatient, victorious longing: the desire to suffer and to die, the sublime folly of the cross (1 Cor 1:18). *There is a baptism with which I must be baptized,* he exclaimed in the moment of supreme intimacy, *and how great is my anguish until it is accomplished!* (Luke 12:50).

Why does the love of the Father produce the folly of the cross? Inscrutable mystery! Chained to the cross is the greater glory of the Father, his splendid and definitive glory. And because Jesus loved the Father he sank into the bitterness of Gethsemane, and climbed the bloody slopes of Calvary, and gave the cross the glorious and mortal embrace of love.

And those who, like Jesus, love the Father, feel like him the arduous and pressing passion to suffer and to die.

How much Fr. Félix suffered! Waiting a long time in silence and in peace when the miraculous vocation already filled his soul and engendered in his heart grandiose projects.[3] Who gave him the strength to wait, one of the things most difficult for the poor human heart? The love for the Father; because he loved him, he waited for his hour in peace and martyrdom.

And the fights and torments that are the cost of giving life also came: ingratitude, lack of understanding, hostility, a depressed spirit, the heart that is torn apart, the soul that appears to be crushed under the weight of multiple and incredible difficulties. But in the bottom of that great heart his devotion to the Father burned like an inextinguishable flame, and in the midst of all the martyrdoms he was able to say like Jesus: *But the world must know that I love the Father... Get up, let us go.*

He did not say it, without a doubt—simple souls do not say what they do. At times, they do not even understand it either; but their courageous and burning behavior expresses the intimate mystery with greater eloquence than words. In this way he traversed the extensive and tortuous paths of sorrow in his life; and the end arrived for him, the inevitable end of human life.

The Father, in his inscrutable designs of wisdom and love, set the hour of the sacrifice. Many times he had freed him from death by a singular favor and even by a true miracle;[4] but it was necessary that the Reverend Father die.

Might a life, perhaps, be consummated with death? Is this not the seal of greatness, the crowning of virtue, the glory of love? We fear death because we are unaware of its mystery; the souls that have received the sublime revelation of that mystery desire it with passionate yearnings. They, like the liberation of chained love, like the triumph of insatiable love, like the holocaust of fecund love, need to fall to the earth and die in order to produce their fruit.

I do not know if Fr. Félix would desire death, but I am sure that at the sounding of the hour of God, with the peace of his soul, with the generosity of his heart, with the almost childlike smile of pure souls, he went toward death able to say like Jesus: *But the world must know that I love the Father... Get up, let us go!*

Can we glimpse the mystery of death?

Ah! Let us not say that death is implacable and cruel; let us not say that it wounds without knowing where and what it uproots, without worrying about the catastrophe that it produces. Death is the messenger of God, of his justice and of his mercy, and since love touched it, since it was united to Jesus on Calvary and was anointed with the divine blood, it was transfigured in an ineffable manner, it was impregnated with sweetness and still able to become a poem of love.

Such is the lesson deduced from the death of the Reverend Fr. Rougier.

I have concluded, but it remains for us to fulfill a most sweet duty for those who love the Reverend Father: to pray for him.

Would to God that he no longer needed our suffrages! But... who knows the inscrutable judgments of God? And it is also a necessity for our souls to send to the one whom we love the only thing that we can send him: the perfume of our prayers.

Oh God, who ignited in the heart of your servant Félix a singular love for you and who by casting on him the rays of your goodness and of your infinite fecundity caused new spiritual families to flourish in the Church through him, open to him your infinite and loving bosom and grant him rest in light and peace. Bless his works so that they may live and flourish and produce fruits of life. We ask this through our Lord Jesus Christ, your Son, who lives and reigns with you in the unity of the Holy Spirit, God, forever and ever. Amen.

CHAPTER 15

The Glorious Triumph of Love over Death

FUNERAL ORATION FOR RAFAEL GUÍZAR Y VALENCIA, BISHOP OF VERACRUZ

Fortis est ut mors dilectio.
Love is strong as death.
(Song of Songs 8:6)

How right the divine Scriptures are to affirm that the memory of death is bitter! God chose it to be the punishment for sin, and indeed divine wisdom and eternal justice made death a formidable punishment.

Sin is a monstrous work of egoism, composed as it is of sensuality and pride. And God, in order to punish sin, wanted death to strip, humiliate, and pour into the human heart its incomparable bitterness. For death separates us from all that we possess on the earth. It takes everything from us, and, what is worse, it tears away pieces of our own hearts, separating our dearest loved ones from us, however noble, however legitimate, however holy the bonds that united us with them may be, and it even introduces its destructive scythe into our innermost being and separates and divides the elements themselves that are essentially united in us.

Death pours some kind of bitter absinthe into our heart, dissipates our desires, withers our hopes, and above all humiliates and definitively squashes our pride because it kills all our desires for greatness, because it converts our dreams of glory into a handful of dust. Ah! Truly death is the complete and full defeat of our poor human nature.

And who can compete with death? Who can conquer it? Who can bind it to his chariot of triumph?

Who? Love, love that is as powerful as death; love, which, if it is divine, is more powerful than death. Only love can place a glimmer of light in its dark shadows; only it can change into sweetness the absinthe of bitterness that death pours into souls; only love can change into triumph the inglorious defeat that death inflicts.

For Bishop Guízar, was death a defeat or was it a triumph? Did we see him fall like a damned soul in the abyss, or did we see him arrive like a blessed soul that knocks on the doors of eternity in order to find happiness? Ah! I do not hesitate to answer that for Bishop Guízar death was a triumph. Was his funeral procession not a triumphal march? Did his diocesan brother priests not take him wrapped in tenderness and veneration to his final dwelling place? Perhaps he had never been so vociferously honored as in those supreme moments.

But more than this exterior triumph, I want to emphasize another—the intimate, profound one.

Those of us who contemplate death, did we not see the peace of God, the light of heaven, descend onto his most noble face? Did we not feel infected with the immense sweetness that God poured into his immense heart? Without a doubt, we mourn him; we are right to do so, and we will never mourn him properly enough. But, is it not true that in the midst of the lacerations of the heart we carry in our souls some inexpressible divine hope? Ah! The death of Bishop Guízar was not a defeat: it was a triumph, and it was a triumph because he carried love in his heart, an immense love, a divine love.

And of this love I want to speak, both because it will be so gratifying for the children to take a look into the soul of their father and because it is useful for all to draw from the death of the distinguished prelate this profoundly Christian lesson, this eminently consoling and fortifying lesson: *Love is strong as death.*

Each soul has its spiritual physiognomy perfectly defined; there is hardly a soul, one might be able to say paraphrasing St. John of the Cross, in which half of the features of its physiognomy looks like the other half.[1] Those who look superficially at souls can confuse them, just as those who are not very observant sometimes confuse one face with another. But for those who look carefully, for those who penetrate deeply, each soul is unique and has its own characteristic, singular, unmistakable physiognomy.

Still more: the features that constitute the spiritual physiognomy of a soul are not like the fragments of marble that are united together ingeniously in order to form a lovely mosaic. No, souls are not a mosaic; rather they have a vital unity. There is in them something like a principle that unifies them, that is the cause of their harmony and of their beauty, above all in the great souls, above all in those that have received a glimmer of the divine.

What was the main feature of Bishop Guízar, what was the principle that gave unity to his great soul, to his most fecund life?

There were gifts in him so beautiful that those who did not penetrate to the depths of his soul could easily be confused at first glance. We might be able to say that the characteristic feature of the Bishop of Veracruz, whom we mourn today, was his splendid detachment, his excessive detachment, at least according to limited criteria. Perhaps we can think that Bishop Guízar heard in his youth the austere and sublime word that Jesus told a youth on the shores of Tiberias: *If you wish to be perfect, go, sell what you have and give to the poor... Then come, follow me* (Matt 19:21).

And without a doubt Bishop Guízar heard this word and squandered his wealth in works of mercy. In addition to this wealth, which was considerable, Bishop Guízar squandered all the treasures that charity and justice placed in his hands with a truly remarkable detachment. One can apply to him the word of Scripture: *Dispersit, dedit, pauperibus. Justitia ejus manet in saeculum saeculi. Lavishly he gives to the poor; his righteousness shall endure forever* (Ps 112:9). A man that handled true riches nevertheless carried in his person and in his things a seal of poverty; noble and dignified poverty, without a doubt, but poverty in the end. How many times we saw him with a worn-out cassock of indiscernible color! How even in his pontifical vestments he wore the seal of his poverty![2]

There will be no shortage of those who judge such modesty unworthy of a prelate; I myself believe that episcopal dignity fits with poverty more than pageantry, and, above all, in Bishop Guízar poverty, his very special modesty, was not a dissonant note but was in perfect harmony with his simple and holy way of being.

Ah! But greater and more noble than his detachment was his generosity. What munificence he had! How he found hidden happiness in giving, in giving always, in giving without measure! Like St. Lawrence, he was able to say: "In caelestes thesauros manus pauperum deportaverunt. All the riches, Lord, that you put into my hands, the poor took them to the celestial treasuries."[3]

His compassionate heart could not bear a single misery, and his hand was always extended to the poor, and his treasure was never exhausted; and if we could count all the necessities that he met and all the sorrows that he comforted, if all those who received benefits from his hand were to come here, ah! this church would be too narrow to contain them.[4] The only thing that was saved, if you will allow me another apparently harsh word, the only thing that was saved from his charitable fury were the goods of the Church, and, above all, your goods, seminarians of Veracruz; he guarded what was yours, or rather he gave it to you without measure, because he loved you with all his soul, because you had a place of honor in his immense heart.

But it occurs to me to ask, if he detached himself from everything, if he looked with disdain on the riches of this world, why did the purse of the poor never run out in his hands? Ah! He knew what all generous and detached souls know, that the purse of the poor is filled by God; and he confidently drew from that purse because he knew that however munificent his hand was, how much more munificent is the provident hand of God. And here appears another feature of his physiognomy that attracts us and makes us wonder if it would not be the characteristic feature of his soul: that trust in God, simple and heroic.

He always trusted in providence. He was an optimistic man who always had an expansive heart, an audacious man who approached God and asked his gifts from him in the way that Moses asked them, with a kind of loving authority.

Bishop Guízar did not only have this unlimited confidence concerning alms for the poor, no; he had it in order to extract from the heart of God the graces for sinners. How the lost sheep would run after him! What efficacy he had, let us say almost infallible, for touching the hardest hearts!

And from where did that efficacy come to him? From his confidence in God, from the audacity of his prayer. The prelate of Veracruz asked God what many of us do not dare to ask, what ordinary prayer does not dare to solicit, employing a phrase from the liturgy: "quod oratio non praesumit, what ordinary prayer does not presume."[5] Bishop Guízar dared to ask it, and he extracted from our Lord God special graces for souls. How many times natural laws had to bend their course before the power and formidability of confident prayer! How lovely is this prerogative, how beautiful this feature of the physiognomy of Bishop Guízar![6]

And, nevertheless, it is not his confidence that is the most characteristic part of his soul. Ah! The secret of Bishop Guízar is deeper, we still have not found the key of his soul and of his life. And allow me to say something personal. A holy friendship, for which I give thanks to God with all my soul, allowed me to come closer to the great heart of Bishop Guízar and surprised me with his secret; and do not say that I am being indiscrete when I reveal this, because nothing impedes me, no bond ties my lips.

I have read in the Holy Scriptures that if it is good to hide the secret of the king, it is honorable to reveal the works of God, and I affirm that the secret of Bishop Guízar was love, a tender love, a burning love, an impassioned love for God that he carried in his soul. Do we not remember that every time he spoke of God his voice shook and his soul shook and his body shook?

One might think that all this was the effect of his burning temperament; no, it was the effect of the fire that he bore in his heart. As when the interior fire in the heart of our planet, in the words of the wise, not finding a way out shakes the earth with formidable movements, so Bishop Guízar lived in constant emotion, always shaking, because he bore in his bosom the secret of his love.

I can say more: that for many years the prayer of Bishop Guízar was always the same, it had an admirable simplicity—prayer, that is to say, the most intimate thing that there is in souls, what expresses their true worth, because how many times do we make noise exteriorly, and, nevertheless we have empty and dry hearts. What a soul is worth is known by its interior life. It is by the word, says Fr. Lacordaire, that the soul speaks to itself, or, better yet, by the word it speaks to God.[7] And what was the word that constantly, that in all times, that in all his prayers Bishop Guízar would say to God? "Lord, I love you, and I want to love you like no one on earth has loved you."

I do not remember where or when he came across this expression;

but since then he never abandoned it, he had it on his lips and always carried it in his soul. Fr. Lacordaire, whom I have just quoted, used to say that when we have said to a person, "I respect you," we can say another better word, "I esteem you"; and when we have said, "I esteem you," we can say, "I venerate you, I admire you"; but when we say, "I love you," we cannot say another word to him.[8] The one who has pronounced this divine word has no other recourse but to keep repeating it always.

And this is what Bishop Guízar did; he found the divine formula of his love, the divine formula of his soul in that sublime phrase, and he savored the sweetness of that word every day, and he stirred it in the intimacy of his heart, and his prayer was to say to God always: "I love you, and I want to love you like no one on earth has loved you."

It may seem folly to dream of loving God like no one has loved him on earth. So be it; but is love not folly? And the love that does not lead to these follies, as we call it in a good way, is a narrow love, is a poor love, is a paltry love. True love has no measure. Is the love of our Lord Jesus Christ not a divine folly? Does St. Paul not call it the folly of the cross (1 Cor 1:18)? Ah! If we look carefully at what Jesus did, we cannot help but think that there is no comparable folly with his, divine and indescribable as it is. With it, he filled his heart and his life.

Yes, love never says, "That is enough"; it is never satisfied. A love that says, "This is as far as I go and no further," I will say it again, is a paltry love, and barely deserves that most sacred name.

St. Thomas Aquinas, the genius of indisputable authority, not the audacious mystic, not the poet that gets carried away by outbursts of his fantasy, but rather the man that sees all in the light of the eternal principles, teaches us two things: that love has no measure, and that we will never finish fulfilling the first commandment of the law: *You shall love the Lord, your God, with all your heart, with all your being, with all your strength* (Luke 10:27).[9] If most holy Mary would have lived longer than she did, she would have had other steps to climb on the ladder of divine love, and still she would have been compelled to love God in a more perfect way. Ah! Whoever judges that audacious phrase of the impassioned souls of God to be folly is someone who does not understand love. I could repeat at this moment the phrase of St. Augustine: "Da mihi amantem et sentiet quod dico. Give me someone who loves, and he will understand what I say."[10]

And when we have discovered in the depth of the heart of Bishop Guízar this inexhaustible source of love, we can understand his whole life. How could it be strange that he viewed the things of this world with disdain when he bore in his heart the divine treasure? How could one not have been generous, if he who loves bears in his heart the same sentiments of the Beloved? Bishop Guízar bore in his soul the sentiments of the heart of Jesus. How could he not have been merciful, compassionate, and most generous? He who loves confides; there is no firmer or more solid foundation for confidence than love. Ah! When one loves, when he is familiar with the Beloved, when one knows—like St. Thérèse of the Child Jesus used to say—where he stands with respect to the goodness and mercy of God, it is impossible to place limits to confidence.[11]

But let us not believe that the detachment, the generosity, and the confidence of Bishop Guízar were features that immediately sprouted from his love of God; no, there is something else that we can call essential in his physiognomy and that is the logical consequence, the prolongation of his love of God, and that is the love of souls.

Surely this love we all know. He hid the love of God a bit on account of spiritual modesty. The love of souls, however, he could not contain: it would come out in his words, in his actions, in everything. Do we not remember with what emphasis he pronounced these words: the souls? How he would become inflamed thinking about them! And it was not a vain emotion, no; his whole life was consecrated for souls. Long before he received the fullness of the priesthood, did he not travel throughout the Republic, what am I saying, did he not travel throughout the world evangelizing souls? On the island of Cuba, in various republics of Central America and of South America, was he not bringing about his work par excellence, the work of his heart, the missions?

And how his soul overflowed into them! His simple but anointed and vibrant word, which, like a two-edged sword, reached the depths of hearts, shook souls and converted them to God. That is why he always dreamed of the missions. In them he spent a good part of his life, and when God, in his holy and mysterious designs, invested him with the episcopal dignity, he did not stop being a missionary; he was a bishop and continued to be a missionary, the missionary bishop who transformed Veracruz with his warm, gentle, simple word, but full of light and effectiveness.

And for souls he worked without ceasing; he was tireless! Because for him there is no weariness nor does he know limits; he was untiring in preaching, and teaching doctrine to kids, and hearing confessions, and he passed the days and nights with an admirable strength that was born from his love for God.

But I also have another secret to reveal. Without a doubt, what the world saw is enough in order to understand the love that he had for souls, but even the apostles who worked in an untiring matter yearned for eternal rest. We work today, some used to say, but we have eternity to rest. Yes, we dream of heaven, not because work bothers us, but because there is at the bottom of our souls a desire to rest that we preserve, at least, for the other life.

Bishop Guízar did not have this desire, or better said, he did have it, but he was as it were overwhelmed under the weight of the other desire. He yearned for eternal happiness, he had the hope—and, in this way, he asked God with all the depths of his soul—that when he would close his eyes to the light of this world, he would open them immediately to the splendors of the beatific vision; not by suffering, he would say, but by seeing God, because his love did not have delays or vicissitudes. Yes, he yearned for union with God, but more than for this, he yearned to do good for souls.

He would have preferred to live until the consummation of the ages, giving missions, working for the glory of God and for the good of souls; and even in the sublime follies of his love he dreamed that God would find some means so that after his death he might be able to come again to earth to continue working for them. In the way that St. Thérèse of the Child Jesus used to say that she was going to spend her eternity sprinkling flower petals on the earth,[12] Bishop Guízar wanted to spend his eternity working effectively for souls.

They will tell me: it is another folly. Yes, but another sublime folly of love, of two loves that are really one love: that of God, that spreads, that extends to the love for our brothers, since the apostle St. John teaches us *whoever does not love a brother whom he has seen cannot love God* (1 John 4:20).

That was the secret of Bishop Guízar, the key of his physiognomy, the characteristic feature of his soul: he was a man who bore in his heart an impassioned love for God, an impassioned love for souls, and from the inexhaustible source of that love came everything else, his detachment, his generosity, his confidence, and all the virtues with which we saw him surrounded.

That is why his death was sweet, tranquil, like the dream of a just man; some kind of supernatural light that made us think of heaven appeared on his face. The love that he bore in his heart triumphed divinely over death, and sweetened its bitterness, and bound it to the chariot of his triumph, converting the defeat with which death always afflicts us into a glorious triumph, because love is stronger than death…

CHAPTER 16

Peace, the Fruit of Harmony

FIRST FUNERAL ORATION FOR ARCHBISHOP LEOPOLDO RUIZ Y FLÓRES[†]

Homines divites in virtute, pulchritudinisstudium habentes,
pactificantes in domibus suis.
Men rich in virtue, cultivators of beauty,
and peacemakers in their homes.
(SIRACH 44:6[1])

I do not think I am failing in my duty—to the sacred duty of someone speaking in the name of God—if I water the words of my mouth with the tears of my soul and envelop the divine concepts with which I must feed souls in the bitterness of my torn heart...

† ORIGINAL: Given at the funeral honors that the Archdiocese of Michoacán celebrated on January 14, 1942.

EDITOR'S NOTE: Leopoldo Ruiz y Flóres (1865–1941) served as archbishop of the Archdiocese of Michoacán, later renamed the Archdiocese of Morelia, from 1911 until his death. He ordained Martínez a bishop, and Martínez acted as his auxiliary for several years. For this reason, as this homily demonstrates, Martínez had a great filial affection for Ruiz. In 1929, near the end of the Cristero War in Mexico, which was fought in large part to end the suppression of the Catholic faith in Mexico, Ruiz was appointed the apostolic delegate to Mexico by Pope Pius XI. As the man charged with handling the relationships between the pope, the Mexican bishops, and the Mexican government in this extremely delicate time, Ruiz faced tremendous pressure. He was exiled from Mexico three times, including a period of exile in San Antonio, Texas, in the 1930s after the pope had criticized the Mexican government for continued persecution of Catholics. He died on December 12, the feast of Our Lady of Guadalupe.

Jesus also cried!

Like heavenly rain his tears fell on the Holy City when from the vantage point of Mount Olivet his lips directed words of ineffable tenderness to it (Luke 19:41). Jesus also cried! And he cried when he was going to exercise his omnipotence, when he was going to snatch his friend Lazarus from the clutches of death; before his voice prevailed over death, his tears fell on the tomb of his friend (John 11:35).

Ah, in vain do my eyes and my heart look for the most loving father of my soul in this church that was his cathedral and that is intimately linked with him!

Thirty years ago I saw him full of vigor and enthusiasm traveling around the naves of this cathedral in order to take possession of his Church; many times I saw him enter triumphantly after his many burials; and in the most glorious days for the Church of Morelia, the sweetest days for my heart, many times I saw him on this cathedra or on his episcopal throne; and at least for a month his mortal remains were here... Now even that last consolation does not remain for our hearts!

I repeat, in vain do our eyes and our hearts seek him; nothing remains of him but a memory, a most sweet memory for being that of a father, but austere and bitter for not being more than a memory...

But let us not let the pain fool us. There remains something more than a memory of His Excellency, Don Leopoldo Ruiz, something sweet remains for us, something exquisite, something fecund. He could have said like the Latin poet, "Non omnis moriar. I will not die completely,"[2] not only because we hope that he enjoys eternal life in the infinite bosom of God, but also because here on earth his memory will also be immortal, because something remains of him, the light of his doctrine, the wisdom of his counsels, the example of his virtues—and these things are immortal.

Archbishop Ruiz wrote very few books; but he wrote one, and if you will allow me the expression, he lived one, luminous and fecund: his life, which is a living lesson of unity, of harmony, and of peace.

The great merit of a life is unity.

In the ineffable unity of God, his infinite perfections are consummated. And a reflection of that sublime unity comes to dwell, comes to rest from time to time, on souls and on human lives.

The life of Archbishop Ruiz had a marvelous unity, a stupendous harmony. Archbishop Ruiz could have been many things, because he had notable natural gifts and very particular supernatural gifts; but all those gifts of God were founded in unity.

Archbishop Ruiz was only one thing: he was a bishop.

His thoughts, as far as we are able to glimpse them, were episcopal; his words were episcopal, full of prudence and of light; his works were episcopal, fecund and holy; even his exterior demeanor was episcopal, as if the character that he bore in his heart put a seal even in the details of his exterior.

But being a bishop is not a small thing for him who bears a tremendous dignity with decorum and holiness. Being a bishop is one of the best compliments that can be paid to a man. St. Thomas Aquinas teaches that the most perfect state in the Church of God is that of the bishop.[3] The bishop is a man consecrated forever, totally, and to the point of heroism. The ring that we bear is a symbol of commitment and of fidelity because we are perpetually united to our Church and totally consecrated to our faithful. One day we heard in the intimacy of our hearts the divine word of Jesus: *Do you love me more than these?* And when this sincere cry of our love sprung forth: *Lord, you know that I love you!* Jesus Christ said to us: *Feed my lambs* (John 21:15).

The proper virtue of the bishop is charity toward his neighbor. The same Angelic Doctor teaches that, as religious go to perfection by means of the evangelical counsels of poverty, chastity, and obedience, the bishop walks to the highest perfection to which he is called by the heroic exercise of charity towards his neighbor.[4] The bishop is a man who loves souls in an exclusive way, so perfect, so heroic, that he devotes and consecrates himself totally for them.

In this way, Archbishop Ruiz, whose death we mourn, devoted himself to souls. In the forty-one years of his holy and fecund episcopate, that is, in the greater part of his life, he did nothing else: he consecrated himself to souls, he gave them his time, his word, his wisdom, his sorrows, his tears, and his blood... The active and firm charity of Archbishop Ruiz could be expressed with the words of the apostle: *Ego autem libentissime impendam, et superimpendar ipse pro animabus vestris. I will most gladly spend and be utterly spent for your sakes* (2 Cor 12:15). His hand, how it was always open to help! His lips, how they were always disposed to pour out light and counsel into souls! But, above all, how generous was his heart!

That is why I think that the nuance of his own charity was goodness. And goodness consists not in giving many things—you can give nothing and be good; however, one can also give much and not be good. I think that goodness consists in giving the heart, in giving it always, in giving all of it, in giving it gratuitously, in giving it without hoping for payment. And in this way, Archbishop Ruiz gave his heart: who does not remember having received that magnificent gift many times? He used to give it to the child who approached him to kiss his pastoral ring, to the old man or to the beggar who solicited his charity; he used to give it to his friends and he used to give it to his enemies. On his desk in the place of his exile, he had the picture of a persecutor of the Church of Mexico, to pray for him always and to give him his heart in this way.

There is no doubt that goodness was something characteristic of Archbishop Ruiz and one of the principal features of his physiognomy.

And why not say it? Archbishop Ruiz also had his deficiencies. Who does not have them? There is only one who never had them—him of whom the Church sings: "Tu solus sanctus. You alone are the holy one"[5]—and after Jesus, the most holy Virgin Mary, the perfect image of Jesus. Outside of those two, we all have deficiencies. And it does not hurt my heart to speak of the deficiencies of Archbishop Ruiz because they are so heroic; his deficiencies came from his excess of goodness: the only thing that he could be blamed for was that sometimes he was too good...too good, according to our poor human criterion. But only God knows the prize that our father will have received for his charming excesses of goodness.

But St. Paul teaches us that charity takes all forms: *Love is patient, love is kind. It is not jealous, love is not pompous, it is not inflated...it does not seek its own interests, it is not quick-tempered.... It bears all things, believes all things, hopes all things, endures all things* (1 Cor 13:4-7). Therefore, although charity is the characteristic of all holy bishops, each one of them receives from charity a special seal, because "there is hardly a soul that in the middle of its journey looks like another," as St. John of the Cross marvelously said.[6]

In some bishops charity is strength, indomitable strength, like in St. Thomas of Canterbury; in others it is wisdom, deep wisdom, like in St. Augustine; in others it is overpowering eloquence, like in St. John Chrysostom; in others untiring activity, like in St. Turibius of Mogrovejo.

What was the seal that put the episcopal virtue of charity in the soul and in the works of Archbishop Ruiz?

No virtue stood out properly in the heart and in the life of Archbishop Ruiz because the characteristic thing in him was the balancing of all the virtues. It was the most beautiful harmony that existed in his soul and in his life, in the way that in a polyphonic song played magisterially no voice sticks out but, rather, one only feels the harmonious impression of the group. Many can surpass him in wisdom, in eloquence, in strength; but in what perhaps few match him is in the balance, in the harmony, in the unity of all his qualities and virtues.

That is why I have desired to apply the words of Sirach—*Homines pulchritudinis estudium habentes. Men who are cultivators of beauty.*—and not because he had any special concern to cultivate beauty in the ordinary way in which that expression is usually understood—although he may not have lacked artistic faculties, he never had the pretension of cultivating them—but because his life was a great work of art, a work of harmony and of beauty.

Whoever has dealt with him intimately, and even superficially, has felt that impression of harmony, of balance; in him there were no exaggerations, nor extremes, nor dissonances.

There will be no lack of people who object to me that Archbishop Ruiz possessed singular virtues, and they may even enumerate to me his goodness, his equanimity, his simplicity, etc. I also enumerate and admire them; but those singular virtues were only the result of his own balance, the resonances of that harmony, the perfume of the exquisite flower of his moral beauty.

The first perfume that exuded from that harmony was his serenity, a serenity that accompanied him always. Whether in moments of joy or in days of tribulation, we always found him the same, the same smile on his lips, the same calmness in his countenance, the same accent in his episcopal voice. Ah! Many times he must have had an immense sorrow in his soul, but he hid all that under the religious mantle of his serenity.

I could multiply the facts that prove this truth. Once he was hiding in a shack in the Bajío; it was a difficult and tragic time for the Mexican bishops. In the middle of the night, he received news that his hiding place had been discovered and that the military was going to take him prisoner. The Archbishop checked his watch and saw that it was three or four hours before the time he used to get up. He understood that the soldiers would not arrive any sooner, and he returned to sleep quietly until it was time to get up and escape.

I saw him, I am a witness that when the storm used to hover over his head, he would talk and relax peacefully with his friends.

From the time when he was apostolic delegate, I keep as a jewel a letter he wrote to me when he was exiled the last time. What lofty ideas! What serenity they reveal! And from the heights where he flew as in an airplane, he had the calm to contemplate the magnificent panorama that unfolded before his eyes…

And let us not believe that his serenity came from his temperament. His character was lively, as evidenced by the speed of his resolutions and his sometimes alarming and perhaps a little exaggerated punctuality. Nor should we think that this equanimity of his soul depended on the insensitivity of his heart. Ah, insensitive Archbishop Ruiz! Whoever says so did not know him. His heart was—dare I say it—almost excessively sensitive. Who did not know the exquisite delicacy of Archbishop Ruiz? In him there was room for all human feelings; he felt sorrow and joy, fear and hope; but, above all, he felt affection: he was so loyal, he was so sincere in the affections of his heart!

The secret of his serenity was in his virtue: because he was so rich in virtue, that is why he was balanced and serene.

But the harmony of his soul had another consequence: simplicity. Archbishop Ruiz was simple, not in the somewhat pejorative sense with which at times this word is taken in the world; no, he was simple in the elevated and spiritual sense, according to which simplicity constituted one of the greatest qualities of his soul. With what naturalness he did everything, whether he was devoutly celebrating Mass or graciously exercising eutrapelia with his friends, whether he was engaged in the great business of his offices or conversing with a poor person, with a beggar, or with a child!

Everything in him was simplicity and naturalness, simplicity that was richness and naturalness that was elevation, similar to the difficult ease of the orator of which so much has been said, similar to that naturalness that the great works of art have by which it seems that anyone could do them and yet they are the fruit of a genius.

And that simplicity accompanied him even to death because he died with the naturalness with which he had lived, because for him sickness and death were one of so many things in life. And he received them like he had received everything, like he received the priesthood, like he received the episcopacy, like he received his exile, like he received sorrow—in this way he received death…

And I think that this simplicity came from the harmony of his soul. Because what breaks simplicity is passion, even when it is noble, passion that overflows, that in the midst of that symphonic song dominates the other voices; but when everything is harmony, everything is naturalness, everything is simplicity… God is simple, because in him everything is harmony.

It only remains for me to consider another marvel that the harmony of his soul produced in Archbishop Ruiz: peace.

St. Augustine, who had among other privileges that of felicitous wording, left us this comprehensive and profound definition of peace: "Peace is the tranquility of order."[7] It is order, it is harmony, but a harmony that shines and resonates, a harmony that makes an impression all around itself.

Friar Luís de León, in order to explain peace to us, makes us observe the marvelous spectacle of the firmament on a splendid night.[8] In the serene sky, the stars twinkle and move with perfect precision and order; it is a harmony that we do not understand but that we sense. And little by little it subtly enters into our interior, and captivates our heart, and makes us forget the vicissitudes of life, and makes us forget our sorrows and our hopes, and it appears that we are sinking into the immense bosom of peace...

The firmament produces peace, because it is order, because it is harmony. There was also in the heart of Archbishop Ruiz a firmament, a marvelous order, a perfect harmony. That is why peace spread around him: his peace was a contagious peace. When we approached him, we felt that something soothing ran through our spirit and our being and put a glimmer of harmony in us, a vestige of that peace.

Archbishop Ruiz was one of those peacemakers of whom the Scriptures speak; he gave peace to souls and peace to the diocese. Wherever he was, peace reigned; whatever matter was placed in his hands, we could wonder what resolution he would give it, but we could be sure that in that matter he would put his seal, the seal of peace.

And because he was peaceful and a peacemaker, God gave Archbishop Ruiz in the last years of his life a grandiose mission. It was in the dark days for the Mexican nation: the churches were without Jesus, the abomination, the desolation, to use the word of the Scriptures (Matt 24:15), passed triumphantly over our territory; the bishops exiled, the priests hidden, Christian hearts torn apart. At the most violent part of the storm, the vicar of Jesus Christ, with the intuition that he has by his most high position, by his divine mission, set his eyes on Archbishop Ruiz and named him his representative, made him the apostolic delegate.

And Archbishop Ruiz came to Mexico and put an end to that very sad situation, employing simple and audacious means, so simple that it appeared absurd, so audacious that it appeared incredible.

Certainly, what he did in the memorable year of 1929 was not peace but the germ of peace.[9] It was a tiny and small germ like the grain of mustard seed; and Archbishop Ruiz had the bravery and the strength to take that tiny seed and plant it in Mexican land (Matt 13:31).

Many smiled, others were scandalized, very many, even his friends, reviled him. Archbishop Ruiz did not lose his serenity. The pope had placed the blessed seed in his hands. What did it matter if everyone rose up against him?

That seed began to develop with the slowness of all vital processes, but at the same time with the certainty of all that is divine.

And we have seen the plant grow; and from that tiniest of seeds sprouted a bush that is becoming a tree. Are we not enjoying freedom and peace? In good time they will tell me that this peace and this liberty have not yet reached the fullness of high noon. Wait! Wait! They will arrive very soon. The tree that Archbishop Ruiz planted will be a gigantic tree on whose branches the birds of the sky will come to perch (Matt 13:32). And when we contemplate the fullness of that high noon and sit underneath the fig tree and the vine, like the Israelites (Mic 4:4), to savor the fruits of peace, then the name of Archbishop Ruiz will be great and glorious.

Alius est qui seminat et alius est qui metit (John 4:37). How true it is that one is the one who sows, and another is the one who reaps. God knows to whom it will fall to reap the plentiful harvest; but it was Archbishop Ruiz's task to sow, and I think it is more glorious to sow in sorrow and in tears than to gather in satisfaction and in joy (Ps 126:5-6).

Now Archbishop Ruiz has completed his mission. We watched him decline as we watch the sun sink into the splendid sunset every day. And his sunset was glorious because even though his body was destroyed by a terrible illness, he died like he had lived: in peace, in serenity, in simplicity, in love...

We enjoy his precious lessons in the midst of the tears of our eyes and the sorrow of our hearts. But let us not think that those lessons are only for us bishops, but also for priests and for the faithful because we all must have unity in our lives, harmony in our hearts, serenity in our souls, peace all around us.

Let us enjoy those precious lessons and after having contemplated the glorious sunset of Archbishop Ruiz, let us think about dedicating to him not only the intimate memories of our souls but also the prayers of our hearts.

I have just assured you that Archbishop Ruiz had a glorious end; and it would be enough to justify my assertion to consider that he died on the greatest day for Mexicans: the twelfth of December. Can it be thought that the Blessed Virgin took him on that glorious day for anything other than to make him enter into the joy of the Lord?

I do not know if my filial love deceives me, but I have the sweet hope that since the twelfth of December Archbishop Ruiz has been enjoying the vision of God in sweet eternity.

But what do we know of the other life? How can we boast of knowing God's designs? Ah! We do not know them, and that is why our filial duty is to elevate our prayers to the Lord.

Oh God, who in your most loving designs chose your servant Leopoldo to be bishop with all the greatness, with all the heroism that is proper to such high dignity! Lord, you who enveloped in your charity that heroic soul, who put a divine harmony in his heart, and who covered him with the mantle of serenity, you who made him participate in your divine simplicity and gave him peace for himself and for others, hear the prayers of his children, of those of us who received life, light, strength, counsel, love from that episcopal heart!

Oh all-knowing and merciful Lord, give to your servant Leopoldo the word of the eternal reward—*Come, share your master's joy* (Matt 25:23)—so that there, in your infinite bosom, he will find the sovereign harmony, the eternal peace, and the marvelous simplicity of love that will make him happy forever and ever!

CHAPTER 17

The Prudence of a Man of God

SECOND FUNERAL ORATION FOR ARCHBISHOP LEOPOLDO RUIZ Y FLÓRES†

Consiliarius tibi sit unus de mille.
Let one of a thousand be your counselor.
(SIRACH 6:6[1])

JUST as the sun, when it gloriously sinks into the sunset imbues the firmament with multiple and such beautiful colors, so His Excellency, the Most Reverend Archbishop of Morelia, Don Leopoldo Ruiz, when he sank piously into the sunset of the grave, left a trail of sympathy and kindness and produced an explosion of prayers that have risen to the throne of God for his soul.

Without counting the innumerable persons who on the occasion of the death of the most illustrious prelate mourned him, praised him, and eulogized his virtues, those of us who loved him have seen with intimate satisfaction that in many parts of the Republic in an official way solemn funerals were held for the soul of the His Excellency the

† ORIGINAL: From the funeral oration proclaimed by His Excellency, the Most Reverend Luis M. Martínez at the solemn funeral honors that the venerable Mexican episcopate celebrated in the Basilica of Tepeyac on April 16, 1942, in suffrage for the soul of His Excellency, the Most Reverend Leopoldo Ruiz.
EDITOR'S NOTE: For more biographical information on Ruiz, see the note at the beginning of the previous homily.

Archbishop: the dioceses he governed, those who had spiritual ties or debts of gratitude to him, have expressed their love and gratitude by celebrating solemn funeral honors for the soul of Archbishop Ruiz.

But the current solemnity has a more important significance and a deeper meaning. This solemnity is not the fulfillment of a filial duty, as in the dioceses that he governed; nor is it only a manifestation of gratitude, as in the other dioceses of the Republic; nor even is it simply a tribute of fraternal love that Archbishop Ruiz knew how to earn with his fine manners and his great heart. No, this solemnity is a tribute that the venerable Mexican episcopate renders to His Excellency, the Most Reverend Archbishop of Morelia, Don Leopoldo Ruiz, and a testimony that such an illustrious prelate had a most efficacious influence on the entire venerable Mexican episcopate for a long time.

I want, with the grace of God, to consider on this occasion this facet of the most fine diamond that was the soul of Archbishop Ruiz and expound this thought: how Archbishop Ruiz was for a long time the counselor of the venerable Mexican episcopate.

And it is my purpose not only to point out the fact, but rather to scrutinize the reasons for which Archbishop Ruiz exercised this influence on his brothers in the episcopate—more than to praise him, to draw from his life a most useful lesson and to explicate, with regard to this exemplary life, something of the spiritual doctrine of Holy Church, since this always has to be the end that must be proposed by all who speak in the name of God.

The fact is undeniable.

Many of us received episcopal consecration from his hands and a decisive influence in our lives from his soul. That is why we consider him like a father.

Others, without having such close ties, were united to him by a holy friendship; so many came to him demanding counsel in their difficulties and problems, and everyone recognized and praised the qualities of Archbishop Ruiz: his grand spirit, his immense heart, his boundless generosity.

For many years, from the founding of the Episcopal Committee until the death of Archbishop Ruiz, he was the president of that Episcopal Committee and therefore the one who directed the collective activity of the venerable Mexican episcopate.[2] And he was the president of the Episcopal Committee by a free and enthusiastic general election, and each time it was necessary, we elected him again with the same unanimity.

Furthermore, before the Sovereign Pontiff had named him the apostolic delegate, he had already rendered remarkable services to the apostolic delegation with his information and his advice, as two representatives of the Sovereign Pontiff testified.

How can we explain this very efficacious influence in the Mexican episcopate for many years? What was the virtue that served as the base of that work that Archbishop Ruiz carried out among his brothers? Why were his words so full of wisdom? Why did we receive decisive and valuable directions from him?

Because Archbishop Ruiz possessed in a singular way a valuable virtue, a rare virtue, a virtue that directs the rest, that points out their course, marks their degree and coordinates them in an admirable way. Have we understood it? I am referring to prudence. And not to that prudence that we must all have for the sanctification of our souls, since without prudence there is no perfect virtue, but instead to that rare and precious prudence that serves to direct others.

Yes, lovely, because it is a profoundly aesthetic virtue, the virtue of harmony, the virtue of marvelous unity. And it is a most rare virtue, as the words of Sirach assure: *Consiliarius tibi sit unus de mille.*

Let one of a thousand be your counselor.

For, in truth, such are the qualities and prerogatives that are needed in a soul to be able to counsel rightly, without which it is not possible for counselors to be multiplied in the world. The Scriptures, I repeat, have said it admirably: *Let one of a thousand be your counselor.*

It might be thought that prudence, being an intellectual virtue, needs nothing more than a clear intelligence and right judgment. But prudence, although it is a virtue of light, nonetheless has like the rest of the virtues its deep roots in the heart. To be prudent it is not enough to be intelligent or erudite, but one also needs to be calm, to have in one's soul the silence of serenity that is indispensable for hearing that omnipotent word that does not descend from its royal throne except into the midst of the august silence of the soul (Wis 18:15).

For the word of God to come to us, the passions of our hearts must be quieted. Do we not know that most of our errors come from our passions? Even noble passions can disturb the clarity of our spirit.

For our vision to be clear and profound, for us to be right in our resolutions, peace and tranquility must be established in our hearts. Let me repeat it: the word of God does not descend to earth except into the midst of the august silence of the soul.

Our Lord Jesus Christ expressed this doctrine marvelously in those well-known words of the Holy Gospel: *Discite a me, quia mitis sum et humilis corde. Learn from me, for I am meek and humble of heart* (Matt 11:29).

The commentators say that this expression does not mean that Jesus Christ invites us to imitate him in those two virtues of humility and of meekness, but rather he invites us to be his disciples because he has the qualities needed to be a master. The qualities of the master must be humility and meekness. Therefore, the meaning of this evangelical phrase is: Be my disciples because I am meek and humble of heart.

It is truly so: to be a master, one has to be meek and humble. To be prudent, to direct others, to counsel them, it is indispensable that the passions have been silenced in our hearts. And that is why Jesus Christ says in a very significant way: *Discite a me, quia mitis sum et humilis corde.*

And Archbishop Ruiz possessed those virtues in the highest degrees. His meekness was well-known. Always serene in the midst of the vicissitudes that he suffered, tender and sweet with his own, generous and so delicate with his enemies, Archbishop Ruiz was a model of meekness.

I had the good fortune to know him personally for many years, and I can testify before God that I never saw him become irritable. He had an unfailing meekness. Yes, in the forty-one years of his episcopacy—and what difficult and tragic years!—in the midst of the vicissitudes of his eventful life, in the midst of the dangers of those fateful years of our history, Archbishop Ruiz always kept calm.

He found himself in unending difficulties; he had bitter enemies; but neither the great sufferings of his life, nor the dangers to which he found himself exposed, nor the privations which he had to bear played a part in disturbing the calm and the serenity of his soul.

As for humility, in the life of Archbishop Ruiz we find indisputable manifestations of that virtue, from details that at first glance have no importance but are precious because they reveal a great soul, to the admirable features that sometimes verge on the heroic.

How many times did Archbishop Ruiz help many priests at Mass! And when they, embarrassed, wanted to prevent it, Archbishop Ruiz, with naturalness and grace, repeated the words of Pius X: "I received the order of the acolyte; I can perfectly help at Mass."[3]

At first glance it is an unimportant detail; but is it not true that these details sometimes reveal the mystery of a soul?

His humility was splendidly manifested in the government of his diocese. His government, if I may use the expression, was an impersonal government, wonderfully impersonal. Archbishop Ruiz only took into account the interest of his diocese. Many times he sacrificed his opinion, his preferences, his personal tastes, to submit to the will of his collaborators; he forgot about himself, he disappeared totally to search always with rectitude and generosity for the glory of God and the good of souls.

Archbishop Ruiz practiced that form of humility that is the most difficult and the rarest: humility of intelligence, humility of judgment, sacrificing your opinion, subjecting your judgment to the opinion of others when you are aware of your vast studies, your extensive experience, your profound knowledge of men, subjecting it when you have, at the same time, a clear intelligence, an energetic will. This is a marvel of humility that verges on heroism. And Archbishop Ruiz had it, he knew how to subject his opinion to the opinion of others quickly and easily, naturally and with gentleness.

Thus, because he was humble and meek, his soul had that constant serenity that allowed the word of God to enlighten his soul.

Because tranquility of soul is nothing more than a preliminary of prudence. In a calm soul the light of God descends, because prudence springs from divine light and signifies a clear, profound, exact vision of life and of its very complicated problems.

But that clear and exact intelligence is not enough to be prudent. There are many truly wise men who move with incredible ease in the heights of speculation but who fail to plant their footing in this mundane and miserable world. If I may use a current word, I will say that there are spirits who can soar, but who do not know how to land, who fly and easily stay in the heights, but who never descend from them and feel embarrassed in the extremely complicated netting of the concrete.

There are other spirits who live on earth and no detail of reality escapes them; they see everything, they touch everything. Ah! But they do not know how to fly, they do not know how to understand reality deeply. They see it in a superficial and fragmentary way, but they do not fly, they do not climb to the heights, they do not see human things from the lofty vantage point of the principles, which is where the complete vision of reality is found.

If you will allow me again a comparison taken from current things, I will say that the prudent man must be like those powerful airplanes that fly in lofty regions, but that have enough flexibility to descend quickly near to the earth, and after carrying out their work, launch themselves gallantly and victoriously up to the heights.

That is how the prudent man is: he knows how to fly and he knows how to land; he lives in the heights and has enough flexibility to descend quickly to human things.

Such was the spirit of Archbishop Ruiz. He lived with as much naturalness in the lofty heights as he walked on the mundane and miserable earth. He never lost sight of the principles; his eyes, the eyes of his spirit, were fixed on God. He did not fail to see the eternal notions of justice and truth, but with the same ease with which he flew in the heights, he descended to the earth and made contact with human reality.

Even when nearing his end, Archbishop Ruiz retained that marvelous adaptability. In those long hours of solitude and of suffering that preceded his death, he lived in the heights. "What is Your Excellency doing?" someone asked him. "I am reviewing the years of my life in the sorrow of my soul." But thirty hours before he died he was still giving provisions in accordance with the reality of the moment, speaking about who had to stay at his house and what had to be prepared for the next day.

That ability to live in the heights and to see what is human according to reality served him admirably in carrying out the mission the Sovereign Pontiff wisely entrusted to him.

He captured the Mexican reality marvelously. No, he was not like so many who want to apply to our homeland the norms and procedures that have been successful in the most cultured nations of Europe. No, Archbishop Ruiz knew his homeland, he knew perfectly well what the Mexican reality means, and he never tried to forge illusions or let himself be blinded by vain mirages, no matter how attractive they were. He knew how to capture reality, because without leaving the heights of the principles, he did not lose a single one of the mundane details of life.

But neither the serenity, nor that light, nor that very clear vision are enough for someone to be prudent.

How many there are who think admirably, but who cannot execute. It is not enough to know our difficulties: it is necessary to overcome them. It is not enough to know what must be done: it is also essential to bridge the distance that separates the idea from practice. How many there are who, due to cowardice or timidity, cannot carry out what they think!

The prudent man not only knows what he should do; he also knows how to put it into practice. And Archbishop Ruiz was like that. He had a holy daring, a simple audacity, that sometimes made those who saw him shudder.

They called him the bishop without difficulties because, in fact, he beat them all, in the public order as in the private order, in his diocese as in the rest of the Republic. When Archbishop Ruiz was apostolic delegate, he had all the qualities of a counselor. He did not stop in the face of any difficulty; he was prudent and at the same time audacious, because he was a man of God.

Nothing detained him in his purposes because he did not seek the applause or approval of others; he looked toward the sky, and with all the rectitude of his soul he went toward the proposed end, whatever happened.

Those who saw Archbishop Ruiz as acquiescent and as a pacifist believed that he had an accommodating spirit and that he gave in for comfort, so as not to suffer. Ah! Archbishop Ruiz did not tremble in the face of suffering. He gave clear evidence of it. He endured three exiles; he had the courage to protest against the laws contrary to the Church; and in difficult moments he spoke with the precision that the circumstances demanded and with the integrity of a man who fears nothing.

If he was obliging, it was not because his heart, full of faith, was afraid; it was that he saw reality, because he knew what was advantageous for his nation.

And he had the courage to be acquiescent.

In a certain way the gallant attitude of intransigence and combativeness has its flattery; but when prudence demands that gallantry be put aside, then it is necessary to have the courage to appear to others as weak. To acquiesce and to have the necessary fortitude to appear weak before others when duty demands it is a glorious fortitude, verging on the heroic. Archbishop Ruiz possessed such qualities.

But they are not yet enough to understand the marvel of his prudence. The apostle St. Paul had a strange phrase: *Nolite esse prudentes apud vosmetipsos. Do not be wise in your own estimation* (Rom 12:16). Prudence should not be selfish; prudence should be charitable like all Christian virtue. There are those who are prudent in what concerns them. They think about what is their own and reflect and make the right decisions, but they do not worry about others.

Archbishop Ruiz was not like that, he was not prudent for himself, but rather carried in his heart a treasure of generosity. He was concerned about other dioceses, he was concerned about everyone, and he wanted to do good to everyone, even his enemies. I am a witness to the delicacy and even the tenderness with which he treated his enemies and the yearning of his soul to do good to them. All the more reason why he was generous to the point of self-sacrifice with his friends and with his brothers.

Let us imagine that Archbishop Ruiz had thought of nothing more than his diocese, abandoning the others; he would not have been the counselor of the episcopate. But, on the contrary, anyone who was thirsting for advice and light had only to approach Archbishop Ruiz, who felt any problem that was presented to him as his own.

And just as he was kind, he also inspired great confidence. Everyone would pour out their confidences into that big heart, would empty their hearts, avid for consolation, into Archbishop Ruiz's soul. Archbishop Ruiz had lived so much, had loved so much, had suffered so much, that he understood all the problems.

Clear and deep vision, holy boldness and generosity of heart were the qualities that made Archbishop Ruiz become the counselor of the Mexican episcopate.

I have expounded in broad strokes the reasons why Archbishop Ruiz had such exquisite prudence. But I think that in Archbishop Ruiz there was something more. The Holy Scriptures, in a brief and succinct sentence, like all of them, make us aware of the difference between divine prudence and human prudence: *Cogitationes mortalium timidae et incertae providentiae nostrae. For the deliberations of mortals are timid, and uncertain our plans* (Wis 9:14).

The difference between human and divine prudence could not be better expressed, because, even though the virtue of prudence is a precious gift, it is handled by our poor reason, which always puts the seal of its weakness on its actions.

But there is a divine prudence, the gift of counsel.

The gift of counsel, superior to the virtue of prudence, is a marvelous instrument of the Holy Spirit, whose thought is neither timid nor his foresights uncertain. Directed by the Paraclete, this heavenly gift is profound in its intuitions, accurate in its dispositions, quick and efficient in its activity.

I suspect that this precious gift guided the soul of Archbishop Ruiz. I believe it for the ease with which he solved all the problems, for the success with which he got to the bottom of the issues, for the very wise way he had of finding the most appropriate resolution; because he was very quick in his resolutions, quickness that did not come only from his temperament, but was the fruit of the light of the gift of counsel.

How many times, when others examined a matter after much study and reasoning, they reached the same conclusion that he had quickly seen with his clear and profound vision!

Oh! It was not the uncertain, timid, human prudence that governed his soul: it was the Holy Spirit with his gift of counsel.

And I can even expand my observation and ensure that the serenity of his soul was not simply the peace achieved by the victorious struggle against his passions; it was the divine peace that emanates from the gift of wisdom. And his boldness came from the gift of fortitude, and his whole life and all his virtues were the fruit of the gifts of the Holy Spirit, who possessed and governed the soul of Archbishop Ruiz.

I am confirmed in my judgment of the intensity and depth of his inner life. His soul was intimately united to God, and from the abundance of his contemplation proceeded his outward activity.

What long and devout prayers Archbishop Ruiz made! How silent and devoted he remained before the tabernacle! With what unction he spoke to us of divine things! What a love so fervent for Jesus Christ! What tenderness towards the Blessed Virgin! What fervor of his soul!

Someday the very beautiful pages that Archbishop Ruiz wrote about divine things will be known, pages that will have neither the elegance of great writers nor the finery of human eloquence, but that have the enchanting charm of simplicity, the sweetest unction of humble and peaceful souls.

To express in two words this new aspect of Archbishop Ruiz, I will repeat what an illustrious prelate, His Holiness Pius XI, said on several occasions: he is a man of God.

The pope said it. We were able to verify it.

And because he was a man of God, that is why he had that exquisite prudence, that rare and precious prudence, that made him the counselor of the venerable Mexican episcopate.

This solemnity has that transcendental meaning. It is a testimony that his brothers in the episcopate give him; it is a tribute that we pay to him who was our counselor for many years.

I thank God that he has granted me to be the bearer of the episcopate on this solemnity. But we have not only met to meditate on the precious lessons of the life of Archbishop Ruiz but also to raise our prayers to heaven, our collective prayer, the prayer of the pastors and the faithful, for the eternal rest of such an illustrious prelate.

Let us kneel down and lift up our hearts to God to pray for him.

Oh Lord, who enriched the soul of your servant Leopoldo with graces and heavenly gifts, whom you gave peace and light and boldness to be the counselor of the Mexican episcopate and to do good to many souls, to many dioceses, and to the entire Mexican nation, accept our prayers, the prayers of his brothers and the prayers of all the faithful, who, forming one heart and one soul, raise them to heaven to ask you to pay your servant Leopoldo for what he did for us, what he did for all.

Give him fulfilled peace, give him infinite light, give him eternal happiness. Be you, oh Lord, his splendid reward, keep him in the region of light, love, and happiness, keep him in your infinite bosom, through Jesus Christ, your Son, who lives and reigns with you in the unity of the Holy Spirit, forever and ever. Amen.

CHAPTER 18

The Peace of the Kingdom

FUNERAL ORATION FOR POPE PIUS XI[†]

Laudemus viros gloriosos et parentes nostros in generatione sua...
pulchritudinis studium habentes, pacificantes in domibus suis.
Let us praise the glorious men and our ancestors in their time...
cultivators of beauty, and peacemakers in their homes.
(SIRACH 44:1,6[1])

I do not know when God appears greater before the astonished gazes of men: if it is when from the treasures of his wisdom, from his power and his love, he draws exceptional souls, uniquely gifted to carry out on earth a most noble and fruitful mission; or if it is when, making use of his sovereignty, God collects these souls from the earth and takes them to his bosom precisely when we thought they were at the full maturity of their mission, when we believed they were going to produce their richest and most opulent fruits.

The former is a manifestation of his power; the latter seems to me an ostentation of his inexhaustible fecundity: he erases great men from the earth so that we know that his power is in need of no one,

† Born Ambrogio Damiano Achille Ratti (1857–1939), Pius XI reigned as pope from 1922 until his death. During the periods of intense persecution against the Church in Mexico, Pius XI wrote to the Mexican people multiple times.

that his action is not inextricably linked to any instrument, and that when he needs them he knows how to forge them and, as Scripture says, *can raise up children to Abraham from these stones* (Matt 3:9).

Seventeen years ago, God gave his Church the magnificent gift of an exceptional pope. Pius XI appeared in the Vatican with a profound gaze, a vast vision, an immense heart, a bold will. We do not know if posterity will call him the Pope of the Missions or the Pope of Catholic Action. We are not yet able to determine whether his greatest glory was to sign the Lateran Treaties or to give the world the wonderful teachings of his encyclicals.

And when it seemed that he had reached the fullness of his action, when we had learned to know and love him, when all the peoples of the earth told him, as the disciples of Emmaus did to the divine Master, *Mane nobiscum, Domine. Stay with us, for it is nearly evening* (Luke 24:29), our Lord God snatches him from us, leaving sorrow in our hearts and tears of pain in our eyes.

It is true that our Lord God has already given us a devout pope, very prudent, appropriate for our time[2]; but the righteous joy of the pope's coronation, which was yesterday, the assurance we have that God always gives his Church the men it needs in every age, cannot heal the deep wounds of our filial hearts; and here we come, the clergy and the people, with the representatives of the friendly nations, to render to Pope Pius XI the homage of our filial love; here we are with tears in our eyes, sorrow in our hearts, and prayers on our lips.

And it fulfills my duty to evoke in these solemn circumstances the colossal figure of Pope Pius XI and to make his work and mission known—that work and that mission that have already been consecrated and anointed by the majesty of death.

What was the characteristic trait of His Holiness Pius XI? Was it, by chance, his soul, a soul of light, one of those souls that shine in heaven and illumine the earth with their celestial splendors? Or, was he rather a man who carried fire in his heart and spread torrents of tenderness and love around himself? Was Pius XI a man of firm character, of bold will, of intrepid faith, who undertook the most heroic actions, the undertakings that seemed the most adventurous?

I think that the characteristic feature of His Holiness Pius XI was none of these that I have just enumerated: it was his balance, it was the precious harmony that all these traits had in his soul. His life was a masterpiece of beauty, his life was true harmony; that is why I have dared to apply to him the words of Ecclesiasticus: *Laudemus viros gloriosos et parentes nostros in generationes sua...pulchritudinis studium habentes, pacificantes in domibus suis.* He had the eagerness and solicitude for beauty in his own life. His life was a harmony, in his soul splendid intelligence and delicate love and firm character come together. Let us examine with the grace of our Lord God this marvelous harmony of the soul and life of Pius XI, who spread peace all around himself.

I

In the pope's youth, and even in his maturity, he liked the exquisite delight of climbing to the heights and feeling the joys of mountaineering. How many times has Monsignor Ratti watched from the exalted peaks of the Alps how immense horizons stretched out before his eyes and how magnificent panoramas unfolded beneath his feet! Then he learned to look at things from above, to encompass them as a wonderful whole. And when our Lord God placed him on the exalted vantage point of the Vatican, he looked out like a spiritual mountaineer as the horizons of the world expanded before his eyes and the panorama of his time with all its details appeared before his vision, clear and vast with all its harmony.

Do we not remember that, in the same year of his exaltation to the throne of St. Peter, Pius XI in his encyclical *Ubi arcano* gave us a marvelous description of the world at that time? The Great European

War had just passed.[3] Among the smoking ruins that the terrible catastrophe had left in Europe, the hatred had not yet died down, the logical consequences of the great conflagration remained: economic crises, political problems that took and will take a long time to be resolved. But, in addition, due to one of those phenomena that is difficult to explain in history, the Great World War caused doctrinal currents and transformations of customs to appear and develop in the world that came to change the face of the world.

It seems that after the Great War a new humanity was emerging from some mysterious bosom. History changed its course; it was a new stage in the life of the human lineage. So we can ascertain now, but Pius XI saw it then. He saw how doctrines were appearing on earth that were guiding humanity along new paths, doctrines that, taken to their exaggeration, seemed to unhinge the world, changing the very foundations of society, and at the same time how those horrid doctrines were spreading throughout the land. He saw that customs were changing and the home and youth were transforming. Everything seemed changed; it was a streak of ice that stretched across the world and that seemed to wither the precious flowers of our saints, of our glorious ancestral customs.

Pius XI saw it from his lofty vantage point and described to us in the aforementioned encyclical the ills of the world. What precision to describe it to us, what fineness of analysis, what a profound sense of reality!

And Pius XI was not satisfied with expressing to us superficial phenomena and their immediate causes. His deep gaze penetrated deeper and revealed to us that all men and peoples have turned away from our Lord Jesus Christ, from Jesus Christ who is life, and light, and love, and peace. And because men have distanced themselves from Jesus Christ, that is why there are so many worries and so many evils on earth, that is why from the bottom of all hearts a cry arises, a longing, which Pius XI knew how to capture and carry in his heart: the longing for peace.

To satisfy the yearnings of the world, it was necessary to lead souls to Jesus Christ. It was necessary to restore, to perfect, to solidly establish the kingdom of Jesus Christ on earth. From that reign, peace would spring. And in his mind he drew up his glorious motto, and from the bottom of his heart came that cry that resounded over the earth: *Pax Christi in regno Christi!*

"The peace of Christ in the kingdom of Christ" was the motto of His Holiness Pius XI, and rarely in history has such perfect and great fidelity to his motto been seen as his. His life, his work, his mission was simply the carrying out of that motto that appears in the first of his encyclicals: *Pax Christi in regno Christi!*

If the kingdom of Jesus Christ is the remedy for all the ills of the world, it was necessary for Pius XI to work in his pontificate to reestablish, to restore, to perfect that heavenly and divine reign, and so he did.

In the Holy Year of 1925, Pius XI in a wonderful encyclical, *Quas Primas*, presents Jesus Christ the King to us, lifts him up on the shield, places him on the throne: Jesus Christ is the King of the world, and thus he presents him before the astonished eyes of the earth. There is the remedy for all ills, there is the satiation of human aspirations, there is the sovereign of love and peace who comes to bring men the satisfaction of their immense aspirations: peace.

And in another encyclical, *Miserentissimus Redemptor,* Pius XI reveals to us the spirit of this most sacred kingdom of Jesus, he speaks to us of the heart of the King, and in it two heavenly realities appear: love and sacrifice, which are what constitute the spirit and soul of that heavenly kingdom.

Pius XI does nothing other than expound the doctrine of Jesus Christ in his encyclicals.

The encyclicals of Pius XI! How many times it has seemed to us on reading them to find in them an echo of the luminous encyclicals of Leo XIII! But the encyclicals of Pius XI have—I do not know how to express it—a practical spirit, a wonderful adaptation to current affairs.

Pius XI does nothing other than expound the doctrine of Jesus, the old, the eternal doctrine, the one that is nineteen centuries old, the one that does not change, the one that does not age, the one that does not wither. But Holy Church has the exceptional privilege of taking old things and adapting them to new times in such a way that they appear with the perfume of spring, with the charm of youth. Jesus Christ already said it in the Gospel: *Then every scribe who has been instructed in the kingdom of heaven is like the head of a household who brings from his storeroom both the new and the old* (Matt 13:52). Ah! What Pius XI taught the world is very old, it is the truth of nineteen centuries ago; but what Pius XI taught the world, I say it again, has the perfume of spring.

How wonderfully do the Roman pontiffs know how to adapt the doctrine of Jesus Christ to the needs of each time! The encyclicals of Pius XI are proof of this. In them he speaks of Christian marriage, of the Christian education of youth; he touches on the great social problems of our time by commemorating the encyclical *Rerum Novarum* by Leo XIII; and then, making a marvelous synthesis of all modern errors, in his encyclical on atheistic communism he defines with admirable precision the risks of that great danger that afflicts humanity and reveals the most effective and powerful remedies that the Church of Jesus Christ possesses against communism.

The kingdom, the spirit, the legislation of the kingdom. Pius XI looked at all this with admirable precision; but as the great pontiff contemplated the problem of the earth from above and compared the situation of the world with the ideal traced out in the divine Gospel, I think he felt more and more his own impotence and the need for our Lord God to come to his aid. He understood that the undertaking was gigantic, that to carry it out a multitude of vassals of Jesus was needed, or, rather, of soldiers of Christ, and then God came to his aid, and from the intimacy of his heart the new army sprang up, the most noble army of the kingdom of Jesus Christ: Catholic Action.

Catholic Action is nothing more than that. The kingdom of God must be restored; peace will spring from it. But to restore it, will we priests suffice? Will the hierarchy suffice? Ah! The work is colossal, and even if the hierarchy were enough to carry it out, it is glorious for the Christian faithful to share the fatigues and triumphs of the apostolate with their hierarchy.

And from the heart of Pius XI sprouted the new army, a peaceful army that fights in the immaculate battles of the Church of God, that will go throughout the world carrying in its heart the spirit of Jesus Christ, on its lips the doctrine of Jesus Christ, that will go everywhere carrying the good news of the eternal Gospel, restoring everywhere the spirit of Jesus, re-Christianizing the world, establishing that kingdom of Christ from which the peace of Christ will sprout. How I would like to dwell on each one of these so important points of the work of the pope whom we mourn!

Forming that noble and glorious army that is Catholic Action did not satisfy Pius XI. His immense heart looked into the distance…

He saw how there are still regions on earth to which the good news of the Gospel has not reached, in which the sweet name of Jesus has not yet resounded… And the pontiff must have felt in his heart what Jesus Christ felt nineteen centuries ago, when, sitting on the edge of Jacob's well, he contemplated the crops that were already close to maturity and told his apostles with an inexpressible intimate emotion: "Look, look at the crops; the harvest will come very soon.

Ah! Beg the Father of families to send laborers to his estate" (Luke 10:2).

What Jesus felt then when contemplating the multitude of souls awaiting light, and love, and consolation, and life, Pius XI must have felt when, from the beginning of his pontificate, he turned his gaze to those regions where there are still souls who do not know God and his Christ.

In the same year of his exaltation to the pontifical throne, when commemorating the third centenary of the establishment of the Congregation *De Propaganda Fide*, Pius XI made known his missionary program, a broad and complete program.

With what emotion, with what lyricism did Pius XI in that Pentecost address of the year 1922 express what his soul felt when looking in the distance at that multitude of confessors who work to take souls to heaven, that multitude of martyrs who give their blood and their lives for the spreading of the kingdom of God, those innumerable virgins who sacrifice themselves in the works of the most heroic charity!

And he saw at the same time how millions of souls left the darkness and shadows of death where they lay to return into the arms and to enter into the heart of Christ our Lord. And he felt a divine enthusiasm in his soul, and he began to give very pertinent orders so that the missions could be developed with greater determination and in a more perfect way.

And the truth is that perhaps in no pontificate as in that of Pius XI have the missions been so extensively developed. It is enough to study the statistics to be astonished. But it was that Pius XI had his heart there. That is why he promoted a magnificent missionary exhibition, that is why he put his hand in all the missionary works, particularly in the Missionary Union of the Clergy, that is why he raised a monument in Rome, the new Congregation for the Propagation of the Faith—so that it could be seen that truly in the heart of the pope, in the heart of the Church, there was an immense longing to encompass in a colossal embrace all the souls that exist on earth, so that all of them might come to form a single flock under the direction of a single shepherd (John 10:16).

If I were not afraid of going too long, I would talk about how Pius XI extended his august hand to the easterners. How he took advantage of the centenary of the canonization of an eastern saint to attract all those of the East and make them fix their sights on the Catholic Church! How in the same Basilica of St. Peter the pope wanted to commemorate the Council of Nicaea with eastern rites! How the vaults of St. Peter resounded with Byzantine chants, and how the Sovereign Pontiff, with an eastern rite, celebrated the august mysteries! But it is impossible to say everything; the pontificate of Pius XI is so great and so fecund, his work is so marvelous, that it is not possible to describe it in a few words.

II

From the vantage point of the supreme pontificate, he contemplated the whole of his time, as from the snow-capped peaks of the Alps he looked at the marvelous scenes in the days of his youth.

But was Pius XI just a man of clear vision and profound sight? Did he not have a heart, and a burning heart, and an immense heart?

We are inclined to think ordinarily that intellectuals are cold; it seems to us that a man like Pius XI, who spent years of his life in the silence of libraries with his eyes and attention fixed on old parchments, should not have a heart, should not feel the sweetness of human affections. This suspicion grows in us when we consider the character of Pius XI, manly, austere. Would love and sweetness fit in the heart of that man?

Ah, yes! And he had them in abundance, in wonderful abundance. Pius XI was a man of the heart. Without losing an iota of the virility of his character, Pius XI carried exquisite tenderness in his heart.

Will we have to go and look elsewhere for evidence of this truth, when we ourselves have been the object of that incomparable tenderness?

Ah! It is enough to know how he loved Mexico. We are a monument of his tenderness and his love. It is not a patriotic illusion that makes me think that Pius XI loved us. It was the august lips of the pontiff himself who said it: tell them that Pius XI is perhaps the pope who has loved Mexico the most. And we received the precious message, and we kept it in our hearts, and we spread it around us.

Yes, Pius XI was the pope who loved Mexico the most! The constant concern that he had for us in the dark times we have been through manifested, first, in an apostolic letter and then in the encyclical *Iniquis afflictisque*; later, in a speech at the Consistory in December 1926; in 1932 in the encyclical *Acerba animi*; and in 1937, in the apostolic letter that we all know.

And how in those documents Pius XI raised his furious voice at the mistreatment of which we were victims, how he poured into our hearts the sweet consolation of his paternal love, how he marked out the paths that we should follow with precision, with a solicitude, not simply that of a teacher but, above all, that of a true father. And so that we do not doubt his love, there we have the unequivocal proof: in 1933, in the Basilica of St. Peter, the pope celebrated with us the feast of the Blessed Virgin of Guadalupe on December 12. I had the immense satisfaction of contemplating that unique spectacle: the pope, with all the insignias of his power, surrounded by the cardinals of the Roman Church, by a multitude of bishops who had come there for the Holy Year, by all the religious orders, was there in the Basilica of St. Peter, and during Bernini's *Gloria* we looked at the sweet image of the Blessed Virgin of Guadalupe, ours, the one we love, the one who especially loves us. There the two loves of our heart were fused together in the great basilica: love for the Blessed Virgin of Guadalupe and love for the Vicar of Jesus Christ.

And last year, the pope granted us an exceptional Jubilee, a Guadalupan Year with privileges similar to those that the pope usually grants during the Holy Year.

And now, shortly before he died, the pope agreed that we Mexicans should erect a monument to the Most Blessed Virgin of Guadalupe in the Vatican, so that in that blessed city, which is the center of our faith and piety, those two loves of which I spoke to you before will be united forever: the love of Mexico for the Virgin of Guadalupe and the love of Mexico for the Vicar of Jesus Christ. Is this not enough for us to admire the tenderness of the heart of Pius XI?

Ah! And his sufferings! The sorrows of his soul! He suffered, and suffered bitterly. He could say with the apostle St. Paul: *Quis infirmatur et ego non infirmor? Quis scandalizatur et ego non uror? Who is weak, and I am not weak? Who is led to sin, and I am not indignant?* (2 Cor 11:29-30). The pope felt the evils of all peoples, he felt the evils of all humanity. His heart was filled with sorrow, especially in the last days of his life, when our Lord God, with a most loving and remarkable providence, wanted to express in the heart of the pope the divine sorrow of the heart of Jesus.

But I do not want, when speaking of the pope's heart, to fail to say a word about the one who, according to what has been said, was the star of his pontificate. I am referring to St. Thérèse of the Child Jesus.

The pope, with extraordinary enthusiasm, canonized her. He especially entrusted his pontificate to her, he always invoked her, he kept her close to him, and in the last years of his life, when illness came, he entrusted himself to her and to her he attributed that relative relief that lasted more than a year and that allowed him to do so many wonders.

Why did he choose St. Thérèse of the Child Jesus as his patron, as the star of his pontificate? Why not St. John Bosco, the tireless apostle? Why not St. Robert Bellarmine, the untiring polemicist? Ah! Let us not look for the reason for this choice in the pope's mind: let us look for it in his heart. He chose St. Thérèse, the one who wrote, "My vocation is love. I, in the heart of my Mother the Church, will be love."[4]

III

One last word about the great pontiff. Not only did he carry in his spirit the light of heaven, not only did he have an immense heart, full of love, but his character was firm, he was active, he was passionate.

His activity is well-known. How he worked the seventeen years of his pontificate! The last period of his life draws attention in a very special way. Seriously ill, when the doctors prescribed rest, he said: "Our pastoral duties do not allow us to take vacation days." And tirelessly, in the midst of his ailments, he worked; it could be said that if something hurt him from the disease, that if something made him suffer that last trial that our Lord God sent him, it was not precisely the inconvenience of the disease but that the disease made it impossible for him to continue his work.

It causes admiration to know everything Pius XI did during the time he was ill.

But his activity was not only tireless: as a characteristic of his action, Pius XI had audacity, daring.

What adventures he undertook! We have a momentous and very important one: the Lateran Treaties. How many years had the

Roman question been unresolved; how many upheavals for the pope, how many for the Catholics!

It was not, we know very well, it was not the ambition of temporal authority that made the popes constantly protest against the usurpation of the Papal States, no; what they yearned for was independence, the freedom of the Sovereign Pontiff in the spiritual government of souls. It was necessary for everyone to see that the pope is not even materially subject to another man, that he enjoys full freedom, that he has a piece of land of his own, that in that piece of land he is sovereign, even if with no other force than the spiritual and divine force.

The question was unresolved; our Lord God granted to Pius XI the privilege of resolving it, and he resolved it masterfully and prudently. Perhaps after we have read the Lateran Treaties we admire the wisdom and prudence with which they were made, but before that arrangement was made, who would have thought of such a solution? There the firmness, the audacity of the pope was revealed. He does not need territory: a piece of land is enough for him as long as a spiritual sovereignty can be built on that piece of land.

And the boldness he had to sign those treaties was the boldness he has always had, the colossal firmness to defend his rights, and above all the rights of his children. When they hurt Catholic Action, they hurt him in the heart; and like the lion that defends its cubs, the gentle Pius XI stood up and, facing the mighty of the earth, defended his little children so that they could continue their most meritorious work in the freedom and peace of Jesus Christ.

We have seen him: Pius XI, the one with the immense heart, the one who looked at things from above, also had admirable strength to face all the great men of the earth, to tell the truth when it was necessary to tell it. His strength and character were proportionate to the vastness of his gaze and the tenderness of his heart.

His soul and his life is harmony, is beauty; and that soul—balanced, harmonious—spread peace throughout the world. Peace will sprout from that kingdom of Christ, restored by the pontiff Pius XI; peace will sprout from his luminous encyclicals, from his Catholic Action, from his missionary works, from the Lateran Treaties, from all the work of the pontiff. Pius XI fully carried out his motto: *Pax Christi in regno Christi*. Did he by chance see peace? No; God had not made him to enjoy peace, but to work for it. He was a peacemaker, and even though he is dead, his work endures: his successors will see peace.

Perhaps the current pope, Pius XII, is the first to see peace as the precious fruit of the efforts of his predecessors, and especially Pius XI. Who knows the future? But whenever peace comes to the world, the world should know that Pius XI contributed powerfully to bringing it about. He did not enjoy it; just as Moses contemplated the promised land from Mount Nebo (Deut 34:1), so Pius XI glimpsed peace in the distance... But he must have died peacefully, because he saw it in the distance and offered his own sufferings and his own life for the peace of the world.

Laudemus viros gloriosos et parentes nostros in generatione sua... pulchritudinis studium habentes, pacificantes in domibus suis. Let us praise, let us praise our pope, let us weep before his tomb the tears of our filial love and, above all, let us pray for him:

Oh Jesus, King of peoples and individuals, King of peace, King of love, King of light, have mercy on your servant Pius, who consecrated his life to the establishment of your kingdom, so that from that divine kingdom the peace that the world longs for may spring forth. Oh Lord, open the immense arms of your love to the one who sought your kingdom on earth; give your glory in heaven to the one who worked to seek it on earth; grant him in your most loving bosom peace, divine peace, eternal peace, the peace that is nothing other than the outpouring of God in hearts and souls!

CHAPTER 19

Jesus, in the Eucharist and in the Papacy

A DISCOURSE ON THE PAPACY

Ego autem rogavi pro te ut non deficiat fides tua
et tu aliquando conversus confirma fratres tuos.
I have prayed that your own faith may not fail; and once
you have turned back, you must strengthen your brothers.
(Luke 22:32)

In the fullness of time, Jesus came to earth, the gift of God, the fount, the crown of all the divine gifts, and St. John could say: *And we saw his glory, the glory as of the Father's only Son, full of grace and truth* (John 1:14). Yes, Jesus came to earth and said heavenly words to us, carried out stupendous wonders, taught us by his own example the way of heaven, and consummated his life with an august sacrifice, dying out of love for us on the cross.

And Christ's visit was not fleeting. Although he has ascended to sit at the right hand of the Father, although our mortal eyes do not behold him, nor our fleshly ears hear him, nor our hands can touch him, Jesus has not gone away, he lives with us, fulfilling the divine promise he made to us: *I am with you always, until the end of the age* (Matt 28:20). We could say, as never before, that since he ascended to heaven, Jesus is with us and lives in his Church, spreading his light everywhere, warming hearts with his love, pouring into souls the magnificent streams of his life.

We possess him, of course, in the ineffable sacrament of the Eucharist. There Jesus is really present, with his body, with his soul, with his heart, with all that he is. He is within reach of our hands, he is within reach of our hearts.

But it was not enough for Jesus to remain with us in the Eucharist, and, to tell the truth, neither was it enough for us. However great, however rich the Eucharist is, it was not sufficient for the necessities of our hearts. It was necessary for him to remain in another way, and Jesus Christ, in the excess of his love, found that way of remaining with us. Jesus remained also in the Church, in the Supreme Pontiff, in the pope.

Such are the two principle ways that our Lord Jesus Christ lives on earth: in the Eucharist and in the pope. And I want to treat both of these in this last chapter; or, better, I want to make known how Jesus Christ lives in the pope, comparing that marvelous existence of Jesus in the Supreme Pontiff with that marvel of love that our Lord carries out by living with us in the divine Eucharist.

Without a doubt, the Eucharist is something wonderful; there we find the intimate Jesus, the Jesus of Nazareth, hidden and silent, who has heavenly contact with our souls, who enters without a sound in our hearts, who warms us with his heavenly and divine fire. But, is it not true that Jesus in the Eucharist lacks something, or better, that we would lack something if we did not have more than the Eucharist?

What would we lack? His word, because in the Eucharist Jesus does not speak, he is silent. Undoubtedly, he speaks in that ineffable manner to which St. Thérèse of the Child Jesus refers when she says that he was a teacher who taught without words.[1] The word of Jesus in the Eucharist is the intimate word, the word of love, that which is said to the ear, that which is received in the midst of the delights of an intimate secret. But in the Eucharist the solemn word, the official one, that which Jesus pronounced in the midst of the multitudes during the three years of his public life, is not said. In the Eucharist is the intimate Jesus, but we will not find there the supreme Teacher, who had words of eternal life and who captivated the multitudes with the spell of his supreme word.

But Jesus provided for this deficiency, if you will permit me the audacity to call it so, perpetuating that teaching that he exercised during the three years of his public life, establishing a solemn, official, infallible teaching; and this supreme teaching he conferred on the pope.

In such a way, as like under the Eucharistic accidents, in the sacrament of love, Jesus is really and truly present, so also Jesus is present under the fragile humanity of the pope: Jesus, the unfailing light; Jesus, he who did not stop announcing on earth the words of life, the words that save, transform, and sanctify and that bring humanity towards happiness.

To human eyes, the pope is no more than a fragile man, as we all are, who is subject to the vicissitudes of human life, whose life has an end, and who, like the rest, descends into the tomb.

Those who do not have faith will be able to think that he is a man with an immense authority, who is at the head of millions of Catholics—an exceptional man, but nothing more than a man.

But the pope is not simply a man: he is Jesus, because under the human accidents is Christ, the Teacher who taught in an infallible way, the Teacher who is repeating to men in the course of the centuries the divine teachings that were scattered on the shores of Lake Tiberias and in the synagogues of Judea.

One day, Jesus Christ said to Peter: *Satan has demanded to sift all of you like wheat, but I have prayed that your own faith may not fail; and once you have turned back, you must strengthen your brothers.* Do we understand the extraordinary gift that our Lord gave to St. Peter by saying to him these words that the Gospel has preserved for us?

The faith of Peter can no longer fail. The faith of all souls has vicissitudes. How many times have geniuses been seen to vacillate and to sink into the depths of error! It is so easy for the poor human spirit to lose its way! But if all men can go astray, if even geniuses can rush into error, there is a faith that never fails, there is a word that never errs, a magisterium that has the solidity of a rock: the magisterium of Peter, because under the accidents, as it were, of the man, Jesus is there, the divine Teacher, he who said: *I am the way and the truth and the life* (John 14:6).

You are Peter, he said to him on another occasion, *and upon this rock I will build my church, and the gates of the netherworld shall not prevail against it* (Matt 16:18). The Church is founded upon the teaching of Peter, upon his unfailing word, upon his immortal word. All of our words have deficiencies; sometimes they are brilliant, they captivate and seduce the soul; but after an ephemeral triumph, how many times the word of man is brought down to the abyss of ignorance and error! The word of Peter is not like this. It is the unmoved rock, the firmest rock, where we are able to have the certainty that we will find the truth.

In the Eucharist, we find without a doubt the truth, an intimate and most sweet truth. How many times being close to the tabernacle have we learned profound things, divine things! Yes, because in the tabernacle Jesus speaks to us the sweetest word of love. But, can we have the certainty that what we hear in the intimacy of our hearts comes from Jesus? It is so easy to have illusions! Could not our spirits attribute to Jesus what is a product of our ingenuity or of our initiative? If we wanted to guide ourselves in our lives by the intimate word that we believe to hear at the foot of the tabernacle, we would be subject to illusions, we would not have the absolute certainty of being in the truth. And it is necessary to be certain. Whereas if we do not only draw close to the Eucharist but also to the pope and listen to his voice, and study his teachings, and subject ourselves to his infallible teaching, we can be sure that we will never err: *Heaven and earth will pass away, but my words will not pass away* (Luke 21:33). The teaching of the pope cannot have deficiencies nor eclipses, because he has received from our Lord Jesus Christ the privilege of infallibility.

In the Eucharist, Jesus is present, but silently; in the pope, Jesus teaches us. In the Eucharist, the intimate Jesus is present; in the pope, Jesus the Teacher is present, he who makes resonate through all the centuries those words of eternal life that illumine our spirits and inundate our souls with light.

But that is not the only deficiency of the Eucharist, if you will allow me that audacious word again. In the Eucharist, Jesus does not rule us, Jesus does not govern us. Of course, he efficaciously influences the depths of our hearts, but in the Eucharist our Lord does not make known to us in a clear and precise way, without fear, that we will not make mistakes, what is the path we have to follow, what is the holy will of God. In the Eucharist, Jesus soothes and softens our hearts, he disposes them for everything and propels them to accomplish the divine will. But, how many times we debate with ourselves in the midst of the perplexities of our spirits, not knowing precisely what is the will of God, what we should do! Of the problems so complicated and so difficult that are presented to us in life, how could we find the exact and sure solution if we did not have more than the Eucharist?

Without a doubt, in the Eucharist we find strength, love, and also light. But we need something absolutely sure that is not subject to the vicissitudes of illusions, something that reveals to us in a clear and precise manner the divine will. We need, so to speak, a kind of sacrament of the will of God.

And all of that we find in the infallible magisterium of the pope. In him we find he who rules us, he who governs us, the shepherd of our souls. He speaks, and when he orders, we know that it is God who orders, because Jesus said: *Whatever you bind on earth shall be bound in heaven; and whatever you loose on earth shall be loosed in heaven* (Matt 16:19). His regulations, his commands, are regulations and commands of Jesus. We, when the pope speaks, do not have to hesitate: we are sure, supported on that most firm rock upon which Jesus Christ raised the marvelous edifice of his Church.

The pope rules us and governs us in the name of God, or, better, Jesus, who lives in the pope, governs us and rules us through him. Because Jesus does not live in the pope only to teach us the truth but also to make known to us the holy will of God, to ordain for us what we should do, to point out to us the paths where we must find the sanctification of our souls and the happiness of our lives.

In the Eucharist, we have life. Ah, yes! It is the sacrament of life. There we are united to Jesus in an ineffable way; and united to us, Jesus pours into our souls marvelous torrents of his own life. For this reason he said: *Unless you eat the flesh of the Son of Man and drink his blood, you do not have life within you* (John 6:53). The sacrament of the Eucharist is the sacrament of life.

And, nevertheless, so that we can live fully that life that Jesus brought us and about which he spoke with his own lips—*I came so that they might have life and have it more abundantly* (John 10:10)—so that we might live that life fully, which is a participation of the same life of God, the Eucharist does not suffice: we need the pope.

One radiant morning, on the shores of Lake Tiberias, a sublime, charming scene took place (John 21:15-19). Jesus directs himself to Peter, who has moved away from the rest of the disciples, and he asks him a strange question three times: *Simon, son of John, do you love me more than these?* To each of these questions, St. Peter gives the same answer, an answer mixed with certainty and fear: *Lord, you know that I love you.*

Without a doubt, the apostle was remembering the denials of the Passion, and he was feeling humiliated for having dared on that disastrous night to deny the Teacher. Ah! But above all his fears was the sincerity of his love that flowed from his heart when his lips said the magnificent phrase: *Lord, you know that I love you.* And every time that Peter gave this answer, Jesus gave him a charge, gave him a mission, was pointing out to him an undertaking—*Feed my lambs,* he told him the first time—and he repeated it to him after St. Peter made the second confession of love, and when for a third time Jesus Christ directed to him the same question, *Simon, son of John, do you love me more than these?* St. Peter said to him: *Lord, you know everything; you know that I love you.* And then Jesus answers him: *Feed my sheep.*

What does that mysterious scene signify? It signifies that Jesus conferred a mission on Peter, that of feeding the lambs and sheep, that is, the shepherds and the faithful. Peter has to feed all: bishops, priests, and the faithful. All have a shepherd, all receive the divine breath of our souls from the hand of Peter.

To feed is not to give but to nourish life. But the pope does not only nourish it but also gives us that same life. Whenever we receive the gifts of heaven, there is the influence, mysterious but real, of the Supreme Pontiff. We receive the nourishment of our souls from priests. They, in the name of Jesus, lavish us with the mysteries of the kingdom of heaven, pardon our sins, nourish us with the divine Eucharist. Priests, in turn, receive the Holy Spirit from the hand of our bishops. They extend their consecrated hands, and the Holy Spirit descends on the elect to give them light, strength, and life. But, do we not know that without the pope there would be no bishops nor priests? Do we not know that all that the bishops and the priests do, they do in intimate communion, in close dependence on the Supreme Pontiff?

If the bishops and the priests were separated from the pope, if they broke the holy and supernatural bonds that united them with him, ah! their priesthood would be sterile and they would no longer be feeding the lambs of Jesus Christ, because from the pope we receive all in an ordered and most wise way.

Jesus Christ established in his Church that perfect unity, we could say an organic unity, a vital unity, more admirable than the unity that exists in an organism. In such a way, the principle of unity, the principle of life in the Church of Jesus is the pope, is Jesus, who is hidden in the pope, who lives in him.

Because of this, I have said that Jesus Christ, in order to carry out his divine promise of staying with us until the consummation of the age, found two ineffable ways of living in the midst of us: in the Eucharist and in the pope.

And the two ways complement each other mutually.

But these considerations are not just a simple explanation to entertain the ears or simply to instruct the spirit, no; my goal is to ignite piety and devotion to the pope in hearts, devotion that should exist in Christians but particularly in those who form that enthusiastic, vigorous group of Catholic Action.

Because Catholic Action, being as it is profoundly Christian and eminently hierarchical, should distinguish itself by its piety, by its devotion toward the august person of the Supreme Pontiff.

And, let us understand it well, piety toward the pope is nothing other than a prolongation of the love that we should have for our Lord Jesus Christ. How rightly did the apostle Paul exclaim: *Omnia et in omnibus Christus. Christ is all and in all* (Col 3:11).

In the Eucharist, we find Jesus. The illumined eyes of our hearts discover, under the Eucharistic accidents, the majesty, the love, the charms of Jesus. In the same way, in the pope the humble eyes of our hearts also discover Jesus, Jesus who is hidden there, who lives there, who works there. But just as our hearts go towards the Eucharist because Jesus is there, so it is necessary that our hearts go towards the pope, because Jesus is there. To love the pope is to love Jesus. The love of the pope is a prolongation of that ardent, tender, delicate love that should exist in hearts toward our Lord Jesus Christ.

St. Paul said: *Si quis non amat Dominum nostrum Jesum Christum, sit anathema. If anyone does not love the Lord, let him be accursed* (1 Cor 16:22). It is a duty, the first Christian duty, or, better said: the whole of our Christian duties is summed up in the love of our Lord Jesus Christ. And that love that we should have for Jesus Christ has as a logical consequence, as a natural prolongation, the love, the piety, the devotion that we should have towards the Supreme Pontiff.

The duties that we have toward the Supreme Pontiff can be reduced to three principle ones: first, to look at him supernaturally; second, to love him with the most excellent parts of our hearts; third, to enter into intimate communication with him.

In the end, are not these the three duties that we have with the Holy Eucharist? The Eucharist is a mystery of faith, as the Holy Church says in the Canon of the Mass: *Mysterium fidei*. And the first duty that we should fulfill with the Eucharist is to believe in that divine mystery. The first duty that we have when dealing with the pope is to look at him with the eyes of faith. We were saying that men see in the pope the exterior, that which shines, that which appears. No, we have a mysterious eye in our soul that teaches us to forget all those human things and to find the divine mystery that is hidden underneath them. In the pope, we see Jesus. Before the eyes of our hearts, the pope is transfigured, is Peter, or, better, Christ.

The second duty that we have with the Eucharist is to love it. Ah! If it is a sacrament of love, how is it possible that our hearts do not burn when we draw close to the Eucharist? The disciples of Emmaus, after they recognized Jesus Christ in the breaking of the bread, said, *Were not our hearts burning within us while he spoke to us on the way* (Luke 24:32). When Jesus draws close to us, our hearts always burn. If Jesus is also in the pope, it is necessary that we feel our hearts burn when in some way we draw close to him, at least spiritually, across the distances, because there is Jesus.

The second duty we have towards the pope is to love him, to love him not for his natural gifts but for the supernatural title that he has to our love. The popes, even seen from the human point of view, are great, are admirable. How many reasons we have, above all we Mexicans, to love the Supreme Pontiff for his special tenderness toward us, for the solicitude that he has always had for us, for the compassion he has for our sorrows and vicissitudes! The last magisterial letter he addressed to us, in which our problems and the happy solutions to them are perfectly noted, that letter, not only very wise and full of prudence but warmed with the fire of a paternal love, would be enough to make us love Pius XI with all our hearts. But, no: above all those reasons so just, so noble for us to love the pope, there is another deeper and more divine, if you will allow me the expression. We love him because he is Jesus, because Jesus lives in him, and speaks through his mouth, and governs through him, and feeds his sheep and lambs.

The third duty that we have with the Eucharist is to put ourselves in ultimate contact with it through communion. Through communion we allow Jesus to penetrate our souls, to share his life with us. Also with the Supreme Pontiff we have to be in close and mysterious communion: communion of faith, because our faith must be the faith of Peter, the unfailing faith, that for which Jesus prayed would never fail. We should always be in close communion of thought with him, to believe what he believes, to teach what he teaches, to think what he thinks, according to the limits of his infallible magisterium; communion of wills, in such a way that what he wants, what he decrees, is for us a sure and most firm rule that comes to serve as a norm for our will. To be in intimate communion with him, that is the third of our duties with respect to the pope.

Let us thank Jesus for his magnificent gifts. Let us give him thanks because he gave us the Eucharist, because he gave us the pope. Let us know how to fulfill our duties, let us see the pope with the illumined eyes of the heart, let us love him with the love that the Holy Spirit has put into our souls, let us work in intimate communion with him. In short, let us cultivate in our hearts devotion toward the pope so that the word of our Lord is accomplished, so that in the world there will be one flock under the staff of one shepherd (John 10:16).

NOTES

Notes for Chapter 1

1. "L'amour n'a qu'un mot, et qu'en le disant toujours, il ne le répète jamais" (Henri-Dominique Lacordaire, *Vie de Saint Dominique*, huitième édition [Paris: Librairie Poussielgue Freres, 1882], 116–7). "Love has but one word, which, because ever on its lips, is never repeated" (Henri-Dominique Lacordaire, *Life of St. Dominic*, translated by Mrs. Edward Hazeland [London: Burns and Oates, 1883], 95). Fr. Henri-Dominique Lacordaire, O.P., (1802–1861) re-established the Order of Preachers (the Dominicans) in France after the French Revolution. He was also a renowned preacher, for which reason Martínez as a deacon studiously read many of his homilies. As Treviño notes, "In his free time Reverend Mr. Martínez devoted himself to study and to reading. During that period, he aimed to read and to assimilate all the works of Lacordaire. This accounts for Lacordaire's influence upon his oratorical flights in later years. From time to time he even quoted Lacordaire literally" (Joseph G. Treviño, M.Sp.S., *The Spiritual Life of Archbishop Martínez*, translated by Sr. Mary St. Daniel Tarrant, B.V.M [St. Louis: Herder Book Co., 1966], 11).
2. In the *usus antiquior* of the Roman Rite, after purifying his fingers after his Holy Communion the bishop would use John 15:15 as part of a responsory before continuing with aspects of the ordination of the new priests, particularly placing his hands on their heads a second time to invoke the Holy Spirit and their expression of obedience to their bishop (*Pontificale Romanum* [Paris: Jouby, 1859], 55–6).
3. St. Augustine, *Homilies on the First Epistle of John*, 7.8 (1 John 4:4-12). For the complete work, see *Homilies on the First Epistle of John*, Vol. III/14, translation and notes by Boniface Ramsey, edited by Daniel E. Doyle, O.S.A, and Thomas Martin, O.S.A (Hyde Park, New York: New City Press, 2008).

4. St. Ignatius of Antioch, *Letter to the Romans*, 4.2. For the complete work, see *The Apostolic Fathers in English*, translated by Rick Brannan (Bellingham, WA: Lexham Press, 2012).
5. In the last year of his life, St. John of the Cross related to his brother Francis de Yepes that when the Lord asked St. John what he wanted for all his labors, St. John replied with these words (Crisógono de Jesús, O.C.D., *The Life of St. John of the Cross*, translated by Kathleen Pond [New York: Harper & Brothers, 1958], 268).
6. "Martyrdom was the dream of my youth and this dream has grown with me within Carmel's cloisters. But here again, I feel that my dream is a folly, for I cannot confine myself to desiring one kind of martyrdom. To satisfy me I need all" (St. Thérèse of Lisieux, *Story of a Soul, The Autobiography of Saint Thérèse of Lisieux,* translated by John Clarke, O.C.D., edited by Marc Foley [Washington, DC: ICS Publications, 2016], 300).
7. See the Benedictus antiphon for the feast of St. Andrew: "Salve, crux, pretiosa, suscipe discipulum eius, qui pependit in te, magister meus Christus" (*Liturgia Horarum*, vol. 1 [Città del Vaticano: Libreria Editrice Vaticana, 2000], 963).
8. Treviño recounts an episode from Martínez's installation as Archbishop of Mexico City: "When all the canonical prescriptions had been fulfilled, His Excellency ascended the pulpit to speak to his flock for the first time. The faithful filled the cathedral to capacity. Scarcely had he begun to speak when an unfortunate accident occurred. The wood floor, deteriorated by time, yielded to the weight of the multitude and caved in near the sanctuary on the Epistle side. The confusion and alarm were great, although the collapse had no consequences of importance; but the Archbishop's sermon was ruined. When calm was restored, it seemed fitting to him to limit himself to these words: 'I am here only to promise you one single thing: "I come to give you my life."' In truth, the whole episcopate of Archbishop Martínez was reduced to fulfilling that promise" (Treviño, *The Spiritual Life of Archbishop Martínez,* 218).
9. Martínez originally writes, "hay que hacer el sacrificio supremo sobre *el monte de la visión*," which could be translated literally as, "one must make the supreme sacrifice on *the mountain of vision*." The note in the NABRE on

Gen 22:1-19 could account for why Martínez says "mountain of vision": "The word 'Moriah' is a play on the verb 'to see' (Heb. *ra'ah*); the wordplay is continued in v. 8, 'God will provide (lit., 'see')' and in v. 14, Yahweh-yireh, meaning 'the Lord will see/provide.'"

Notes for Chapter 2

1. The antiphon for the Invitatory for the Solemnity of the Nativity of the Lord in the Divine Office.
2. St. Ambrose of Milan, *On the Death of Satyrus* II, 102. For the complete work, see *St. Ambrose: Select Works and Letters*, Nicene and Post-Nicene Fathers, Second Series, Vol. 10, translated by H. de Romestin, E. de Romestin, and H.T.F. Duckworth (Buffalo, NY: Christian Literature Publishing Co., 1896).
3. Thomas à Kempis, *The Imitation of Christ*, Book 2, Ch. 8. For the complete work, see, for example, Thomas à Kempis and Dennis J. Billy, *The Imitation of Christ: A Spiritual Commentary and Reader's Guide*, translated by William C. Creasy (Notre Dame, IN: Christian Classics, 2005).
4. "Supplices te rogamus..." The current translation of the Roman Canon (Eucharistic Prayer I) of the Mass is used here.

Notes for Chapter 3

1. "Amor sacerdos immolat" is the last line of verse 2 of the hymn *Ad regias Agni dapes* (At the Lamb's High Feast We Sing). This hymn was found in the Roman Breviary and was sung during the Easter season.
2. St. Ignatius of Antioch, *Letter to the Romans*, 5.3. "Now at last I am beginning to be a disciple. May nothing visible or invisible envy me, so that I may reach Jesus Christ. Fire and cross and battles with wild beasts, mutilation, mangling, wrenching of bones, the hacking of limbs, the crushing of my whole body, cruel tortures of the devil—let these come upon me, only let me reach Jesus Christ!" (Michael W. Holmes, *The Apostolic Fathers: Greek Texts and English Translations*, 3rd ed., [Grand Rapids: Baker Academic, 2007], 231).

Notes for Chapter 4

1. These words were said after the consecration of the wine in the Roman Canon of the *Missale Romanum* used in Martínez's time.
2. St. Thomas Aquinas, *Summa Theologiae* II-II, q. 188, a. 6; III, q. 40, a. 1, ad 2.

Notes for Chapter 5

1. See above, note 2 to Chapter 1 (p. 243).
2. The *Gloria* in the Mass of the Roman Rite.
3. Martínez originally writes, "pero como dijo Isaac al subir al *monte de la visión*," which could be translated literally as, "but as Isaac said upon ascending the *mountain of vision*." The note in the NABRE on Gen 22:1-19 could account for why Martínez says "mountain of vision": "The word 'Moriah' is a play on the verb 'to see' (Heb. ra'ah); the wordplay is continued in v. 8, 'God will provide (lit., 'see')' and in v. 14, Yahweh-yireh, meaning 'the Lord will see/provide.'"
4. Thomas à Kempis, *The Imitation of Christ*, Book 2, Ch. 8. For the complete work, see, for example, Thomas à Kempis and Dennis J. Billy, *The Imitation of Christ: A Spiritual Commentary and Reader's Guide*, translated by William C. Creasy (Notre Dame, IN: Christian Classics, 2005).
5. St. Thomas Aquinas, *Summa Theologiae* I-II, q. 113, a. 9, ad 2.
6. St. John of the Cross, *The Spiritual Canticle*, stanza 5. Translation taken from *The Collected Works of Saint John of the Cross*, translated by Kieran Kavanaugh and Rodríguez Otilio, 3rd ed. (Washington, DC: ICS Publications, 2017), 472.

Notes for Chapter 6

1. This is reminiscent of both the *Anima Christi* ("Ne permittas me separari a te. Do not permit me to be parted from you.") and the ending of the *Domine Jesu Christe* said before the priest's communion ("et a te numquam separari permittas; and never let me be parted from you"). It is hard to say if Martínez was thinking of one over the other.
2. Sophie Swetchine, *The Writings of Madame Swetchine*, translated by H.W. Preston, edited by Count de Falloux (Boston: Roberts Brothers, 1869), 7.

Notes for Chapter 7

1. See above, note 2 to Chapter 1 (p. 243).
2. "Homo sum: humani nil a me alienum puto" (Terence [*Publius Terentius Afer*], The Self-Tormentor [*Heauton Timorumenos*], Act 1, Scene 1, Line 77 in *Terence*, edited by John Sargeaunt, The Loeb Classical Library [London: W. Heinemann, 1959], 124).

Notes for Chapter 8

1. "'What then is true joy?' [Brother Leonard asked. St. Francis replied,] 'I return from Perugia and arrive here in the dead of night; and it is winter time, muddy and so cold that icicles have formed on the edges of my habit and keep striking my legs, and blood flows from such wounds. And all covered with mud and cold, I come to the gate and after I have knocked and called for some time, a brother comes and asks: "Who are you?" I answer: "Brother Francis." And he says: "Go away; this is not a proper hour for going about; you may not come in." And when I insist, he answers: "Go away, you are a simple and a stupid person; we are so many and we have no need of you. You are certainly not coming to us at this hour!" And I stand again at the door and say: "For the love of God, take me in tonight." And he answers: "I will not. Go to the Crosiers' place and ask there." I tell you this: If I had patience and did not become upset, there would be true joy in this and true virtue and the salvation of the soul'" (St. Francis of Assisi, *Francis and Clare: The Complete Works*, translated by Regis J. Armstrong and Ignatius C. Brady, edited by Richard J. Payne, The Classics of Western Spirituality [New York: Paulist Press, 1982], 165–66).
2. Jacques-Bénigne Bossuet, *Oeuvres de Messire Jacques-Bénigne Bossuet*, tome huitième (Paris: Boudet, 1778), 639.
3. St. Thérèse of Lisieux, *St. Thérèse of Lisieux, Her Last Conversations*, translated by John Clarke, O.C.D. (Washington, DC: ICS Publications, 1977), 123.

Notes for Chapter 9

1. See above, note 2 to Chapter 1 (p. 243).
2. St. John of the Cross, *Living Flame of Love*, stanza 3, commentary no. 59. "God leads each one along different paths so that hardly one spirit will be

found like another in even half its method of procedure" (St. John of the Cross, *The Collected Works of St. John of the Cross*, translated by Kieran Kavanaugh and Otilio Rodriguez, 3rd ed. [Washington, DC: ICS Publications, 2010], 697).

3. This Scripture verse is taken from the Douay-Rheims translation. It captures why Martínez uses "substantial" in this homily.

Notes for Chapter 10

1. St. John Vianney, *The Little Catechism of the Curé of Ars* (Rockford, IL: Tan Books, 1987), 34.
2. See above, note 2 to Chapter 1 (p. 243).
3. This Scripture verse is taken from the Douay-Rheims translation. It reflects Martínez's original Spanish and his continued reflection on paternity and fatherhood in this homily.
4. St. Thomas Aquinas, *Summa Theologiae* III, q. 82, a. 1, ad 4.
5. The current Code of Canon Law (1983) gives priests and deacons the faculty to preach everywhere (can. 764). The 1917 Code of Canon Law stated that priests and deacons were granted the faculty to preach from the bishop (can. 1337).
6. What was known as Extreme Unction is currently called the Anointing of the Sick. The Anointing of the Sick is a sacrament not only for immediate preparation for death but also for those who because of sickness or old age have some serious health impairment.
7. St. Thomas Aquinas, *Summa Contra Gentiles* IV, c. 76. See also, *Summa Theologiae* II-II, q. 185, a. 1, ad 2.

Notes for Chapter 11

1. Dante Alighieri, *Inferno*, Canto III, lines 5-6. For the complete work, see, for example, Dante Alighieri, *Inferno*, translated by Anthony M. Esolen (New York: Modern Library, 2002), 23.
2. St. Thomas Aquinas, *Summa Theologiae* II-II, q. 184, a. 6.
3. Nicene-Constantinopolitan Creed.
4. See above, note 5 TO Chapter 10.

Notes for Chapter 12

1. See above, note 1 to Chapter 1 (p. 243).
2. In the *usus antiquior* of the Roman Rite, the priest says this antiphon when he first arrives at the altar for Mass (cf. Ps 43:4).

Notes for Chapter 13

1. On May 25, 1754, in the papal bull *Non est Equidem*, Pope Benedict XIV named Our Lady of Guadalupe patroness of New Spain. He also approved an Office and Mass for Our Lady of Guadalupe. The Communion Antiphon at the Mass was, and still is, taken from Ps 147:20.
2. During the periods of intense persecution against the Church in Mexico, Pope Pius XI wrote to the Mexican people in *Iniquis afflictisque* (1926) and *Acerba animi* (1932).
3. On October 12, 1895, a canonical coronation of the image of Our Lady of Guadalupe was carried out with the permission of Pope Leo XIII. Our Lady of Guadalupe was then called Queen of Mexico and Patroness of the Americas.
4. Martínez refers to the parochial school for girls that Plancarte founded.
5. Take, for example, Blessed Concepción (Conchita) Cabrera de Armida (1862–1937). Blessed Conchita was a Mexican mother of nine, a widow, and a mystic, for whom Martínez acted as spiritual director for the last twelve years of her life. Blessed Conchita was an extremely prolific writer, and her works can be found in English and Spanish. For an overview of her life and writing, see *Conchita: A Mother's Spiritual Diary*, translated by Aloysius J. Owen, S.J., edited by Marie-Michel Philipon, O.P. (New York: Alba House, 1978).
6. Martínez refers to the Institute of the Sisters of Mary Immaculate of Guadalupe that Plancarte founded.
7. This Scripture verse is adapted from the Douay-Rheims translation, which is closer to the Latin Martínez knew.

Notes for Chapter 14

1. See *María*, published by Editorial La Cruz.

2. This Scripture verse is taken from the Douay-Rheims translation. It reflects Martínez's original Spanish and his continued reflection on paternity and fatherhood in this homily.
3. Rougier was asked to wait ten years by his superiors in the Society of Mary (the Marists) before founding the Missionaries of the Holy Spirit. Philipon recounts how "the Father General of the Marists...made him stay in Europe. There Father Félix, with heroic obedience and faith as unshakeable 'as that of Abraham,' waited, in silence, for God's hour....When, not having seen [Conchita] for ten years, Father Félix met her again, his first words were simply: 'I have not changed my opinion about the Works of the Cross'" (*Conchita: A Mother's Spiritual Diary,* translated by Aloysius J. Owen, S.J., edited by Marie-Michel Philipon, O.P. [New York: Alba House, 1978], 56).
4. Martínez refers to the miraculous healing of Rougier's arm before his ordination to the priesthood. The serious condition of his arm would have prevented his ordination, but due to the intervention of St. John Bosco his arm was healed.

Notes for Chapter 15

1. See note 2 to Chapter 9 (pp. 247–48).
2. ORIGINAL: His pastoral ring had cost him the laughable sum of two pesos and fifty cents, as he himself graciously affirmed when he complained of having lost it. When he was consecrated, he was presented with a magnificent pectoral cross by popular acclaim on the island of Cuba. As soon as he was consecrated, he sold it, and with its proceeds he had his Catechism printed, with a print run of half a million copies.

   EDITOR'S NOTE: Guízar was consecrated bishop of Veracruz in Havana, where he was exiled because of persecution by the Mexican government.
3. See the Magnificat antiphon for Second Vespers on the Feast of St. Lawrence: "Beatus Laurentius, dum in craticula superpositus ureretur, ad impiissimum tyrannum dixit: Assatum est, jam versa et manduca: nam facultates Ecclesiae, quas requiris, in caelestes thesauros manus pauperum deportaverunt."
4. ORIGINAL: Periodically he would distribute to bashful families all that was necessary in order to stock their pantries.

5. From the Collect for the 11th Sunday after Pentecost (according to the *usus antiquior* of the Roman Rite): "Omnipotens sempiterne Deus, qui, abundantia pietatis tuæ, et merita supplicum excedis et vota: effunde super nos misericordiam tuam; ut dimittas quæ conscientia metuit, et adicias quod oratio non præsumit" (*Missale Romanum* [Vatican City: Typis Polyglottis Vaticanis, 1962]). In the *Novus Ordo*, the same collect is used for the 27th Sunday in Ordinary Time: "Almighty ever-living God, who in the abundance of your kindness surpass the merits and the desires of those who entreat you, pour out your mercy upon us to pardon what conscience dreads and to give what prayer does not dare to ask" (*The Roman Missal*, Third Typical Edition [Washington, DC: United States Conference of Catholic Bishops, 2011]).
6. Original: Here is one of the many features of his life that show it. Bishop Guízar was going to give a mission in Villahermosa, Tabasco, taking advantage of the winter season, when the temperature was bearable and it was possible that the Tabascan people would come. But he received a telegram from his bishop (then Bishop Guízar was a canon of the cathedral of Zamora), saying that he should call him immediately. When he returned from his trip, winter had already passed and the tremendous heat was passing over Villahermosa. In such circumstances, the attendance at the mission would have been nothing. Bishop Guízar did not give up but, rather, and accompanied by the other priests, went before the tabernacle, knelt down, and, taking the thermometer in his hands, said full of faith: "We will not get up from here until the thermometer lowers so many degrees." And the thermometer lowered, and the temperature stayed that way the whole time of the mission, which was very well attended and fruitful.
7. Henri-Dominique Lacordaire, O.P., *Conférences de Notre-Dame de Paris et Conférences de Toulouse*, Oeuvres du R.P. Henri-Dominique Lacordaire, Vol. 5 (Paris: Librairie Poussielgue Frères, 1881), 115. For more on Lacordaire, see above, note 1 to Chapter 1 (p. 243).
8. Henri-Dominique Lacordaire, O.P., *Conférences de Notre-Dame de Paris et Conférences de Toulouse*, Oeuvres du R.P. Henri-Dominique Lacordaire, Vol. 6 (Paris: Librairie Poussielgue Frères, 1884), 360.
9. St. Thomas Aquinas, *Summa Theologiae* II-II, q. 27, a. 6.

10. St. Augustine, *Tractates on the Gospel of John*, 26.4. For the complete work, see *Homilies on the Gospel of John 1–40*, translated by Edmund Hill, edited by Allan D. Fitzgerald and Boniface Ramsey, Vol. 12, *The Works of Saint Augustine: A Translation for the 21st Century* (Hyde Park, NY: New City Press, 2009), 453.
11. "We can never have too much confidence in the Good God, He is so mighty, so merciful" (St. Thérèse of Lisieux, *The Story of a Soul*, edited by T. N. Taylor [London: Burns and Oates, 1912], 213).
12. St. Thérèse of Lisieux, *The Story of a Soul*, edited by T. N. Taylor (London: Burns and Oates, 1912), 212.

Notes for Chapter 16

1. Translated directly from Martínez's Spanish, here and throughout this homily, to capture his use of this verse in this homily.
2. Horace, Ode 3.30. See Horace, *The Odes and Epodes*, translated by Charles E. Bennett, revised edition, The Loeb Classical Library (Cambridge: Harvard University Press, 1964), 278–9.
3. St. Thomas Aquinas, *Summa Theologiae* II-II, q. 184, a. 7.
4. St. Thomas Aquinas, *Summa Theologiae* II-II, q. 184, a. 5.
5. From the *Gloria* in the Mass.
6. See note 2 to Chapter 9 (pp. 247–48).
7. St. Augustine, *De civitate Dei*, 19.13. For the complete work, see *The City of God*, translated by William Babcock, edited by Boniface Ramsey, Vol. 7, *The Works of Saint Augustine: A Translation for the 21st Century* (Hyde Park, NY: New City Press, 2012–13), 368.
8. Luis de León, *The Names of Christ*, Bk II, Prince of Peace. See *Luis de León: The Names of Christ*, translated by Manuel Durán and William Kluback, edited by Richard J. Payne, The Classics of Western Spirituality (Ramsey, NJ: Paulist Press, 1984) 212–4.
9. In 1929, Emilio Portes Gil, the president of Mexico, agreed to a more lenient enforcement—but not the repeal—of the anti-clerical laws violently enforced by his predecessor. Ruiz had a hand in these negotiations.

Notes for Chapter 17

1. This Scripture verse is adapted from the Douay-Rheims translation.
2. The Episcopal Committee was the forerunner to the Mexican Episcopal Conference. Even when Ruiz was in exile in San Antonio, Texas, he remained president of the Committee and kept in constant contact with the bishops of Mexico ("Historia de la CEM," *Conferencia del Episcopado Mexicano*, https://cem.org.mx/historia-de-la-cem/).
3. Forbes recounts this story of Pope St. Pius X: "An intimate friend of the Cardinal's, who was staying with him at the episcopal palace, asked one day if he might say Mass at an early hour next morning, as he had to catch a train. 'Why not?' was the answer. 'I will see that all is ready for you.' What was the astonishment of the priest when he went to the private chapel of the Patriarch at an early hour to find his illustrious host himself preparing everything for the Mass. 'But who will serve?' asked the celebrant. 'I,' answered the Cardinal very simply. 'Oh, Eminence!' protested his guest, quite aghast at the suggestion. 'What!' exclaimed the Patriarch smiling. 'Do you imagine that a Prelate of my rank does not know how to serve Mass?'" (Frances Alice Forbes, *Life of Pius X* [United Kingdom: R&T Washbourne, 1918], 58).

Notes for Chapter 18

1. Translated directly from Martínez's Spanish, here and throughout this homily, to capture his use of this verse in this homily.
2. Pius XII was elected pope on March 2, 1938, and his coronation took place on March 12.
3. World War I.
4. St. Thérèse of Lisieux, *Story of a Soul, The Autobiography of Saint Thérèse of Lisieux,* translated by John Clarke, O.C.D., edited by Marc Foley (Washington, DC: ICS Publications, 2016), 302.

Notes for Chapter 19

1. St. Thérèse of Lisieux, *Story of a Soul, The Autobiography of Saint Thérèse of Lisieux,* translated by John Clarke, O.C.D., edited by Marc Foley (Washington, DC: ICS Publications, 2016), 276.

Designed by Fiona Cecile Clarke, the Cluny Media *logo depicts a monk at work in the scriptorium, with a cat sitting at his feet.*

The monk represents our mission to emulate the invaluable contributions of the monks of Cluny in preserving the libraries of the West, our strivings to know and love the truth.

The cat at the monk's feet is Pangur Bán, from the eponymous Irish poem of the 9th century. The anonymous poet compares his scholarly pursuit of truth with the cat's happy hunting of mice. The depiction of Pangur Bán is an homage to the work of the monks of Irish monasteries and a sign of the joy we at Cluny take in our trade.

"Messe ocus Pangur Bán,
cechtar nathar fria saindan:
bíth a menmasam fri seilgg,
mu memna céin im saincheirdd."

Made in the USA
Columbia, SC
01 July 2024

37940214R00153